# ARMED POLICE

# ARMED POLICE

## THE POLICE USE OF FIREARMS SINCE 1945

## MICHAEL J. WALDREN

SUTTON PUBLISHING

First published in the United Kingdom in 2007 by
Sutton Publishing Limited · Phoenix Mill
Thrupp · Stroud · Gloucestershire · GL5 2BU

British Library Cataloguing in Publication Data
A catalogue record for this book is available from the British Library.

ISBN 978-0-7509-4637-7

Typeset in 11.5/15pt Goudy.
Typesetting and origination by
Sutton Publishing Limited.
Printed and bound in England by
J.H. Haynes & Co. Ltd, Sparkford.

# CONTENTS

# LIST OF PLATES

# FOREWORD

This book begins with the *Blue Lamp* image of an unarmed 'P.C. George Dixon' confronting an armed violent thug, and terminates in the context of mass casualty terrorism on the streets of contemporary London. In between it narrates the evolution of the specialists in armed policing in the capital. Where London ventured, other police forces throughout Britain followed.

This is controversial terrain and we see in this account how nervous were senior officers at the prospect and realities of arming their officers. What may appear with hindsight to have been extraordinary timidity had its origins in the very creation of the Metropolitan Police in 1829. Insofar as policing existed before Sir Robert Peel created the Metropolitan Police it was invariably armed: the famous Bow Street Runners carried weapons and so too did others. Insisting that his 'New Police' would venture onto the streets unarmed was a conscious decision by Peel to break with the past and was expressly designed to generate respect for this new force. The historic antipathy of the British to a standing army had aroused suspicion about the very idea of a professional police force, leading several previous attempts to introduce a professional police force to founder. By attiring his 'New Police' in non-military dress (blue rather than red was their colour) and equipping them only with a truncheon, Peel intended that they should give an impression of vulnerability, rather than the formidability that was characteristic of Continental Napoleonic policing.

Peel's formula proved a great success and was widely emulated, especially in the English-speaking world, but almost nowhere else was policing unarmed as it was in Britain. Increasingly the unarmed

British bobby took on iconic significance: a distinctively British institution that demonstrated the remarkably settled character of British society. It contributed to the sense of superiority enjoyed by successive generations of the British.

It was always a manufactured myth: police had access to weaponry and if all else failed (as it occasionally did) there was recourse to the military. But it was a myth that served the police well, engendering the respect and even affection of the public, and generations of senior officers sought to preserve it. Yet, in the second half of the twentieth century society changed. Crime increased markedly and with it came the threat of armed criminality and later the scourge of terrorism, at first domestic and more recently international. This is the story of how the Metropolitan Police struggled to come to terms with this changing reality while attempting to retain the myth of the unarmed 'bobby'.

The story is told with affection, occasional humour, sometimes with grief, but always with commitment. This is truly an 'insider's' account. A career spent very largely at the forefront of specialist armed policing has given Mike Waldren unparalleled knowledge and insight into how 'the Unit' evolved. It goes beyond the dusty memos and minutes of sometimes subterranean official decision-making to reveal the voices of those who served. Very few could have elicited so much from so many. It is testimony to the enormous respect and affection in which Mike Waldren is held by those who served with him that they have given so freely of their memories.

*Professor P.A.J. Waddington*
*August 2006*

# PREFACE

On 7 July 2005 at just before 9 o'clock in the morning, explosive devices detonated on London Underground trains at Liverpool Street, Edgware Road and Kings Cross stations and on a double-deck bus in Tavistock Square. Fifty-six people were killed and over 700 injured. Suicide bombing had come to Britain for the first time. Two weeks later London was again thrown into chaos when attempts were made to set off another four explosions – three on the Underground and one on a bus – although this time the devices failed to detonate.

The Commissioner of the Metropolitan Police, Sir Ian Blair, said his force faced 'its largest operational challenge since the war' and security in London was stepped up to an unprecedented level. The sight of heavily armed police officers on the streets became a regular feature of television news programmes, leaving an enduring impression that the face of policing in Britain had changed for ever – a far cry from the kindly image of *Dixon of Dock Green* and the notion of the unarmed British bobby.

The growth in the police carrying of arms since the Second World War has been controversial – unarmed policing is the hallmark of the British police tradition. Some commentators have described it as a drift towards paramilitary policing that has now crossed the line between the respective roles of the police and the army. To others it represents nothing more sinister than the end of 'the amateur phase of policing', but both views are over-simplistic. To begin with, to most people after the war the concept of being an amateur with a firearm would have had no meaning – you either knew how to use one or you didn't. Many people in Britain had been taught how to use a gun during the war years but most of them would have had little or no shooting practice, particularly those on the Home Front, police officers included. Initially this was due to the scarcity of ammunition but gradually a collective opinion evolved that you could be considered proficient with a firearm without ever actually firing one. Although incredibly naive from today's perspective, this belief remained conventional wisdom for many years after the conflict had ended and the myth still persists that, until fairly recently, the police in Britain did not even have firearms. This is because, for what were considered to be perfectly sound reasons at the time, the carefully crafted postwar image of the police was one of a benign unarmed service that could cope quite adequately without them.

There is no doubt that today's police service is vastly different from the one found in postwar Britain, with the most visible change being that of officers now openly carrying firearms. This is the previously untold insider account of that change.

The story spans more than half a century and includes examples of extraordinary heroism, tragedy, controversy, comedy, intrigue and occasional farce. Each police force in Britain has its own story to tell, but at the forefront of developments has been the section of the Metropolitan Police known variously over the years as D6, D11, PT17, SO19 and now CO19. Initially created out of the need for postwar contingency planning in the event of another war, this branch has evolved into a world-famous operational and training unit in the front line of the fight against armed crime and terrorism.

*Mike Waldren*
*July 2006*

# ACKNOWLEDGEMENTS

Extracts from *Crime in London* by Gilbert Kelland, first published by Bodley Head, are reprinted by permission of The Random House Group Ltd; from *McNee's Law* by permission of HarperCollins Publishers Ltd © Sir David McNee 1983; from *Dr Iain West's Casebook* by permission of Little, Brown Book Group and Mr John Pawsey; from *The Blue Lamp* by Canal+Image UK Ltd; and from *Police Review* by permission of Jane's Information Group – *Jane's Police Review*. Unfortunately, the original contractual information required for formal permission to include extracts from *Scotland Yard* by Sir Harold Scott, first published by Andre Deutsch in 1954, and from *In the Office of Constable* by Sir Robert Mark, first published by William Collins Sons in 1978, cannot now be traced.

I am particularly grateful to Arthur Batten, Kris Freeland, Bob Wells, Jim White, Alex Moir, Ian Chadburn, Bert Harris, Ron Parrish, Colin Bulley, Mick Weight, Ron Jarrett, John Nunn, Peter McDonald, John Warner, Pete Sidebotham, Dave Tilley, Tony Gray, Dave Chambers, Tony Long, Bryan Galley, Peter Harris, Terry Webster, Clive Rawlings, Pete Bradley, Jonathan Ferrari, Dwight Atkinson, Bill Rowlinson, Sandra Perry, Doug McConnachie, Roger Gray, Norman Mackenzie, Stan Conley, Colin Burrows and a few others who have asked not to be named, whose willingness to share their experiences has made this account possible.

The critique of the early drafts of this book by P.A.J. Waddington, Professor of Social Policy at the Policy Research Institute, University of Wolverhampton, has been invaluable. Last, but by no means least, my thanks go to my wife Sue for her encouragement and support.

# ABBREVIATIONS

| | |
|---|---|
| ACA | Assistant Commissioner 'A' department |
| ACB | Assistant Commissioner 'B' department |
| ACC | Assistant Commissioner 'C' department |
| ACC | Assistant Chief Constable |
| ACD | Assistant Commissioner 'D' department |
| ACPO | Association of Chief Police Officers (Commander rank and above) |
| ACPO JSC | ACPO Joint Standing Committee on the Police Use of Firearms |
| ACPT | Assistant Commissioner Personnel and Training department |
| ACSO | Assistant Commissioner Specialist Operations department |
| ACTO | Assistant Commissioner Territorial Operations department |
| AFO | Authorised Firearms Officer |
| ARV | Armed Response Vehicle |
| CID | Criminal Investigation department |
| COBRA | Cabinet Office Briefing Room |
| CPS | Crown Prosecution Service |
| DAC | Deputy Assistant Commissioner |
| DACA (ops) | Deputy Assistant Commissioner 'A' department (operations) |
| DC | Detective Constable |
| DCI | Detective Chief Inspector |
| DCS | Detective Chief Superintendent |
| DI | Detective Inspector |

| | |
|---|---|
| DPG | Diplomatic Protection Group |
| DS | Detective Sergeant |
| HMIC | Her Majesty's Inspectorate of Constabulary |
| IPCC | Independent Police Complaints Commission |
| JSP | jacketed soft-point (bullet) |
| MoD | Ministry of Defence |
| MPA | Metropolitan Police Authority |
| NWGFI | National Working Group of Firearms Instructors |
| PC | Police Constable |
| PCA | Police Complaints Authority |
| PERME | Propellant and Explosives Research and Monitoring Establishment |
| PIRA | Provisional Irish Republican Army |
| PSD | Property Services department |
| PSDB | Police Scientific Development Branch (Home Office) |
| PSNI | Police Service of Northern Ireland |
| RIB | rigid inflatable boat |
| RSAF | Royal Small Arms Factory |
| RUC | Royal Ulster Constabulary |
| SAS | Special Air Service |
| SB | Special Branch |
| SBS | Special Boat Service |
| SFO | Specialist Firearms Officer |
| SOE | Special Operations Executive |
| SPG | Special Patrol Group |
| SRDB | Scientific Research and Development Branch (Home Office) |
| TSG | Territorial Support Group |
| UKU | UK Police Unit (Cyprus) |

*Chapter 1*

# THE GOOD OLD DAYS

### THE BLUE LAMP

In 1949 Ealing Studios in England made a film based on the London Metropolitan Police. In the opening scenes a police car drove out of what used to be Paddington Green police station's yard and began the high-speed chase of a sports car. When this vehicle eventually crashed the driver attempted to escape on foot and before unarmed officers could overpower him, he shot a bystander who tried to stop him.

The next scenes were of newspaper headlines such as 'Murder in the street' and 'Father of six children is killed by gunman', while a voice-over told the audience that: 'To this man, until today, the crime wave was nothing but a newspaper headline. What stands between the ordinary public and this outbreak of crime? What protection has the man in the street against this armed threat to his life and property? At the Old Bailey, Mr Justice Finnemore in passing sentence for a crime of robbery with violence gave this plain answer: "This is perhaps another illustration of the disaster caused by insufficient numbers of police. I have no doubt that one of the best preventives of crime is the regular uniform police officer on the beat."'

The audience was then introduced to 'veterans like George Dixon, with twenty-five years' service, now Police Constable 693 attached to Paddington Green'. The film was called *The Blue Lamp* and starred Jack Warner as Dixon and Jimmy Hanley as a new recruit. Dirk Bogarde played the criminal who shot and killed the hapless Dixon in order to escape after being caught in the act of robbing a cinema box office. Dixon, again played by Jack Warner, was brought back to life in 1955 for a television series. There were over 350 episodes of *Dixon of Dock Green*, and even today the character provides the quintessential classic image of the traditional British bobby who is prepared to accept the price that may have to be paid for policing unarmed.

For Sir Harold Scott, Commissioner of the Metropolitan Police 1945–53, the film was a triumph. In his book, *Scotland Yard*, first published in 1954, he wrote:

> We cooperated with Ealing Studios in making *The Blue Lamp*, which gave a faithful picture of the policeman's life and work in the form of an exciting crime story, much of the detail of which was taken from actual happenings in recent crimes. This film has been shown all over the world and has been a valuable means of spreading a knowledge of the efficiency and high traditions of the Metropolitan Police.[1]

The reason for the cooperation had a great deal to do with Scott's efforts to resolve two problems – a desperate shortage of manpower and a rising crime rate. His force had been reduced from 19,500 regular officers and 25,000 full-time auxiliaries in the early days of the war to some 12,000 officers and fewer than 2,000 auxiliaries by the end of 1945. He needed more officers and to get them he had to persuade the general public and the Home Office that more constables patrolling the beat were a worthwhile investment that could stem the rise in crime. However, he played down stories of criminals with guns, saying: 'The number of armed robberies [per annum] . . . since the war has varied between ten and forty-six, and although great publicity has been given to this subject in the last year or two, the figures for 1950, 1951 and 1952 – nineteen, ten and nineteen respectively – are in no way abnormal.'[2] The rise to forty-six had come in 1947.

Scott was anxious not to give the impression that his officers wanted to carry firearms:

> [Well-publicised cases] lead to a suggestion that the police should be armed. The police themselves do not wish it, believing that if they were there would be an increased tendency for the criminal to be armed also and to shoot on sight. In eight years, only two Metropolitan policemen have been shot dead and four or five

wounded by firearms. . . . We train our policemen in unarmed combat, and this is almost invariably successful in disarming an armed opponent without injury to themselves.[3]

The two Metropolitan policemen shot dead, and for whom the 'unarmed combat' had evidently proved ineffective, were Constable Nathaniel Edgar in 1948 and Constable Sidney Miles in 1952.

Police firearms were not mentioned at all in The Blue Lamp, probably by design, and anyone seeing the film could be forgiven for believing that the Metropolitan force did not have any, particularly after watching the arrest of Dirk Bogarde's character at the end. Unarmed officers, all with a look of grim determination, overcame their armed and dangerous adversary by sheer weight of numbers. Even Dixon of Dock Green would not include an episode showing a police officer being issued with a gun until 1974, by which time, as will be seen, the cat was already out of the bag.

## THE REALITY

Despite the image created by the film, the Metropolitan Police did have firearms and Sir Harold Scott was not being entirely candid in his book. According to an internal memorandum issued in 1938, pistols had been 'held on charge for very many years. In addition to [protection duties] it happens quite often that police have to act as escort to bullion, when they are armed. Also from time to time officers have information that some criminal for arrest has arms and they quite rightly, therefore, arm themselves before going to arrest him.'[4]

The force had been formed in September 1829 and records show it bought fifty pairs of flintlock pocket pistols in December the same year.[5] By 1868 a supply of revolvers was kept at police stations throughout London, but after two officers were shot and killed in the early 1880s there were calls for the police to be armed. In London's outer divisions, 4,430 out of 6,325 officers voted in favour but the Commissioner decided instead that officers 'who desire to have them when employed on night duty' could carry a firearm as long as they could be 'trusted to use them with discretion'.[6] Essex Constabulary was probably just one of several other forces to make identical provision within a year or so.[7] Full arming was avoided, but it had been close.

At the turn of the century it would have been common to see Metropolitan Police officers openly carrying firearms, supplied by the Admiralty, while guarding various navy dockyards, a practice that would continue until 1925. In 1936 the regulations were changed, making it a requirement that a constable had to give a 'satisfactory reason' before a firearm could be issued.[8] It would be 1985 before female officers could carry a firearm on the same basis as their male counterparts.

During the Second World War the force had some 25,000 revolvers and pistols and 3,600 rifles. Most of these were supplied by the War Office, seized from London gun dealers or surrendered by their private owners, and they were mainly used for the protection of buildings and vulnerable points thought likely to attract the attention of saboteurs. At the end of the war most of these weapons were returned to the sources from whence they had come.

Arrangements to be put in force in the event of another war were agreed on 30 July 1948 at a special meeting of the Central Conference of Chief Constables, Police War Duties Committee, held at the Home Office in London. The War Office agreed to keep 4,000 rifles and 8,000 revolvers for the police and to store them at fourteen anti-aircraft ordnance depots around Britain. The chief constable with a depot in his area would then, on receipt of the code words 'Polwin Section Two Scat Homeffen Collect', arrange for their distribution to the surrounding forces.

By 1952 the arrangements were complete and the depot holding the weapons for the Metropolitan Police, and for the forces of Berkshire, Hampshire, Kent, Surrey, Sussex West, Sussex East, Brighton, Eastbourne, Hastings, Portsmouth, Reading and the City of London, was located in Mill Hill in north-west London. Thirty-four per cent of the weapons for all British police forces were kept there, 25 tons of them, and the Home Office asked the Commissioner what arrangements he intended to make for their dispersal. The Deputy Commissioner, Sir John Nott-Bower (Commissioner of the Metropolitan Police 1953–8), wrote back on 23 May to say that he was 'not at all happy about the proposed arrangements'. Collection and distribution would be a major undertaking. However, he was eventually persuaded and the superintendent in charge of the Metropolitan Police training school at Hendon, 2 miles from the depot, was given the job of working out how the weapons would be sent to those who needed them. Splendid though the eventual plan undoubtedly was, it was never tested, and in 1956 it was discovered that the War Office had moved the guns without letting police forces know. All that remained at Mill Hill was rifle ammunition – the rifles and revolvers were in Essex.

This did not mean that the Metropolitan Police had been left with no firearms of its own. Officers were still permanently armed for protection duties and over 1,000 Webley and Scott .32 calibre self-loading pistols had been on general issue and available in all the force's stations since 1911. However, *The Blue Lamp* certainly presented 'a faithful picture of the policeman's life and work' by not showing any of the officers at Paddington Green training with weapons. Because of wartime ammunition shortages, training had been stopped in 1939 and, other than for a few officers employed on protection, it does not seem to have occurred to Sir Harold Scott that there was any need to restart it.

In May 1953 the condition of some of the pistols was described as being 'wretched' and seventy second-hand Beretta pistols in 9mm (.380) calibre were purchased in 1955 for use in central London. Webley and Scott Mark IV revolvers in .380 calibre replaced the Webley and Scott pistols in 1956, and the Beretta pistols were then replaced by new Walther Model PP 9mm (.380) self-loading pistols in 1960.

At the time the film was made the Metropolitan Police covered an area of 700 square miles with a population of about 7 million people. It was divided up into four districts, each under a commander, and subdivided into twenty-three divisions, each under a chief superintendent. The divisions, identified by a letter of the alphabet, were split into three or four sub-divisions each under a superintendent, and most of these were again divided up into as many as five sectional stations. Scotland Yard housed the Commissioner's office and was the headquarters of departments 'A' (operations and administration), 'B' (traffic), 'C' (crime) and 'D' (training). A separate force, the City of London police, covered the 'Square Mile' of the financial district at the city's heart.


## INSTRUCTIONS

In March 1955 Sir John Nott-Bower, now Commissioner, decided that it was time to update the force instructions.[9] The circumstances under which an officer could use a firearm, the equivalent of 'rules of engagement' in the armed forces, were given as being: 'In case of absolute necessity, e.g. if he or the person he is protecting is attacked by a person with a firearm or other deadly weapon and he cannot reasonably protect himself or give protection when he (as well as a private person) may resort to a firearm as a means of defence.'

Weapons could be 'issued only to officers who have been properly instructed in their use', although a liberal interpretation would be placed on the term 'properly instructed'. Former army experience was considered adequate, as Constable, later Sergeant, Ron Jarrett found out:

I joined the Metropolitan Police in 1955 and when I came out of training school in the October I was sent to 'A' division. There were plenty of protection posts on 'A' division and they were all armed posts. I remember we carried the 1934 model Beretta and that the training I had was nil – at least I don't remember any. The fact that I had just left the Marines seems to have been sufficient. The weapon was carried in a pocket – no holsters were issued. We had the long straight mackintosh at the time and we'd put the gun just inside the pocket. 10 Downing Street [the official London home and office of the Prime Minister] had an armed post at the front and I remember that when you were relieved for your refreshments, you used to hand the Beretta over to the bloke who was relieving you. He'd stick it in his pocket and sometimes when you got back you would find the Beretta laid out on the step in front of you. The bloke had stripped it down and you had to put it back together again.

The new instructions required that twenty-four men in each division (those in central London were allowed more) attend an 'annual firing practice and proficiency test', although this was not a new idea. An annual practice (of six rounds) had first been introduced in 1885 and, as its name suggests, it took place once every year thereafter. In 1914 the ammunition expended was increased (to twenty-four rounds) and, for the first time, a proficiency test was introduced. Although the format was revised again in 1936 (to thirty-two rounds), the war intervened in 1939 and it had to stop. The new regulations therefore only reintroduced what had once been a regular event, albeit it had not taken place for a decade and a half. The main new component was that it now had to be carried out in accordance with a booklet produced by the Metropolitan Police Shooting League, an umbrella organisation for divisional clubs that encouraged shooting as a recreational sport for police officers. Since 1914 the Receiver (the person responsible for police finance, buildings and equipment) had even provided indoor pistol ranges in a few police stations and supplied the league with .22 calibre ammunition at a reduced price. The league in turn sold this on to divisional clubs with the benefit to the force being that it provided a cheap form of training for the annual test, although not all divisions had a club and it was certainly not a requirement that officers belong to one.

The league produced separate booklets for the Webley and Scott revolvers and the Walther pistols giving details of the weapon, safety precautions and shooting techniques. The weapon was to be held at waist level for 'sense of direction' shooting at 10 yards and raised to eye level so that the sights could be used for 'aimed fire' at 15 yards. Each man was supposed to fire twenty-four rounds as practice with another twelve for the test. This would all have seemed very familiar to anyone who had undergone training with the Special Operations Executive (SOE) during the Second World War. Captain William Fairbairn and Captain Eric Sykes, both former Shanghai police officers, had taught agents how to shoot at the Arisaig SOE training school in Scotland. Fairbairn had then been seconded to Canada where he taught members of SOE's opposite number in the US, the Office of Strategic Services (OSS).

Fairbairn and Sykes believed that using the sights on a gun at close range was a dangerous waste of time. Instead, a person should use their natural 'sense of direction' which enabled them to point instinctively with their finger at an object without having to close one eye to do it. In place of the finger was a gun. Fairbairn and Sykes's book, *Shooting to Live*, is the foundation from which most modern techniques of close-quarter shooting evolved.

The finer points of combat pistol shooting theory would have meant little or nothing to anyone who had not served in SOE or read *Shooting to Live*. Even with proper training, the requirement to hit a target from waist level at 10 yards was expecting a lot and luck would have influenced the result. The 'standard of proficiency' expected was for an officer to achieve two hits out of six for 'sense of direction' shooting and three hits out of six for 'aimed fire'. However, according to the instructions, 'it is not absolutely essential for all selected officers to pass the proficiency test, so long as each proves clearly that he is capable of handling a pistol or revolver'. When combined with the difficulty involved in 'sense of direction' shooting and a lack of understanding of why it was even required, this appears to have opened the door for the test to be ignored, as Constables Kris Freeland and Mick Weight discovered.

### Kris Freeland

When I left the Royal Marines I went back into the docks as I was a stevedore before I enlisted. I joined the Metropolitan Police in 1950 and although I didn't become an authorised shot [an officer authorised to carry a firearm] right away, when I did I thought the system was archaic. All you had to do was to go to a range and fire a few rounds. I used to go to the range at City Road police station and the first time I went it was almost embarrassing. It was just a question of picking up the gun from the table and when the order was given you started to fire. It was very haphazard, although of course it was all that was required in those days.

### Mick Weight

I joined in 1961 and was posted to Earlsfield on 'W' division. Constable Bert Ball, a wartime special who had stayed on after the war, was the 'station gunman' and after I had finished my two years' probation he asked me if I would like to replace him. He arranged for me to go to Imber Court sports club pistol range where an elderly inspector and six constables arrived in a green police coach. We were shown how to open and load Webley revolvers and proceeded to fire a practice. This was six left-handed and six right-handed at about 15 yards – with no earmuffs of course. We then fired six rounds kneeling, right-handed. We then repeated the shoot in order to qualify.

This was considerably more training than was given to another officer, Constable, later Inspector, Alex Moir, who was authorised at about the same time:

In 1964 I was serving at Kensington on 'F' division. Three of us went in a van to Chelsea barracks where an army sergeant greeted us and took us to a small range where there was a large target set up about 5 to 7 yards away. There was a Webley revolver lying loaded on a table in front of us and on the target there was a large photograph of the then Commissioner, Sir Joseph Simpson. I fired the six shots and hit the photograph six times. The army sergeant told me I had reached the required standard and was authorised to use a revolver. I watched as he unloaded the revolver but I never received any instruction in either loading or unloading. I had to work out how to do it for myself. When I paraded for duty that night I was issued with a Webley revolver, a canvas holster and a canvas webbing belt. I was given twelve rounds of ammunition and instructed by the duty officer to go to the parade room and load the gun. I then covered the Russian Embassy protection post for the night.

Matters were no better anywhere else in Britain. In fact, in most cases they were a lot worse as the police service faced the second half of the twentieth century with absolutely no idea of just how much the situation would have to change.

## Chapter 2

# A FIREARMS TRAINING WING

## NATIONAL DEVELOPMENTS

After the Second World War the main preoccupation of the Home Office in London, at least as far as the police use of firearms was concerned, centred on the anticipated role of the police in the event of another war. National discussion on the subject was led by the Central Conference of Chief Constables, Police War Duties Committee, but by June 1957 members were divided. Planners expected any future war to begin with an exchange of thermonuclear missiles. The Deputy Commissioner of the Metropolitan Police, Joseph Simpson, later Sir Joseph Simpson and Commissioner 1958–68, therefore believed that the police's primary functions would be the maintenance of morale and the saving of life. This would be carried out by mobile reserves of officers moved into a devastated area from outside, and he did not believe that guarding key locations, the usual armed police wartime role, would be of much importance. The Chief Constable of Essex, Captain Jonathan Peel, later Sir Jonathan Peel, agreed and suggested that 'this heavy commitment might not be necessary in a nuclear war', although in this he may have been influenced by the previous year's discovery that he was now responsible for distributing weapons should there be an outbreak of hostilities. However, other members argued that 'it may be nuclear rocket warfare will increase the threat of invasion by paratroops or activities by armed saboteurs' and that the need for the police to guard key locations would therefore increase.

The influence of the Cold War continued to have an effect for the next seven years as the various possibilities were argued back and forth, and by August 1964 opinion had swung in yet another direction. There was now 'an almost universal realisation that it would be essential for the police to be armed during the post-attack period if they were to combat looting and if they were to stand a reasonable chance of restoring law and order.'

The idea of mobile reserves, to become known as 'mobile columns', had been devised in 1954 and kept secret. A single police mobile column would be made up of two units, each consisting of a sergeant and ten constables, under the command of an inspector or chief inspector, with 176 police columns covering the whole of Britain. Similar columns would be made up of the Civil Defence Corps, the Auxiliary Fire Service and the National Hospital Services Reserve. It now looked as though the police contribution would need firearms. However, not only had the columns not existed when weapon supply was agreed in 1948, the handguns and rifles were no longer in Essex – and no one knew where they were. In December 1964 the Home Office wrote to Sir Joseph Simpson, now Commissioner, to tell him that a small working party would be formed to resolve the matter once and for all.

The Working Party on Arming the Police in Time of Emergency held its first meeting on 24 January 1965. The Assistant Commissioner 'D' department (ACD), Tom Mahir, represented the Metropolitan Police at the first meeting, after which he handed this responsibility over to Superintendent Lesley Williams who was from a small branch at Scotland Yard referred to simply as D6 War Duties. This 'D' department branch had been formed in June 1952 after a postwar force reorganisation and made responsible for contingency planning in case of another war. Its remit included anything that involved the weapons and ammunition that had been put into store at Mill Hill the previous month. By 1965 D6 consisted of a chief superintendent, three superintendents and a civilian higher executive officer. Superintendent Williams would be promoted to chief superintendent and made the head of D6 in August.

The first meeting was told that the War Office, by now renamed the Ministry of Defence (MoD), had 10,000 rifles and 20,000 revolvers available for the police if war broke out, but this did not satisfy 'Jess' Browne, the Chief Constable of Nottinghamshire. He had served from 1958 to 1960 as the Commissioner of the fully armed UK

Police Unit (UKU) in Cyprus. For the five years of the 'EOKA Conflict' the UKU had consisted of about 150 police officers drawn from forces around the UK on a voluntary two-year posting, and seven of their number had been killed by terrorists. He could therefore argue with some authority that: 'Rifles were out of date; this, no doubt, was why the Ministry of Defence were disposing of them. . . . Sten [sub-machine] guns should be provided for use by the personnel of the mobile columns and for guarding vulnerable points.' As a result, the meeting agreed that: 'The scale of issue should be a revolver for each man, automatic weapons [Stens] for 15%–25% of the strength [of each force] and possibly a supply of tear gas grenades for use in controlling unruly mobs.' For the mobile columns, each man should have a handgun and 'there should be one Sten gun to a sergeant and ten men'.

The meeting then turned to training, but John Inch, the Chief Constable of Edinburgh, expressed concerns over the expense involved and the 'alarm that could be caused if the public heard of this training during the current anxieties about the activities of armed thugs'. Eventually the meeting settled for agreeing that: 'If arms were to be provided, men must be trained in their use; even infrequent training spells, although they would not produce marksman, would suffice to enable weapons to be used to some effect. Training could inconspicuously and conveniently be carried out at airfields or army establishments, during mobile column visits.'

The Sten sub-machine gun had by now been replaced in the British Army by the Sterling and the news that there was a potential customer for some of its obsolete weapons must have been music to the ears of the MoD. The following May, members of the working party were told that although the MoD could not supply enough revolvers, it might be able to provide 20,000 Stens at a cost of £50,000.

Having to pay for weapons was not what the police members of the working party had in mind at all. In 1914 and 1939 the War Office had offered weapons free of charge and the working party saw no reason for this happy arrangement to change. The MoD did not agree. The Home Office then announced that there were only about 250 tear gas grenades in the UK. These were held by the army and: 'Tear gas grenades require skilful handling and if circumstances warranted their use it is likely that the army would be summoned in any case. It would be politically very embarrassing if large quantities of grenades were issued to the police to store in peacetime and this became known.'

This more or less put an end to the discussion on wartime arming, but, since March, Her Majesty's Inspectorate of Constabulary (HMIC) had been conducting a survey to discover 'the arrangements for the provision of firearms in peacetime and for the authorisation of their issue and use'. Of the 122 forces then in existence, only the Metropolitan Police relied on weapons it had bought. Another twenty-five held a combination of purchased weapons and weapons acquired during the war. Ten did not hold any firearms at all and the rest had only acquired weapons in assorted calibres, many of which had last seen active service in the First World War. No question appears to have been asked about the condition of the ammunition available for these weapons, although on reflection this was probably just as well.

Sixty-five forces required the personal directions of the chief constable or the deputy chief constable before firearms could be issued. The Metropolitan Police and forty-three other forces issued weapons on the authority of the officer in nominal charge of the place where the weapons were kept, usually a sergeant or an inspector. Presumably the other three forces either had no directions or did not respond to the HMIC's question. Four forces claimed to have all of their men trained – Nottinghamshire, Oxfordshire, Bristol and Liverpool – although in the case of the last two, there was no further training after officers had been shown how a gun worked. Only forty-two forces gave their officers the opportunity actually to fire a weapon, and in most cases this was with .22 calibre ammunition, a practice that was to continue in some forces well into the 1980s.

Her Majesty's Chief Inspector of Constabulary, Sir Edward Dodd, considered this chaotic situation to be 'far from satisfactory' and suggested that the working party be used to standardise weapons, training and procedures. The Home Office agreed and on 30 June it circulated a draft 'Interim Report on the Arms for the Police in

Peacetime', followed by a slightly revised version on 20 July. The authorship of these reports is uncertain, although they undoubtedly came from HMIC, but they identified three main requirements to be met – arms to be carried on the person as a regular precaution; arms to be available for rapid issue; and arms to be held in reserve. Circumstances in which firearms might be needed were identified as: 'guarding important and threatened persons, searching for or apprehending dangerous lunatics and criminals, guarding special premises and, in certain cases, manning roadblocks designed to catch dangerous criminals.'

The only types of firearm considered necessary for the police were 'the "hand-held gun" – normally to be carried unobtrusively' and the rifle. It was thought that most forces would be able to enlist the help of the army in giving instruction to police officers but that the larger forces might wish to appoint their own instructors who would require expert training. The shooting standards suggested were those in use at the Royal Military Academy at Sandhurst which, with a disregard for the opinions of Fairbairn and Sykes, were four hits out of six at 10 yards (aimed) with a handgun and 63 per cent hits at 300 yards with a rifle.

On the subject of the authority required to issue firearms, the reports proposed that an officer of the rank of superintendent was appropriate but that normally this should only be after consultation with the chief constable or, in his absence, the deputy. This reflected the views of the majority of chief constables that only they should be entrusted with such a decision, but at the time most forces had fewer officers than would be found in an average Metropolitan Police division. In London, superintendents rarely spoke to the Commissioner, let alone consulted him on anything, and even superintendents were hard to pin down. The Home Office was therefore told that: 'We [the Metropolitan Police] cannot guarantee that a superintendent . . . of a sub-division will be immediately available at all times.' In the third draft of the report, circulated the following August, an additional sentence was included: 'We recognise that the special organisation and circumstances of the Metropolitan Police will influence the degree and manner in which our recommendations might be applied in that Force.'

The representatives from Scotland, still concerned about anxiety and expense, did not want any of this to apply to forces north of the border. In the fourth version a sentence was therefore added: 'Although the Working Party included Scottish representatives, their main interest lay in the war emergency aspect. The Scottish position of peacetime arming of the police is being reviewed separately.' To some extent the divide continues to this day.

The final draft was agreed on 10 November by a preliminary meeting of the Central Conference of Chief Constables and then circulated to all forces as the first national guidance on the subject of the police use of firearms in peacetime. Although it was referred to as an interim report, there was no final report. It has to be remembered that the guidance went out to more than 100 chief constables, most of whom were fiercely independent and resistant to outside interference. Any suggestion, particularly by the Home Office, that they should all follow the same procedure on anything was automatically treated with considerable caution, if not actual resentment. The approval of the Central Conference was no more than window dressing and there is little evidence that chief constables took much notice of it.

This reaction must be seen within the context of the attitudes of the time. Many chief officers shared the views of the Chief Constable of Edinburgh and expressed their fears about the possible public reaction to any development in such a controversial area of policing. Most forces did not even publicly admit that they had firearms – hence the need for the otherwise inexplicable reassurance that training could 'inconspicuously and conveniently be carried out at airfields or army establishments'.

### THE SHEPHERDS BUSH MURDERS

On 12 August 1966 at just after 3 o'clock in the afternoon, a Standard Vanguard motorcar drove along Braybrook Street, near Wormwood Scrubs prison in London. The driver was John Witney and sitting in the back was John Duddy. In the front passenger seat was Harry Roberts, an armed robber who had recently been released from prison after serving five years of a seven-year sentence. Also in Braybrook

Street was an unmarked Triumph 2000 police vehicle, known as a 'Q'
car, being driven by Constable Geoffrey Fox. With him were
Detective Sergeant Christopher Head and Detective Constable David
Wombwell. The vehicle, radio call sign 'Foxtrot-one-one', was on a
routine anti-crime patrol in the Shepherds Bush area and the officers
thought that the three men in the Vanguard were acting suspiciously.

Constable Wombwell walked over to them and as he looked inside
the car and spoke to the driver, Roberts leant across and shot him in
the face. Roberts told Duddy to grab a gun and then went after
Sergeant Head, who had also left the police vehicle. Roberts shot at
the sergeant but missed, and the sergeant tried to use his car as cover.
Roberts walked up to him and shot him as he crouched at the front of
the vehicle. He fell to the ground. Duddy then shot Constable Fox
who was still in the driver's seat. As the constable slumped his foot
relaxed on the brake pedal. The car was fitted with an automatic
transmission and as it crept forward the front offside wheel rolled over
the body of Sergeant Head. As the three killers drove away a witness
made a note of the vehicle registration number – PGT 276.

'Massacred in the Line of Duty' was the front-page headline in the
*Daily Mirror* on 13 August, and a half-page photograph showed
Constable Wombwell in the roadway before his body had been
properly covered. Readers were told: 'Two dead detectives lie in a
street, still, silent symbols of the worst crime London has known this
century. More than murder. It was a massacre. Three policemen
savagely gunned down in the line of duty when, unarmed, they ran
into three gunmen.'

On the next page was a photograph of two officers in plain clothes,
one of whom was holding the butt of a Webley and Scott revolver
that he was in the process of putting into his jacket pocket. The
caption underneath read: 'A detective holds a revolver – a weapon he
has been taught to use expertly', and an article explained that: 'All
Britain's policemen are taught to handle small arms expertly.' At the
time there were many who really believed this to be true.

The car was traced to Witney who was soon arrested. The hunt was
on for the other two, but Duddy had already left London to find a
hiding place in Scotland. A detective inspector in the Glasgow

police, David McNee (later Sir David McNee and Commissioner of the Metropolitan Police 1977–82), later wrote:

> Large numbers of police were mustered at Glasgow Central police station, and formed into squads to seek out Duddy. For obvious reasons, selected officers in each squad carried guns. We had successfully traced Duddy's brother Charles and he told us that John Duddy was hiding in a single apartment in Stevenson Street, Bridgeton. The squad of which I was a member went with Charles Duddy to the premises and he let us into the apartment. There we found Duddy, fortunately unarmed and ready to surrender.[1]

It was discovered that Roberts had caught a bus to Epping Forest the day after the shooting and a search of the forest was conducted by a reported 500 officers, many carrying revolvers. There were also hundreds of reported sightings of Roberts and they all had to be checked. The experience of Constable Tony Gray at Kingston police station was typical:

> After Braybrook Street there were sightings of Roberts coming in hourly throughout the country and the police were at full stretch. Word came in that there had been a very strong sighting of Roberts on Ham Common. They called the entire relief in, about a dozen of us, and the sergeant told us that we had to go up there and get him. Then he asked whether any of us was an authorised shot. Everyone sort of shuffled their feet and looked at each other and asked what an authorised shot was. Next he asked which of us was qualified to carry a pistol. There was more shuffling of feet and we asked what he meant. When the sergeant asked us whether anybody had got any experience of revolvers I said that I had. I had been in the Armoured Corps in the army and in the fifties you trained on a Webley. You fired it once a year and as long as you heard it go bang, or saw a photograph of somebody else who had, then you were qualified.
>
> The sergeant got this Webley out. It was in a cardboard box, still wrapped in greaseproof paper. It had never been issued, never been

cleaned, nothing. I clearly remember his instructions to me. After giving me the gun with a box of ammunition he said: 'Don't you load it whatever you do, but most importantly don't you bloody well use it on anybody. You just go out there and arrest this bloke and then bring that thing back to me and I'll put it away.' I sat in the van with this 'thing' sitting on my knees in its box like it was red hot. When we got to the common the blokes said: 'Don't get out Tony – we'll do it. You just sit there with that and then we'll take it back and give it to the sergeant.' Obviously it turned out not to be Roberts.

On 12 November a camouflaged hideaway used by Roberts was found in Thorley Woods in Hertfordshire, several miles north of Epping Forest.

The trial of Duddy and Witney started on 14 November and on the same day a search of Thorley Woods was mounted involving officers from the Metropolitan, Hertfordshire and Essex police forces, many of them armed. At about 11.45 in the morning two Hertfordshire officers were looking in an old hangar that was full of bales of straw. Pushing aside the bales, one of the men saw a sleeping bag. Giving the bag a good prod with his rifle, the officer was rewarded with the appearance of an unshaven Roberts.

The trial of Duddy and Witney was halted and the Crown proffered a bill of indictment against Roberts, which meant that he could be taken straight to the Old Bailey to join the other two in the dock. A new trial began on 6 December and after all three had been found guilty of all three murders they were each sentenced to thirty years in prison. The judge, Mr Justice Glyn-Jones, described the murders as 'the most heinous crime for a generation or more'.

Public outrage at the shootings was expressed by way of donations handed in to police stations all over the UK. Sir Billy Butlin, the holiday camp pioneer, donated £100,000, and as the total grew it formed the basis for the Police Dependants Trust. This was registered as a charity in January 1967 and it has provided financial assistance to police officers who have been injured or the families of those killed ever since.

## FIREARMS TRAINING

The flaws in the system that had shown up during the searches for Roberts were so obvious that the Commissioner resolved to use the Interim Report to make changes. Even before the trial of Roberts, Witney and Duddy had started, he decided that his force would indeed buy rifles and that the shortage of qualified officers could only be overcome by greatly increasing the divisional allocation. As far as training was concerned, the Commissioner directed that every authorised officer should be properly trained, have a refresher course every four months and re-qualify every year. 'D' department was told to make the necessary arrangements and this instruction was passed on to D6 in turn, probably for no better reason than it had been involved in the national discussions and must therefore know more about the subject than anyone else. On 30 November 1966 Chief Superintendent Williams reported:

> I have contacted the Small Arms Wing of the School of Infantry at Hythe and they have had some previous experience of training police in the use of firearms. . . . I have discussed the matter with the Chief Instructor at the School and he can fit a course to suit our requirements. . . . There would be no cost for the instruction given on this course and the sole cost to police would be the provision of ammunition.

The course was to be for instructors, and in December applications were sought from inspectors, sergeants and constables to go on a 'residential course of five days' duration at the Small Arms Wing of the School of Infantry, Hythe, Kent from 2 to 6 January 1967'.[2]

Finding somewhere that could provide the 'expert training' envisaged by the Interim Report had not been easy. There was no real alternative to using the presumed expertise of Hythe, and it probably helped that the tuition was being offered free of charge, but training someone to shoot was not the same as training police officers how and, more importantly, when to use a firearm. Two of the first officers to go through the process were Constables Arthur Batten and Kris Freeland.

*Arthur Batten*

When I left the RAF Regiment in 1948 I joined the Metropolitan Police and took up competition rifle and pistol shooting. Then 'Foxtrot-one-one' happened and I applied [to join D6] and we went to the old Scotland Yard building on the Embankment for the interviews. There were quite a few that went up and I went in first because the initials of my name were AAB. Going to Hythe was like being back in the forces. They stuck us in a Nissen hut just outside Hythe camp and we did a lot of shooting but I'd already done all that in the services.

They gave us an office in an old brick building in the courtyard at Scotland Yard for a couple or three days and then we were moved to Old Street and we spent several months forming a curriculum. We were split into pairs with each inspector and sergeant having a constable to pair with. Each individual pair was given a subject to work on and to produce what they thought should be taught. The rest of us would then criticise it and the end result was then accepted generally.

*Kris Freeland*

I was a constable at Ilford when there was this terrible hiatus over Roberts. There were lots of people airing their views on what should and what should not have been done. Quite a few officers applied to join [D6] but many never even got as far as the interview boards. From then on it all went through in a rush. The idea of Hythe was that we could then be qualified as firearms instructors. Unfortunately, in the armed forces a handgun was more a badge of office – officers carried a handgun but rarely fired one. A lieutenant who could hit a barn door at twenty paces was on for free drinks in the mess. Hythe was the same and they did not have the experience to teach us anything. With hindsight it was not the best training we could have got.

We all had to do an instructor's course at Peel House as well. They were so concerned about this bunch of outsiders turning up at Peel House – where all the recruits were – that we had to leave a few minutes before they all packed up for the day so that they [the

recruits] didn't see us. The inspector who took us was very honest
and told us at the start that he knew nothing about our subject. In
the very early days we were invited to visit a variety of army and
other establishments. We were very well received everywhere we
went and the general view was one of amazement that we had only
just begun. Due to his ability to organise, [Inspector] Bob Gould was
the lynchpin that pulled the whole thing together and by good
fortune we had a tip-top armourer in [Constable] John Ferguson –
known as 'The Farrier'.

The new instructors had to start from scratch and the
accommodation that was eventually found for them consisted of
several small offices above a garage at the former Old Street police
station in Shoreditch, central London. They wrote their own 95-page
instruction manual, and the first of the new 'basic defensive weapons'
courses started on 3 April 1967. There were ten officers to a pair of
instructors and the course lasted four days. The first morning was
spent at Old Street learning the drills, the technical data and the
safety rules to be observed when handling weapons. The afternoon
was spent firing .22 calibre ammunition on an indoor range. The
second day was spent on an indoor range firing either .380 or 9mm
ammunition, depending on the weapon being taught, and on the
third day students went to Lippitts Hill camp, 20 miles from central
London in Epping Forest at High Beech near Loughton in Essex, to
learn 'fieldcraft'.

The Metropolitan Police had bought the camp from the War Office
in 1960 with additional purchases of grazing land in 1962. The site
totalled about 24 acres and had been used at varying times as an anti-
aircraft battery position, an underground communications centre and
a prisoner-of-war camp. One of the old POW huts was used as an
instructors' office and another as a classroom where students were
introduced to the technicalities of which materials constituted cover
from fire, search techniques and how to take the surrender of an
armed suspect. On the final day the students went back to an indoor
range where, after another practice, they had to pass a qualification
shoot. Unlike the Sandhurst version, this test consisted of using 'sense

of direction' at 7 yards and using the sights for aimed shooting at distances of up to 25 yards.

On 17 May the Home Office gave formal authority for the purchase of twenty army-surplus Lee Enfield No. 4 .303 calibre rifles from the MoD and for an increase in the size of the Metropolitan Police. The latter was for the formation of a Firearms Training Wing consisting of two inspectors, three sergeants, five constables, one executive officer and one clerical officer within D6 Branch. It was a small beginning, but at least it was a start.

Chapter 3

# TEETHING PROBLEMS

### THE TRAINING IS REVEALED

It was not long before rumours about what the Metropolitan Police was up to started to circulate, and representatives of the news media were invited to see what was happening. If the result caused any alarm there was no sign of it when, on 21 April 1967, the *Daily Mail* published photographs of two officers firing Webley revolvers on an indoor range and readers were told: 'These two policemen are training to be crack shots. . . . Men like this, training in the basement at City Road police station . . . will be few and far between. They will become members of a select squad of small-arms experts who will be called on in an emergency.'

In addition to newspaper coverage, a film crew was given access to an indoor range and to Lippitts Hill. In the resulting news item it was explained that for the officers undergoing training:

Their sole justification [in using a firearm] is to save themselves or a civilian from a gunman and to make an arrest. It's the instinctive shooting [as 'sense of direction' shooting was also known] that's most dramatic. They reckon to get off ten rounds in 24 seconds, 1 second faster than the FBI. . . . Extensive training like this started only recently for, with no conscription, the police can't now rely on a large proportion of their men having been trained in the use of firearms by the forces. . . . On the range these students learn to handle weapons and to shoot straight, but it is at Lippitts Hill, a former gun site and prisoner-of-war camp in Epping Forest that they are taught to put the knowledge to use. . . . Responsible for this training is 'D' division [sic] Metropolitan Police, the department in charge of what's called war training. It's not quite as ominous as it sounds. War training in this instance means the special training of police for their slightly different role in the event of a nuclear war.

There is very little in the contemporary records to suggest that the ending of national service in 1960 had been so significant for the level of weapons expertise the police could draw on, and it is more likely that this was just a face-saving explanation given at the time. This introduction was followed by an interview with Chief Superintendent Williams who, when he took command of the War Duties branch just over a year and a half earlier, could hardly have imagined that he would end up on national television explaining why the police had started firearms training in peacetime. When he was asked, 'Does this mean that there is a change of policy; that more policemen are carrying weapons these days?' he replied, 'No, none at all. No change at all.' In response to the question 'Are police officers having to face more criminals carrying weapons these days?' he said, 'Well, it does look as if there is an increase in the use of firearms but this is not the reason why we have done this training. This is something we've thought about for a long time and, well, it just happened to have come along now.'

By October 1967 decisions had been made on the number of officers to be trained and the new arrangements were set out in a complete revision of the standing instructions.[1] The twenty-four authorised officers in each division were increased to sixty and 'such officers of Special Branch as ACC [Assistant Commissioner 'C' department] may direct' were also to be trained. In May 1969, almost as an afterthought, '115 officers of the Traffic Division' were added to the list, bringing the total in London by the end of 1972 to 2,097.[2]

Just because formal firearms training had started this did not mean that the practices of the past died out overnight. Officers authorised under the old system were still issued with firearms until sufficient numbers had gone through a course, and the two systems worked in parallel for several years, although there were no more annual practices.

## THE TRAINING

The instructors soon settled down to a routine of basic and refresher training courses, and they made changes when they found that their initial ideas did not work out. For instance, officers were initially taught to fire a handgun one-handed when using it at 7 yards. This practice had been adopted as a result of a visit the new instructors paid to one of the old forts still used by the MoD on the south coast near Lee-on-the-Solent in Hampshire when they were looking for ideas in early 1967. The site was used to give firearms training to non-military personnel who were travelling abroad on clandestine business for Her Majesty's government.

*Kris Freeland*
It was all very hush-hush and we were sworn to secrecy about the place. To my surprise we met up with a chap who had been the SAI [small arms instructor] who took me on my course in the Marines. This way of shooting was his brainchild and ideally you would be facing slightly to your right. On the command 'make ready' you did this little jump and landed square on to the target in a slightly crouched position with both arms out in front of you and with the gun at eye level. The non-gun hand was held parallel to, and alongside, the gun hand. At the time it was really new, but there's no doubt about it, it did have limitations.

To understand why the instructors passed on this way of shooting despite its 'limitations' it must first be realised that there was (and still is) no definitive method of shooting at close quarters. The ideas pioneered by Fairbairn and Sykes had spread but, as they were passed from instructor to instructor, small changes had crept in. Fairbairn and Sykes had advocated that a handgun should be fired one-handed for close-quarter shooting, but neither the placing of the other hand alongside the gun hand nor the 'little jump' had come from them. Nevertheless, the derivatives all still retained the same basic principles, and the variant chosen by D6 at least had the advantage of being home-grown. As if to illustrate the point about making changes, the 'little jump' was omitted from the police version, but even Sir John Waldron, Commissioner of the Metropolitan Police 1968–72, had trouble mastering the technique.

### Kris Freeland

One day I had occasion to take the Commissioner on the range but he was inclined, as was very common, to try to fire the gun by gripping tighter with his whole hand rather than by just using his trigger finger. It suddenly flashed through my mind that I had heard he liked to play squash and so I asked him whether he played any sports such as tennis or badminton. He told me that he prided himself on playing a lot of squash and that gave me the chance to say that, in my opinion, he was suffering from having one sport competing against another and that he had an over-developed right arm. It made his day and it got me off the hook.

### Arthur Batten

After we had started the training we realised that with the single-handed grip they [the students] seemed to pull the weapon to the right. Most of us had quite a lot of experience with pistols and could just up and shoot, but to the complete novice we found that they weren't capable of doing it and so we then incorporated the double-handed grip.

The two-handed shooting stance eventually adopted would be described in textbooks as the 'isosceles position' (the two arms forming the sides of the triangle with the chest forming the base).

The instructors were learning valuable lessons and their services were soon in demand abroad. In 1970 Sergeant, later Chief Superintendent, Bob Wells was seconded to the Malawi government to train the bodyguard of the President, Dr Hastings Kamuzu Banda:

I arrived at Chelika airport, Malawi, on 18 September and was met by two Special Branch officers from the Malawi police who drove me to Zomba, my base for both accommodation and work. The first week of actual involvement with the guard consisted of watching their methods and noting their degree of success with all the weapons they used. These included Smith and Wesson revolvers, Stirling sub-machine guns, shotguns, and rifles. From the second week as many of the guard as could be spared from guard duty received an adapted form of Metropolitan Police training to increase their accuracy with their short-barrelled revolver.

It was our first involvement with overseas training and it really was 'Darkest Africa' stuff a lot of the time. I provided some drawings and with bits of string and springs the local police transport depot produced 'pop-up' targets. They [the students] had a preoccupation with snakes (understandable to a degree). You could make a protection drill interesting by shouting 'njoka' (snake) loudly, which brought about a starburst reaction by the 'close protection' squad, leaving a startled 'principal' looking around at nobody at all. Once the initial minor difficulties were overcome with regard to equipment and methods, training progressed steadily and a total of eighty-five men were trained, including both the guard and the Special Branch police officers.

Having learned from the experience of going to Hythe, the instructors ran their own instructors' courses to make up for shortages in their number and they also trained officers from other forces in the UK. The Royal Ulster Constabulary (RUC), now the Police Service of Northern Ireland (PSNI), had been armed since its formation in 1922 and from the beginning it had a duality of function. In addition to normal police duties, it was also responsible for the security of the state, but the recommendations in the 1969 Hunt Report resulted in a reorganisation of the force to bring its rank structure and organisation into line with those on the mainland. Colin Burrows, later a Chief Superintendent in the RUC, remembers:

At my recruitment interview in January 1971 I was asked by one of the selection panel how I felt about joining an unarmed police force. The disarmament and reorganisation of the RUC had started a few months earlier as a result of the recommendations of the Hunt Committee. I entered the RUC training centre in Enniskillen in

September 1971 and in October a number of police officers' homes in Belfast were the subject of gun and bomb attacks by the fledgling Provisional Irish Republican Army [PIRA]. It was clear that officers were becoming the subject of terrorist attack both on and off duty and it was decided that it was necessary to issue side arms for personal protection. I recall seeing the training centre instructors all going to the armoury on a Friday evening to be issued with .38 Webley revolvers before going on operational weekend duties.

The following week, all the officers in training were told that there was to be a change to our training programme and that following our passing out parade in December we were to go to Belfast for a one-week 'weapon training course'. The course was held in the old Belfast ropeworks where the long rooms used to lay out ropes had been converted to form two indoor ranges. The course was conducted by former RUC weapon instructors who had just returned from a firearms instructors' course run by the London Metropolitan Police. The intention was that weapon training would be brought into line with that being provided in London and elsewhere, and they would train 10 per cent of the RUC in the use of firearms. Instead, the course that I attended in January 1972 became the forerunner of basic, refresher and specialist firearms training provided to all members of the RUC.

## OLD ATTITUDES

A phenomenon that the instructors in London had to learn how to deal with was having their training disregarded. For example, officers were trained to comply with a regulation that 'when a weapon is issued to an officer, it will be loaded by him and placed in a holster'. This order had been in existence since 1936 (before then the weapon had to be loaded by a supervising officer), but some officers in London were still being issued with firearms with instructions not to load them, as Constable Ron Parrish discovered:

During the late sixties and early seventies many Christmas clubs were subjected to raids by armed criminals. To combat this, some officers were armed and were carried on ordinary patrol in local police cars. Authorised officers were also used on bank days – those days when substantial amounts of cash were to be withdrawn or delivered to various banks. We were issued with a .38 Webley revolver and given twelve rounds of ammunition, and our usual instruction was to load the weapon with six rounds and keep the remaining six in a pocket. However, our superintendent at the time forbade us to load the weapon.

A few senior officers, particularly those on the outer divisions, found it hard to accede to their men carrying firearms under any circumstances, irrespective of what the regulations allowed. For them, *The Blue Lamp* provided the policing model to which their officers should adhere, and as guardians of the Dixon image, their ludicrous solution was to issue firearms and then direct that they must not be loaded. In this way the senior officer could claim that his men were not really armed because the weapons were useless, at least until they had been loaded, thereby making possession of them virtually meaningless.

## THE USE OF CS

Although the Home Office had expressed concern that for police to hold a 'supply of tear gas grenades for use in controlling unruly mobs' would be politically embarrassing, the Home Secretary, Sir Frank Soskice, did in fact give authority for police to acquire CS. It was for a different purpose and a statement to that effect was made in the House of Commons on 28 May 1965. Members were told that the CS would 'be used only in circumstances similar to those in which the issue of conventional firearms to police is authorised – that is to effect the arrest of armed besieged criminals or violently and dangerously insane persons'. CS (o-chlorobenzylidene malononitrile) had been discovered by two American scientists, Carson and Stroughton – hence CS – and developed in the 1950s by the MoD for use by the army for riot control.

In April 1967 the instructors were put on a rota to be available in case the use of CS was required, and so began their combined training and operational role, a practice that would be replicated by most other forces in the years to come. In July, an internal reorganisation of the force changed D6's designation to D11 and 'War Duties' became 'Home Defence Training and War Planning'. From May 1971 the personal authority of the Deputy Assistant Commissioner 'A' department (operations) (DACA (ops)) was required before D11 officers could be used operationally and two months later a request for such authority resulted in CS being used for the first time in London.

On 29 July at just after 10 o'clock in the evening police were called to 17 Olive Road, Cricklewood, in north-west London, where they found the bodies of Winston McKenzie and his wife Edna. The body of their American son-in-law, Richard Simms, was discovered at the bottom of the garden. All had been stabbed to death. The couple's daughter, Candy, was seriously injured and both she and her young child, who was unhurt, were taken to hospital.

The person responsible was the McKenzies' son, Michael, and he had barricaded himself into an upstairs bedroom. He was armed with two carving knives and was described as being 'obviously demented and berserk'. With the authority of the DACA (ops), two instructors were sent for and they brought with them a supply of CS. One was Sergeant Jim White:

> When we arrived we found that the man had barricaded himself in a first-floor rear bedroom of a terraced house. I had a long discussion with the local commander who initially wanted me to fire a round of CS through the bedroom window from the back garden, but I decided it was best fired into the bedroom from the loft space. Trying to explain to the local armed officers that when the CS went in the suspect would come out had been difficult. They all lined up on the landing outside the bedroom door and when I fired the CS the suspect smashed the only window in the room. When the officers on the landing heard the sound of breaking glass they started to force the door, despite my telling them to wait for the suspect to come out. Then the suspect pulled away the barricade on the inside of the bedroom door and ran along the landing. He had a knife tied to each hand with tea towels and

he lashed out as he ran along the landing. At the top of the stairs was Detective Constable Fred Arnold who grabbed at the knives and caught the blades, one in each hand. Both men then tumbled down the stairs, and [Constable Jack Parkes] went into the barricaded room, which was now on fire, and put the fire out with a bucket of water.

McKenzie tried to escape 45 seconds after the CS was fired and in the struggle to get him into a straitjacket, several officers lost their respirators. The CS affected nearly everyone, including a doctor who went into the house to attend to the injuries sustained by the detective constable. The doctor reportedly felt better later after being given a cup of coffee laced with whisky at Harlesden police station.

Early the next day a chief inspector and an inspector from the D11 went back into the house. When they entered the room used by McKenzie neither could feel the effects of the CS until they disturbed the carpet and moved the curtains. They were then obliged to leave rather rapidly.

*Jim White*
Between 8 and 9 the next morning the telephone rang and I was told to report to Scotland Yard in my best uniform as soon as possible. Jack had been told to do the same. At Scotland Yard we were interviewed by the press. Later that same day Chief Superintendent Lyons [the officer now commanding D11] interviewed Jack and myself, and after a full debriefing told us that the local authority had refused to decontaminate the room. He was looking for two volunteers and as Jack and I were the only two present, it was us. We spent the next couple of days scrubbing curtains, clothes and carpets to get rid of the CS. The national press found out about this and took great pleasure in referring to us as 'The Mrs Mops of the Met'.

On 31 July the *Daily Express* told its readers: 'An assurance that CS gas will never be used by police under riot situations was given yesterday after a canister was used in London for the first time to flush out a man in a death house siege. A spokesman said the incident perfectly demonstrated the purpose for which the gas is intended.'

## LEAD POLLUTION

As early as January 1971 the instructors had started to express their concerns about the lead-filled atmosphere in which they had to work. None of the indoor ranges had been designed for the regular heavy use to which they were now being subjected, and Chief Superintendent Lyons asked the force Medical branch to arrange for the officers to have a check. This was carried out in April 1972 and the results showed that some instructors had an unacceptably high level of lead in their bloodstream. The use of indoor ranges therefore ceased (with a few rare exceptions) and the training was transferred to the MoD ranges at Rainham and Purfleet in Essex. These were two of three outdoor rifle ranges on the Thames estuary, downstream from London. The third was at Milton near Gravesend in Kent.

Moving the training had the disadvantage that students had to travel some distance before any instruction could start, but it also had an unexpected benefit. It gave officers the opportunity to fire hand-guns outdoors and at distances greater than 25 yards. It surprised the instructors to see how accuracy suffered when some students, who had only ever used indoor ranges, tried to acclimatise to shooting in ordinary daylight. However, when the instructors were tested again in August they showed another increase in blood/lead levels and all training was suspended in November.

## RIFLES

Of course, the Metropolitan Police was now the owner of some army-surplus .303 calibre rifles in addition to its handguns, but there had been little in the Interim Report to indicate what they were actually for. Although no one can now remember why, by August 1970 there were two at each of the divisional stations of Richmond, Golders Green, Ilford, Brixton and West Drayton (the last probably because of its proximity to Heathrow airport). Finding officers with rifle experience gained in the armed forces had not been difficult, and a handful from each station had been given a few days' training to remind them of the basics. It soon became apparent, however, that the guns had not been such a bargain after all. The North Atlantic Treaty Organisation (NATO) had adopted the 7.62mm as the common rifle calibre in the early 1950s and the .303 rifle cartridge was becoming obsolete.

It was also gradually realised that a police officer was likely to use a rifle under circumstances entirely different from anything expected of the average soldier and that his training should be more akin to that given to a sniper using a rifle fitted with a telescopic sight. The force therefore decided to cut its losses and start again. Volunteers with previous 'competition and/or target shooting experience' were sought from all divisions and there were hundreds of applicants. The number had to be whittled down to a manageable figure and the solution was to introduce a test.

### Ron Parrish

The preliminary tests were carried out at Purfleet. Each participant was given a Lee Enfield No. 4 rifle together with five rounds and told to fire a group of five rounds from a distance of 100 yards at a target. The idea was to group shots on the target, not to achieve any particular score, and it had to be done without using a rest or a sling. The group for the first five rounds was measured and the 'pass' was, I think, a 4-inch group. Any firer with a larger group was eliminated and the remaining officers were again required to fire a further five rounds. The best twenty were accepted for further training. Surprisingly, many excellent shots with .22 calibre rifles couldn't cope with the larger calibre.

Another officer who applied was Constable Bert Harris.

We did the test at Purfleet Ranges. I think we did two lots of groups and a 4-inch group or less was required. Using the No. 4 rifle with no slings or rests proved difficult for all the .22 shots who were not used to shooting like that and when combined with the greater

recoil of the rifle, they failed. I had spent twenty-two years in the
army with a greater part of that time being in the regimental rifle
team. With the TA battalion I was the permanent staff instructor
and my company team became the battalion champions, but it was
only when I did the Metropolitan Police rifle course that I really
started to learn how to shoot.

Those selected were given their two-week course in February 1971
and the weapons used were 7.62mm Lee Enfield L42A1 sniper rifles
borrowed from the MoD. The qualification tests took place in the
middle of the second week and involved distances of 300–600 yards
with a pass mark of 80 per cent.

In February 1972 the force was told that the .303 rifles were being
withdrawn and that 'district rifle officers' would be distributed
throughout the force instead. At the scene of an incident they would
come under the command of the senior officer present, although it was
emphasised that 'it must be left to the discretion of the specialist officers
whether or not to fire'.[3] This is the first mention in writing of the
principle that a police officer, whether armed with a rifle or a handgun,
cannot be ordered to shoot. In most cases this still remains true today,
although the terrorist atrocities in the US in September 2001 would
result in new tactics being devised to deal with 'determined and deadly
attacks' and these would call this axiom into question.

## NATIONAL DEVELOPMENTS

By 1970 the wide variations between forces had attracted the
attention of the Police Federation. This body represents police officers
from the rank of constable to chief inspector. The *Guardian* reported
on 9 April 1970: 'The Police Federation is asking the Home Secretary
to establish a standardised, nation-wide system of weapons training for
police. They want all policemen given intensive training in the use of
guns and want the Home Office to select a standard-issue handgun for
issue to all constables.'

The result of this lobbying was the creation of the Working Party
on Firearms for Police Use in Peacetime. It was chaired by HMIC and

in July 1971 it acquired an advisory body to help it with its work. This was known as the Consultative Panel of Firearms Instructors, and the panel and the working party were to change the face of British police firearms training more than any other group before or since.

In April 1972 the main working party published a report produced by the panel on weapons suggested as being suitable for police use. The Smith and Wesson Model 10 revolver in .38 Special calibre was put forward as the future general-purpose police revolver. Under the heading 'Guns for the Continuously Armed Police Officer' were listed the Smith and Wesson Model 36 revolver in .38 Special calibre and the Walther PP self-loading pistol in either 9mm (.380) or 7.65mm (.32) calibre. The recommended police rifle was a modified L39A1 military target rifle in 7.62mm calibre, later to become known as the 'Enfield Enforcer', which was about to go into production at the Royal Small Arms Factory (RSAF) in Enfield. The Metropolitan Police took delivery of the first batch of the new rifles in December 1973 and some officers still have fond memories of them.

*Arthur Batten*
They made a special sniper rifle for us at Enfield. It didn't have a name when we got it but we were fortunate because we had the rifle even before the army had it. I had a beautiful weapon – it was beautifully balanced and we were issued with them as a personal issue. They were all marked in their boxes and nobody else could use them because of their telescopic sights; we worked the sights out to suit ourselves. I used to get hold of mine quite often and get Joe Lyons' permission to take it and I'd go away shooting with it.

Next the panel turned its attention to training. A survey of all forces in England and Wales (by now reduced by amalgamations to about seventy) found that nearly 40 per cent of all police firearms courses lasted one day or less and only thirty-two forces included any form of tactical training. In September 1972 the panel proposed that the basic training course should be a minimum of five days long and that it should include both handgun shooting and tactics. Three-day seminars on tactics were suggested for all senior officers. Importantly, the panel believed that instructors should be police officers trained within the police service and that a new National Police Firearms Centre should be created for their training. As the panel was to discover, although most of its recommendations would eventually be accepted, the creation of a single point of firearms expertise for the police would be a step too far and the opportunity to do so would be lost, probably for ever.

*Chapter 4*

# CRIME AND TERRORISM

### SHOTS FIRED IN KENSINGTON

Constable Peter Slimon paraded for duty as usual at Kensington police station in central London on 27 December 1972 at 5.45 in the morning. He was posted to a protection post at the South Gate of Palace Green, a private road containing a number of foreign embassies including those of Russia, Czechoslovakia, Israel and Romania, and at just after 6.30 he booked out a Webley and Scott revolver and twelve rounds of ammunition. As generations of police officers had done before him, he put the loaded weapon into the outside pocket of his overcoat. Having covered the post for the first two hours of his four-hour stint, he returned to the police station and, after having breakfast, he took out several routine messages that needed to be delivered. Then, to pass the time before he returned to the post, he walked along Kensington High Street. As he gave directions to passers-by he could have been in a scene straight out of *The Blue Lamp*.

There was a great deal of congestion in the middle of Kensington High Street with traffic trying to turn into Campden Hill Road, and at the junction on the corner there was a National Westminster bank. As Constable Slimon crossed the road to deal with the traffic congestion, he suddenly realised that a man was putting a ladder across the bank entrance and that everything looked very wrong.

Someone rushed past him saying, 'They've got guns', and Constable Slimon drew the revolver from his pocket. When he approached the doorway of the bank he could see a man standing at the counter. As he moved closer he saw another man to his right, tucked in by the doorframe, and this individual had a gun. Constable Slimon announced that he was an armed police officer and the man at the counter turned to face him with a double-barrelled shotgun in his hands. The robber and Constable Slimon both fired at the same time and the officer had no idea whether he hit his target or not because he was thrown backwards by the blast from the shotgun. As he landed on the pavement, he found that his left arm was bleeding profusely and that he could not use it. He still had the revolver in his right hand but that hand was also covered in blood.

He got up, but as he walked forward three men came running out towards him. When one of them pointed a pistol at him, Constable Slimon found he did not have the strength left in his one good hand to squeeze the trigger of his gun. He managed to fire the weapon using 'single action', that is to say he cocked the hammer manually first, and this reduced the trigger pressure enough to allow him to fire one more shot. The robbers got into a van and Constable Slimon memorised the registration number. He kept saying it out loud so that he would not forget it.

While Constable Slimon was waiting for help and an ambulance, the robbers changed vehicles not far away in Pitt Street. As they were doing so, a police dog van appeared and the robbers left a wounded member of the gang behind in their panic to escape. The dead body of another member of the gang, Robert John Hart, was later found not far away on the fifth floor of a multi-storey car park where he had also been abandoned.

Hart was the first person to be shot and killed by police in Britain in more than twenty years and hundreds of messages of support were received at police stations but, according to the *Daily Mirror* under the heading 'The Police and their Guns',

A new controversy over the arming of Britain's policemen flared yesterday following the cops-and-robbers gun battle at a London bank. . . . Labour's spokesman on home affairs, Mr John Fraser, said 'I think we need to know how many police are now carrying firearms. We want to know how many police guarding embassies carry guns and what is the justification for it.' . . . The Labour MP for Hackney Central warned of the possibility of Britain's police becoming armed through a process of stealth.

There were others who thought that Constable Slimon had been issued with a firearm for the protection of embassies, not so that he could tackle armed robbers. For that he should first have sought permission. The *Daily Telegraph* in its editorial thought otherwise: 'The suggestion that he should have hurried to his post, leaving the staff and customers of the National Westminster bank to their fate, or alternatively that he should have gone to the nearest telephone box to get the approval of his superiors for intervention in the raid is clearly absurd. It belongs to the realms of liberal fantasy.'

## ANNUAL STATISTICS

Having been asked how many of the police guarding embassies were carrying firearms, the Home Secretary, Robert Carr, passed the question on to his staff, who did not know. No one in the police knew either, and so in January 1973 the Home Office conducted a survey of all forces under three headings – the number of occasions when firearms were issued for specific incidents, for the protection of persons and for the protection of property.[1] There had been no central record before because there had never been any reason to keep one. However, to counter the claim that Britain's police could become 'armed through a process of stealth', it would now be necessary to reveal the true extent of police arming and, as events were to show, this would never happen. Only the figures for 'specific incidents' were made public, a practice which continues to this day, and no one seems to have noticed that as a result, the issuing of the weapon to Constable Slimon was not included.

Nevertheless, the results showed that the overwhelming majority of 'specific incidents' were in London and that the numbers were increasing. In 1970 the total for the Metropolitan Police was 803 out of an England and Wales combined figure of 1,072, with the forces of West Midlands, Cumbria, Dorset and Bournemouth, Dyfed-Powys, Gwynedd, Mid Anglia, Teeside, West Mercia and Wiltshire showing no firearms issued at all. Twenty-six other forces did not reach double figures and the highest total after that recorded by the Metropolitan Police was shown by Liverpool and Bootle

Constabulary with thirty-eight. In 1971 the total for the Metropolitan Police was 1,344 out of 1,935 for England and Wales and in 1972 it was 1,712 out of 2,237.

## INTERNATIONAL TERRORISM

The removal of the .303 calibre rifles from West Drayton in early 1972 had left a vacuum in terms of an armed response that could be despatched to Heathrow at a time when airports and aircraft were under threat. As the *Daily Mail* reported on 18 September 1972: 'No one, not anyone, who boards an airliner in this most violent year of 1972 can escape the shadow of the escalating evil of air travel – hijacking. No one can be certain that their plane will not become the target for an air bandit, holding their lives to ransom to further his own cause, political or personal.'

In 1970 the International Air Transport Association had recorded ninety-one hijacks, the most spectacular taking place in September when two airliners were seized over Europe and taken to Dawson's Field in Jordan. A third was hijacked to Cairo and the taking of a fourth, flying from London to Amsterdam, failed when a sky marshal shot dead Patrick Arguello and Leila Khaled was arrested. A fifth was hijacked to Dawson's Field three days later to provide hostages for the release of Khaled, who was duly let go, and this resulted in the use of D11 officers at Heathrow for the first time.

*Arthur Batten*
The arrest of Khaled started it off. At the time Heathrow had its own British Airports Authority police and they had no armed officers. We were directed that we had to cover Heathrow airport and I was there for about six weeks. We worked shift duty so that there were at least two of us on duty covering the full twenty-four hours. I was there with [Constable] Nick Carter and I was directed that I had to take my sniper rifle and sidearm. When I got to the airport Nick was already there and we had to act under the directions of the airport police. We used to patrol with the duty officer at Heathrow the whole time.

Other hijackings included a Lufthansa airliner in February 1972 and in May a Sabena airliner from Tel Aviv was hijacked to Lod airport. In September seven terrorists took control of the Israeli athletes' village at the Olympic Games in Munich, killing two and taking nine hostages. In a subsequent rescue attempt at Fürstenfeldbrück airport, all the hostages were killed along with five of the terrorists and a police officer. The following month a Lufthansa airliner from Beirut to Ankara was hijacked by terrorists demanding the freedom of the two survivors – who were duly released. This international terrorism would lead directly to the creation of the specialist counter-terrorist teams of the Special Air Service (SAS) and to the formation of specialist firearms teams in London. However, while these counter-measures were still being discussed, there was an immediate need to fill the gap in the response to an incident at Heathrow.

In April 1972 Sergeant White and Constable Parkes attended an army sniper's course at Lympstone to increase the size of the pool of qualified rifle instructors, and in January 1973 the duration of the Metropolitan Police rifle course was increased to three weeks. Officers from the Special Patrol Group (SPG), a contingent of uniformed officers formed in 1961 on the principles of the mobile columns, were then selected and trained as rifle officers specifically to undertake any response required at Heathrow.

*Tony Gray*
At the beginning of the terrorist troubles it was realised that to get district rifle officers to the airport quickly might take time. There was an SPG Unit at Hounslow with their own transport, communications, command set up and call out system. It made sense that, if they were to be going to the airport anyway in the event of a major incident, the SPG should have rifle officers. Everyone on 1 and 4 Units went for a shoot at Purfleet and from that they selected a dozen to go on the course, six from each Unit. The assessment was on .303 Mk 4s with open sights, and of the twelve that were selected to go on the course, eight of us passed. They then told us that as we were not authorised to use revolvers

we had to very quickly do a basic course. At first we had the No. 4 Lee Enfield's in 7.62mm with the army scope on them. Then the army wanted all their accurate rifles back and so we had to buy our own. I had Enfield Enforcer number 002 – number two off the production line.

On 4 January 1974 Sir Robert Mark had a meeting with his head of Special Branch and the Assistant Commissioner 'A' department (ACA). They had information that terrorists had access to ground-to-air missiles and that they had undertaken a reconnaissance of Heathrow airport. The Commissioner later wrote:

The likelihood of finding a small team of determined men can never be high. The chances of finding and killing them after using weapons are much better if adequate preparations are made, and this itself is a useful deterrent. All that is necessary is protective armour, weapons capable of penetrating buildings and adequate manpower. In other words, the army.[2]

The following morning, soldiers were seen patrolling Heathrow for the first time and by April the decision had been taken that the Metropolitan Police would take over the policing of the airport.

### INDIA HOUSE

At about 9.30 on the morning of 20 February 1973, three Pakistani youths raided India House, the offices of the Indian High Commission in the Aldwich in central London. Wearing stocking masks and armed with a sword, two revolvers, three knives and a bottle containing nitric acid, they took hostages who were forced to lie on the floor. The first officers to arrive were unarmed and they retreated after being threatened with the guns. One hostage managed to escape by throwing himself through the plate glass window at the front of the building, by which time members of the SPG had arrived. At the time, a unit of the SPG was responsible for providing the 'Central London Reserve' each day. This ensured that there was a mobile group of officers, some armed, available to respond to emergencies. One of the officers that morning was Constable Stan Conley.

Two of us had guns but there was another constable and a sergeant in the carrier who didn't have anything. We were at Vauxhall Bridge when the call went out to the local RT car that there were armed men in the Indian High Commission and we said that we would attend. When we got to India House a chap came running up. He was bleeding from the head and saying: 'They've got guns, they've got guns.' Initially he said that there were five of them but I found out afterwards that he had jumped through a plate glass window to get away from them. It was small wonder that he got his figures a bit addled. My mate and I, with the sergeant and the constable, went in through a side door of the building in Montreal Place.

We went along a passageway and pushed open the doors. There was a lot of screaming and there was one terrorist behind a pillar. He said he was going to kill us and another terrorist ran across the room toward the hostages threatening to kill them. My mate shot him and we stepped back and dropped to the floor. The doors closed and I told my mate to cover me as I went in on my stomach. I pushed the doors open and I looked to the left and there was this man on his knees with a gun that he was pointing at the hostages. I told him to drop the gun and he looked at me, dropped the gun and waved his arms in front of him. It turned out he was one of the hostages. The first terrorist had dropped his gun when he had been shot and this man had run over from the hostages and picked it up. When I saw him, he was pointing the gun at the terrorist in the corner where the hostages were.

Then one of the lifts opened and three people started to walk out. I waved them back inside. I suddenly realised there was a pool of liquid on the floor and that it was giving off fumes. It was from a plastic container with acid in it and we found out later that they were going to spray it in the faces of the hostages so that they couldn't identify anybody. I went round to the left and got between the lift and the stairs. I looked out across the room and there was still this terrorist behind the pillar and his gun was pointing straight at my mate. I told him to drop the gun and he stepped back and put his arm across his chest so that the gun was pointing at me. I fired one shot and he dropped to the floor.

There was nobody doing anything else other than the terrorist in the corner that we could see. He had the hostages and some of the other lads came in from outside through the broken glass window and dealt with him. By that time there were CID with guns starting to come in through the door. The chap on his knees came over afterwards and thanked me for saving his life. From the time that we got the call to the time that it was all over was less than five minutes.

The two men who had been shot were Basharat Hussain and Mohammed Hanif Hussain, both aged nineteen, and they died of their injuries. The third was Dalamar Khan, aged fifteen; his age was only discovered when his stocking mask was removed. When the revolvers were examined it was found that they were not real. They were toys made by the Crescent Toy Company, modelled on a short-barrelled Smith and Wesson .38 calibre revolver. Sir Robert Mark later wrote: 'There was only one possible thing to do. Tell the truth and tell it quickly. This we did and although the press were sympathetic it did not lessen our genuine regret and sadness at our unwitting part in this tragedy. The two constables in particular were much affected by it.'[3] In the House of Commons the Home Secretary supported the action taken at India House.

A major agenda item at the Central Conference of Chief Constables on 3 May 1973 was the issue of firearms to police officers. Prior to the meeting, the Home Office had circulated the results of its January 1973 survey to all of the members, who were also told that:

The Home Secretary has emphasised in Parliament that the increased frequency with which firearms have been issued is a response to the more frequent circumstances in which this has been necessary and that there has been no change in policy. . . . The Home Secretary is anxious to ensure that the increase in the number of occasions when it is necessary to issue firearms should not result in issue coming to be regarded as in any sense routine. . . . Suggestions have been made to the Home Secretary that a police officer issued with a firearm for one purpose should not use it if confronted with some quite different situation where its use might be legally justified. It does not seem practical to suggest that a police officer who happens to have a firearm and is confronted by an armed criminal should be under orders to refrain from using the firearm to protect himself or others. But it seems important to ensure that every officer who may be in this situation understands that he is personally answerable to the law, both criminal and civil, for the way in which he uses a firearm issued to him.[4]

Sir Robert Mark told the meeting that 'the general circumstances in which firearms were issued to police officers had not changed and their issue had definitely not become routine. . . . The issue of firearms to police officers had, in his view, a deterrent effect . . . and he did not himself believe that the use of weapons by criminals would increase if the police were armed.' Nevertheless, the meeting acknowledged that the issue of firearms to police officers should be carefully controlled, that the need was likely to grow, and that the Home Office was concerned to ensure that their use by police officers was kept to a minimum.

## RESUMPTION OF TRAINING

Meanwhile, tests on the instructors in London had shown that the lead content of their blood had returned to normal levels, but installing ventilation in the indoor ranges was going to be an expensive process. Training resumed at Purfleet and Rainham in January 1973 and in 1974 a range at RAF Uxbridge was also taken into temporary use.

*Alex Moir*
Because of the location of the various ranges, instructors who lived near them would travel direct and prepare for the course of fire that was part of the refresher training session for that period. We had six

different refresher courses for students. Some were only for practice and others were for classification purposes. Also at this time we used the 'incident rooms' in the basement at Old Street with wax ammunition that the instructors themselves had to make in a workshop at the back of the rooms.

The 'incident rooms' were a series of spaces put together by the instructors themselves with 'friend or foe' targets appearing from various cupboards or from behind furniture when an instructor pulled on a rope.

Some work was also needed on the MoD ranges.

*Arthur Batten*

I was posted to Purfleet range permanently at the time. We used an old army store behind the range for a stockroom and lying unused was an old set of army metal fittings all linked together to form a turning target system. The range warden and I sorted them out and eventually these were placed on our part of the range. The targets stood in holders that rotated on swivels made of iron. I attached a rope to the left-hand end of the line of target holders and when the rope was pulled the targets all turned to face the students on the firing point. When the rope was released the targets all turned edge on. The instructor on the rope could vary the time between exposures of the targets.

I also had the mushroom concession. Going down very early, I used to go out behind the butts about half a mile or so into the safety zone where they grew in abundance. Some of the students went home with freshly picked mushrooms at the end of the day.

Around the world at this time there was an increasing level of knowledge of the tactics that could be used when dealing with armed criminals and terrorists, particularly when hostages were involved. Perhaps the most noteworthy experience in 1973 occurred in Sweden when a bank siege, during which an escaped convict, Jan-Erick Olsson, took a number of hostages, resulted in the discovery of a phenomenon that would become known as 'Stockholm syndrome'.

Olsson said later that he would not have harmed the hostages because he had grown to know them so well during the siege. In due course it would be realised that the syndrome was not the panacea for dealing with all sieges, but at the time the training of police officers as hostage negotiators became a priority.

Technical advances also meant that increasingly sophisticated equipment could be used to listen in to what was being said inside a building under siege and sometimes actually to see who was saying it. To allow the Metropolitan Police to make use of all of this experience and equipment it was necessary to ensure that senior police officers at least knew of their existence. It fell to Bob Wells, now an inspector, to provide the training.

In 1974 I had to do a complete tour of all the divisions in an ancient J4 van – two divisions a week – and I used films, slides and overheads to teach 'tactics' to supervising officers. It took about ten months to go around once and we had a job getting senior officers to attend. They were always too busy and there was real cynicism in the audience too. It was hard work.

By August 1973 the instructors were running out of .380 ammunition. Future supplies looked doubtful and in January 1974 a meeting was held at New Scotland Yard (the old building had closed in 1967) to discuss the shortage. Chief Superintendent Lyons explained about the April 1972 report on weapons suggested as being suitable for police use and proposed that the force take the decision to change to the Smith and Wesson revolver.

The representative from Special Branch insisted that neither his branch, which had a national responsibility for the close protection of politicians and important visitors, nor officers who had a similar responsibility for members of the royal family, had any wish to change from the Walther pistol. As a result, the meeting agreed that the central divisions and all CID officers would in future be issued with the Model 36 revolver if the need arose. The rest of the force would change to the Model 10 with the exception of the Special Branch, royalty protection officers and the Bank of England escort, which since 1971 had carried Browning 9mm pistols for the protection of large quantities of cash and bullion being moved around Britain. It was also agreed that when the new weapons were issued, the Webley and Scott revolvers would be taken into store as a wartime emergency stock. Accordingly, the Home Office granted authority for the purchase of 800 Smith and Wesson revolvers.

## THE ATTEMPT TO KIDNAP A PRINCESS

Two months after the meeting an attempt was made to kidnap Her Royal Highness Princess Anne. On 20 March 1974 Ian Ball, armed with two revolvers, four pairs of handcuffs, a ransom note for £3 million and a 'free pardon' that awaited a royal signature, drove his white Ford Escort in front of a chauffeur-driven Rolls-Royce in The Mall near Buckingham Palace. The chauffeur was Alexander Callender and in the back were Princess Anne, her then husband Captain Mark Phillips and a lady-in-waiting, Miss Brassey. Inspector James Beaton, the princess's protection officer, was sitting in the front passenger seat and assumed that Ball was an irate motorist. He got out to speak to him but Ball made for the offside passenger door of the Rolls-Royce and tried to pull it open.

Inspector Beaton walked around the back of the Rolls-Royce and then realised for the first time that Ball had a gun. Ball fired three shots and one hit the officer in the shoulder. The inspector fired one shot at Ball using his Walther pistol but missed and the gun then jammed. Ball told him to put down his gun or he would shoot the princess, and so the officer dropped it and joined the others inside the back of the car, trying to keep the door shut.

John McConnell, a freelance journalist, tried to intervene but Ball shot him in the chest. Ball then fired at the princess through the closed window of the car but the shot hit Inspector Beaton in the hand. Constable Hills heard the sound of the shots and ran to the scene. As he approached Ball he was shot in the stomach, but he managed to use his radio to call for help. Ball then managed to force open the door and he shot Inspector Beaton in the stomach. The officer fell into the roadway and it was at about this time that the chauffeur was also shot. Passer-by Glenmore Martin drove his Jaguar car in front of Ball's Escort to prevent it from being driven away, but he retreated when Ball stuck a gun in his ribs.

A taxi driver, Ronald Russell, stopped his taxi and punched Ball, who was still trying to drag the princess from her car. Ball fired at him but missed and the shot shattered the taxi's front windscreen. After retreating for a few moments Mr Russell returned and punched Ball again, and by now further police assistance was starting to arrive. Ball tried to run off but Detective Constable Edmonds brought him down with a rugby tackle. On 22 May 1974 Ball pleaded guilty at the Old Bailey to attempted murder, attempted kidnapping and wounding with intent. He was detained under the provisions of mental health legislation.

The effect of the attempted kidnapping was immediate and twofold. Firstly, Special Branch and royalty protection officers lost faith in their self-loading pistols and now wanted to get rid of them. Secondly, demands were made for officers to be trained in how to deal with the kind of situation that Inspector Beaton had faced in The Mall.

## PROTECTION TRAINING

Initially a crash programme was introduced to train all officers on close protection duty in the use of the Model 36 revolver, but some officers did not find the change easy to cope with.

*Ron Parrish*
When the Model 36 was introduced it immediately gave problems to the students. The shorter barrel meant that in many cases the students couldn't shoot accurately enough to meet the required standard to pass their classification. Also the sharp recoil, not previously experienced by the firer, meant that a degree of apprehension crept in, causing students to 'snatch' at the trigger thus affecting their fall of shot on the target. In one case a student employed as a senior protection officer failed to meet the standards required of him. As this officer was due to perform duties overseas he was given many more rounds to qualify but he still failed and he

was eventually authorised and qualified for 'single action' only. You can imagine how we felt about that!

The 1972 report had recommended the Model 36 with its 2-inch barrel for 'the continuously armed police officer' because it was both light to carry and easy to conceal. However, the .38 Special cartridge was more powerful than the 9mm (.380) cartridge that it replaced and this resulted in greater recoil. In addition, the accuracy of any weapon is largely dependent on its barrel length – hence a rifle is more accurate than a handgun. The shorter the barrel, the more time is required for training if a reasonable standard of accuracy is to be achieved.

To ensure that the instructors were up to date with the latest techniques in close protection, two instructors and four royalty protection officers attended a bodyguard course with the SAS at Hereford.

*Ron Parrish*
This course lasted three weeks and encompassed all aspects of protection. The Met officers were trained with members of the SAS and the training consisted of shooting, car-drills using live ammunition, protection drills, and preparation for arrival and departure to any destination. It also included physical training and much to be looked forward to were the deep hot baths at the end of each day.

We then held bodyguard courses to train both Special Branch and royalty protection officers. The course was for a week and during that time the officers' shooting ability improved considerably. They also got, for the first time, anti-ambush drills and building and room preparation. During the ambushes, with instructors playing the part of the terrorists, thunderflashes were used to simulate grenades. Many was the time that one landed underneath a car – unintentionally of course – thereby giving the car a de-coke of mud. Initially there was a marked reluctance from officers of both departments to involve themselves in the course. Their attitude was one of 'we have been doing the job for many years and so we cannot be taught anything'. The course was not only designed to introduce officers to current thinking in terms of protection but also to provide the instructors with an insight into the problems the students encountered. Once the students entered into the spirit of the course and realised we were not teaching them to suck eggs, the courses went quite smoothly.

## FACILITIES

The bodyguard courses were run at Lippitts Hill camp which was gradually seeing an improvement in facilities. When firearms training had been transferred to Rainham and Purfleet the instructors had suggested that the Metropolitan Police should either purchase or lease Rainham from the MoD since it was no longer being used by the armed forces. The proposal had been turned down and in 1973 it was decided that a range should be built at Lippitts Hill.

The construction of a 50-metre eight-lane outdoor range at the camp was completed in 1975. Built at one end on an outside wall was a small, two-storey house consisting of little more than walls and a tin roof. This became known as the 'fieldcraft house' and over a quarter of a century later it was still standing, although many wondered how this was possible after all the rough treatment it had received over the years. The main range itself did not stand up so well.

*Ron Parrish*
It was a magnificent 50-metre range based on an American model. The whole floor area was covered with grass and it was beautifully mown. It was also open to the elements. An instructors' course was run about six weeks after it opened and by the end the range was so churned up it looked like the Somme.

*Mick Weight*
I joined [D11] at the time when the conversions had just started from the Webley and the Walther to the Smith and Wesson Models 10 and 36. The new 50-metre range with 'indestructible grass'

opened at Lippitts Hill and part of the refresher training was moved there. The grass totally disappeared after being attacked by the boots of forty authorised officers a day.

## DOMESTIC TERRORISM

Mentally disturbed persons trying to kidnap princesses, domestic criminals and international terrorists were not the only menaces facing the Metropolitan Police. Domestic terrorists, in the form of the PIRA, parked four car bombs on London streets in March 1973. Two were discovered and defused but the third detonated while explosives' officers were making preliminary tests and sixty-one people were injured. The fourth, outside the Old Bailey, exploded and there were 162 casualties. A piece of window glass, embedded by the force of the blast into the foyer wall, remained untouched and can still be seen to this day. In August a fire bomb and letter bomb campaign in London, Birmingham and Manchester resulted in thirty people being injured and in December explosives left in two cars and a parcel bomb injured sixty people.

The attacks continued during 1974. On 22 February 1975 Constable Stephen Tibble was off duty when he saw a man being chased by police in Barons Court, west London. The man was William Quinn, an American, who had joined the PIRA and come to England late in 1974. He was just walking away from a PIRA safe house and bomb-factory in Fairholme Road, Hammersmith, when members of a plain-clothes squad looking for housebreakers stopped and questioned him. He ran, and Constable Tibble crouched down with his arms outspread ready to tackle him. Quinn fired three times at Constable Tibble and then stepped over his body. The officer died of his injuries.

Quinn escaped to Ireland and then to the United States, but in September 1981 he was arrested in San Francisco, where he spent five years fighting extradition. In February 1988 at the Old Bailey he was found guilty of murder and sentenced to life imprisonment. He was the first American citizen to be extradited from the United States to face justice in Britain.

## FIREARMS TEAMS

On 6 May 1975, two and a half months after the murder of Constable Tibble, the Commissioner and his policy committee met to discuss whether it was time for the Metropolitan Police to create specialist firearms teams. It was not possible to give a high level of counter-terrorist training to all authorised shots in the force and:

> In the event of terrorists taking hostages, a special military team would be summoned to the scene, but this unit would not arrive for a few hours from the time it was called and it would therefore fall to the police to handle the situation in the meantime. As things stand the police involved would be the local divisional officers who would include some who were armed and who were authorised to use guns. A few might be snipers. In the type of incidents which have been experienced recently . . . such a police capability could prove quite inadequate and a highly trained team, expert in the use of a wide range of firearms would be necessary if the situation deteriorated before the arrival of the military. . . . If necessary this unit could also be employed in cases of serious armed crime.

The proposed new unit would consist of the instructors in D11 and be capable of 'taking effective action against a number of determined and ruthless men armed with automatic weapons possibly barricaded inside a building or an aircraft'. The additional equipment required included transport, Browning self-loading pistols, Heckler and Koch HK93 .223 calibre rifles, Heckler and Koch MP5 and MP5 SD 9mm sub-machine guns, shotguns and body armour.

Although the proposal was fully supported, a caveat was included to ensure that the teams were only called out on the personal authority of the DACA (ops) – an extension of the procedure that had been in place since 1971. The next step was to get formal Home Office approval, not least because of the weapons that would be required, but before this could be given there was an opportunity to try out some of the new ideas on the ground.

*Chapter 5*

# SIEGES

### SPAGHETTI HOUSE

In the early hours of 28 September 1975 three young black men carrying firearms walked into the Spaghetti House restaurant in Knightsbridge. It was the usual practice of the nine managers of the Spaghetti House restaurant chain to meet late every Saturday night to discuss business and to pay their collective takings for Friday and Saturday, which amounted to about £13,000, into a nearby night safe. Realising that they were in the middle of a robbery, the two managers carrying the money managed to hide it unseen under tables on the ground floor. All nine managers were forced down a flight of stairs into a basement, but the first one down was able to cross the basement floor and escape up a flight of stairs that led back to the ground floor. He raised the alarm and when police arrived the three gunmen bundled themselves and the remaining eight managers into a small storeroom.

*Mick Weight*
Chief Superintendent Lyons called us out from home in the early hours of the morning. When we reported to Old Street, two traffic cars were waiting to take the first team to the incident. We loaded up the cars with equipment and I was in the first car to leave with Bob Gould, Arthur Batten and Ron Parrish. Three of us sat in the back and Bob Gould sat in the front with the car totally overloaded. We had all the kit bags on our laps and on reaching Regent Street doing about 70 miles an hour we hit a dip in the road. There was a loud bang and Bob Gould thought that we had lost a rifle box from the boot. The car skidded to a halt but all we had done was lose the rear exhaust box.

We arrived at the restaurant sounding like a jet aircraft landing. Bob Gould reported to the control, did a quick recce, and then we deployed down into the restaurant. Because it was thought at first that it was a terrorist incident, [Constable] Alec Neville, the storeman in D11, had loaded two Stirling sub-machine guns from the museum in with our kit and, along with pump-action shotguns and Browning pistols, we deployed with these at the scene. This raised a few eyebrows but the Commissioner seemed quite happy about it and he told Bob Gould in no uncertain terms that we were to deal with the situation as we saw fit.

The leader of the gang was Franklin Davies who had already served a prison sentence for armed robbery. The other two in the storeroom were Wesley Dick and Anthony Munroe. The reason for the initial belief that the incident was terrorist related was that Davies claimed to be a major in the 'Black Liberation Front'. The three also claimed to be 'militant' and said that they would die rather than surrender. The police worked to discover the true identities of the gunmen. One hostage was released on the first day after he became unwell.

In due course a visual probe gave a live picture of what was happening inside the storeroom and preparations were made to use explosives to blow the hinges off the storeroom door in case a rescue proved necessary. Sir Robert Mark later wrote:

The drill to which we had given so much thought during the preceding two years was then applied in full. . . . We decided to provide accommodation across the road for the relatives of the hostages and I thought it my duty to visit them twice daily to offer what consolation and encouragement I could. It was not easy. One or two clearly thought that we should accede to the gunman's demand for an aircraft and guarantee of safe conduct and found it difficult to accept my view that in no circumstance at all would we agree. To their very great credit, the overwhelming majority of relatives, despite their anguish, were solidly behind us in our determination not to give way.[1]

When a photograph of Davies appeared on the front page of the *Daily Express*, the police wrote across it the name of the person suspected of supplying the guns and that he had received £500 for the photograph. It was not true, but they watched for the reaction as they slipped the newspaper under the door. Davies was asleep at the time and when his two confederates saw the newspaper they tore it up. When Davies woke up the process was repeated and this time the effect was immediate. Davies was furious that someone was making money out of his predicament and just before 4 o'clock in the morning of 3 October, with the siege just entering its sixth day, the gunmen released their hostages.

*Bert Harris*

There were signs of unrest that continued until about 3.55 in the morning. Then there was a knock on the storeroom door and they announced that the hostages were coming out. The hostages left the storeroom first and went up the stairs. The gunmen were told to slide the guns out of the door and there were sounds of things being moved about in the storeroom. The door then opened slightly and they pushed a shotgun out first. They said that they were trying to unload another gun and that a bullet was stuck. Then there was the sound of a shot and they said that Davies had committed suicide. They wanted a doctor to go in straight away.

Dick and Munroe came out and were taken into custody before any officer entered the storeroom. Davies was then removed and he made a full recovery from his self-inflicted injury. In June 1976 at the Old Bailey, Davies was sentenced to twenty-one years in prison, Dick to eighteen years and Munroe to seventeen years. Lillo Termine, who admitted supplying the information that had led to the attempted robbery, was given six years. The jury could not agree in the case of Samuel Addison, the driver of the getaway car, and so a new trial was ordered. In November he was found guilty of attempted robbery and sentenced to eleven years.

It seemed that the police had found an infallible formula. Confine the hostage-takers in a small space, use a negotiator gradually to convince the hostage-takers that their position is hopeless and that they may as well give up, and let nature take its course by relying on the 'Stockholm syndrome' to ensure the safety of the hostages. It was not an appropriate time to point out that there were armed officers right outside the door of the storeroom. The explosive charges were already prepared and the end of the siege could easily have been spectacularly different.

If there had been any doubts within the Home Office about the wisdom of the Metropolitan Police forming specialist teams, the siege at Spaghetti House dispelled them. On 26 November 1975 an official at the Home Office wrote to Assistant Commissioner H.J.E. Hunt saying that he was:

> Sorry to have taken so long to give a formal response to your proposal for the formation of a special anti-terrorist squad comprising instructors from D11. The Home Secretary welcomes this proposal and is glad to approve it. I think we are all agreed that the Spaghetti House incident confirms the value of having these skilled officers readily available and the arrangements you propose seem a sensible means of achieving this.

Thus the instructors became the force's Firearms Unit and, as if providence was keen to put the matter beyond dispute, the Home Office would have further proof of the value of the teams within weeks.

## BALCOMBE STREET

During 1975 there were twenty-nine terrorist incidents in London which killed 10 people and injured about another 169. A major operation was planned to catch those responsible. A pattern of attacks had been identified and on 6 December, four terrorists fell into the trap that had been set for them when they drove down Mount Street in Mayfair at just after 9 o'clock in the evening. They opened fire with a sub-machine gun on Scotts Restaurant and the registration number of the vehicle they were using was transmitted over the local police radio network. An inspector and a sergeant saw the vehicle in Portman Square and they gave chase in a commandeered taxi until the terrorists stopped in Alpha Close several streets away. The four left their vehicle and were chased on foot. As the officers reached Balcombe Street a woman shouted that four men had just run into some flats. The area was cordoned off. The terrorists then helped out by telephoning New Scotland Yard to announce that they were in flat 22B and that they had taken John Matthews and his wife Sheila as hostages.

*Mick Weight*

We were called out very late in the evening and at Old Street we loaded up our new call-out van. I drove with an escort of two traffic cars, one in front and one behind. When we arrived at Balcombe Street the engine was ticking with the heat. I had a Stirling SMG (from the museum) and I climbed an old rotting wooden ladder up to the second floor of a block of flats opposite 22B and sat with an SPG rifle officer who was already in position.

Two officers took up a position outside the front door of the flat and others looked for a way in. Six district rifle officers were called out from home at 4 a.m. and by 8 o'clock the pattern for the siege was more or less established. Sir Robert Mark later wrote:

Contrary to general belief, the operation was quite simple and straightforward once we were sure of the problem. Though we were deeply concerned about the safety of the hostages I did not consider for one moment that they were not expendable. I felt heartfelt sympathy for Mr and Mrs Matthews but felt that human life was of little importance when balanced against the principle that violence must not be allowed to succeed. Fortunately in deciding that policy there was no need to consult anyone, nor did I do so. The four terrorists were common criminals and the responsibility for dealing with them, unless I decided to use the SAS, was mine and mine alone. It was not so much a difficult decision as no decision at all. There was no question of giving the gunmen anything, other than the means to sustain life.[2]

The presence of the SAS was not officially acknowledged during the siege but a privately owned ex-army armoured personnel carrier that happened to be parked nearby served to heighten the media speculation. By 3.30 in the afternoon of the first day it was found that furniture had been piled up behind the front door of the flat but no movement could be detected other than in the main living room. A temporary position found at the back of the flat was now made more permanent.

*Bert Harris*
The position was at the same level as the windows of the flat but separated from it by a dropped courtyard. The problem was that sandbags had to be carried to the position and at first this had to be done while staying behind a very low wall. With Kris [Freeland] hanging over a roof just behind me I got a few bags along and placed them in position, giving myself protection from the windows, but the constable who pulled the remainder of the bags to me had a pretty rough time of it.

Although D11 had been able to stay out of the media spotlight at Spaghetti House it was more difficult to do so at Balcombe Street. The new Firearms Unit became the 'Blue Berets' who had been 'revealed for the first time'. According to the *Daily Mail*:

There are only 20 of them, all mature unflappable men. They are elite policemen who have been trained to use a handgun or a rifle. They are the men in dark-blue battle-smocks and berets . . . who have been noticed for the first time in action. The fact that the siege has made the public realise London has this elite force of professional marksman ready to kill and maim if necessary is bound to raise the question: 'Are we moving too quickly towards other countries which have permanent para-military police units?' . . . On the roof, tubular police spotlights aimed at the windows could blind anyone inside. Each Blue Beret was issued with pictures of Mr and Mrs Matthews taken from the family album. They were told to memorise Mr John Matthews' face in case he is ever pushed out ahead of the terrorists.

The 'blinding tubular spotlights' were actually telescopes which were used on a firing range to see where shots had landed without having to go up to the target to take a look. They had been pressed into service because of the absence of a suitable alternative. There was also little need to memorise the faces of Mr and Mrs Matthews.

### Tony Gray

There was one particular senior officer who came to where we were one night. He asked me whether I would be able to identify one of the terrorists against one of the hostages if necessary. One of the terrorists was continually moving the curtain at the front windows and so I asked the senior officer if he could see what the terrorist was doing. He said that he could and I told him that I could read the time on the terrorist's wristwatch from where I was through my telescopic sight.

The third day of the siege passed quietly and that night a means of gaining access to the flat was built at the back of the building.

### Mick Weight

A Unit of SPG officers went off to a yard somewhere and practised building a tall scaffold tower with a platform on top. Then the same crew built this tower, in darkness and with no noise, in the rear courtyard of the flats. The platform was just level with the rear kitchen window of No. 22B and I went up first carrying a pump-action shotgun and sat on the platform at the top to give cover while Bob Wells and [Constable] Ian Chadburn entered the kitchen.

### Bob Wells

My first sally into the flat itself with Ian Chadburn was not until 3 o'clock in the morning on 10 December. The objective was to place sound probes in the door to the lounge from the hallway. The first few minutes were fairly tense as the technician fiddled with his probe in the keyhole of the door and every sound seemed magnified. I had also been asked to lift and tuck up the front bedroom curtains overlooking the street to give the snipers a view into the flat. It felt strange doing that, knowing that I was covered by telescopic sights, even our own. I remember giving them a wave and feeling foolish for doing so.

We crept out fifteen minutes later, quite relieved. I repeated this kind of entry four times in the next two night shifts with Ian Chadburn, Mick Weight, [Sergeant] Colin Bulley and Ron Parrish. It became more of a routine and less tense, except for the last one at just after 2 o'clock in the morning of 12 December. The negotiators, led by Peter Imbert [later Sir Peter Imbert, Commissioner of the Metropolitan Police 1987–93], wanted the rest of the flat searched. This took nearly forty-five minutes because it was difficult to do quietly at that time of the morning.

A camera looking into the flat through the front door had a view along the hallway, but not of the door to the lounge.

*Colin Bulley*

We weren't too happy that the door opened into the room and so we got this bit of cord. I looped the end of it around the door handle and I think we tied it off in the kitchen but then we realised that you couldn't see the cord if it moved. I suggested that we put a pair of knickers on it but Bob Wells wouldn't have that. Then I found a little witch doll and I went back and tied the witch on to the cord. If the doll moved we would then have an indication that they were trying to open the door.

The small doll soon became known as 'Witchy-Poo' and after the siege Mr and Mrs Matthews gave it to the Firearms Unit as a souvenir. When the end came the four terrorists – Martin O'Connell, Henry Duggan, Edward Butler and Hugh Doherty – left the flat using the balcony window overlooking the street and surrendered to a Firearms Unit sergeant. In February 1977 at the Old Bailey all four were found guilty of various offences including six murders, causing several explosions and unlawfully imprisoning Mr and Mrs Matthews. They were sentenced to life imprisonment with a recommendation that they each serve thirty years.

It was yet another success for the strategy of negotiation. The public certainly did not know that the hostages were considered expendable, and a new phrase was even coined to convey in simple terms what the approach meant in practice – 'Play it Long'.

## NATIONAL DEVELOPMENTS

The Working Party on Firearms for Police Use in Peacetime had circulated the 1972 report of the Consultative Panel of Firearms Instructors to all chief officers and had asked for their comments. It then produced its own report at the end of 1975.[3] This took up the proposal that the basic course should be five days long, but the working party did not support the idea of a national police firearms centre. It feared that it would acquire a 'disproportionate influence over a sensitive aspect of police work'. There were also doubts about whether it would be used to its full potential unless it 'resulted in a greater emphasis on the place of firearms in police work' and this the working party considered 'undesirable'.

Nevertheless, the training of police firearms' instructors did come in for special attention. The number of forces in England and Wales had by now reduced to forty-three and out of the 250 instructors available, about 110 had been trained in or by the armed forces. Of the remainder, the Metropolitan Police had trained 45, Lancashire 30 and West Yorkshire 29. The rest had picked up what they knew at civilian shooting clubs. The working party was most emphatic that from now on an officer's training outside the police service should not be regarded as sufficient qualification. The training of instructors was therefore made the responsibility of the Metropolitan Police and the forces of Lancashire, West Yorkshire and Devon and Cornwall. The working party also believed that the same four forces – ironically, to become known as 'National Centres' – should provide all police rifle training to sniper level. The Royal Ulster Constabulary joined the group in 1987 and West Mercia in 1994.

With one extraordinary exception, chief officers had all accepted that seminars on tactics should be held for senior officers, but the majority felt that a one- or at most a two-day course was sufficient and this became the eventual recommendation. Finally, the working party proposed the setting up of a permanent committee: 'To maintain and develop high and consistent standards of firearms training in the police service; to monitor and assess the development of new weapons, ammunition and training techniques; to provide information and advice on these matters to police forces; and to maintain liaison with other bodies having relevant expertise on these subjects.'

The report eventually reached the Chief Constables Council (the successor to the Central Conference of Chief Constables) where its recommendations were accepted and the Association of Chief Police Officers Joint Standing Committee on the Police Use of Firearms (ACPO JSC) held its first meeting on 16 October 1979. It had representatives from all of the main ACPO committees, F8 division of the Home Office (responsible for operational policy), HMIC and the Police Federation, and one of its first actions was to create the National Working Group of Firearms Instructors (NWGFI) to advise it on technical matters. This was the direct descendant of the consultative panel with membership drawn from the National Centres. The committee would remain in existence until 2002 when a reorganisation of ACPO bodies resulted in the formation of today's ACPO Working Group on the Police Use of Firearms with three 'practitioner forums' in place of the NWGFI.

## Chapter 6

# TEAMWORK

### MYDDLETON PASSAGE

In December 1976 in London, Chief Superintendent 'Robbie' Robbins became the Firearms Unit's commanding officer with an operational and training staff of two inspectors, six sergeants and eleven constables. The instructors were divided into four teams and each team was on full-time stand-by for one week in four.

A blue Ford Transit long-wheel-base van had been specially converted for the Unit and its first use had been to take officers to Balcombe Street. As well as providing transport, it had a ladder-rack that doubled as a firing platform on its roof and purpose-built cabinets for rifles and shotguns fitted into its rear compartment. At this time arrangements were formalised for calling out a team when it was needed.

*Ron Parrish*
The callout system for the team on stand-by was that there would be a ring around, usually initiated by the chief superintendent or superintendent. If possible, traffic patrol cars would be sent to our home addresses to convey us into Old Street or if necessary to get a couple of the team to the incident. Later, the ring around system was abolished and we were provided with pagers.

It was not long before a trailer was needed to carry the increasing amount of equipment that the Firearms Unit was starting to acquire. This included an armoured shield that would stop rifle fire but was so heavy that it had to be pushed around on its own trolley. Trials were conducted using the contraption to carry a stretcher and it was thought that it could be used to rescue a person trapped by gunfire. It was the only one of its kind (although there are records of the police in Liverpool having mobile armoured shields as early as 1929) and its main drawback was its weight. On a downhill slope it developed a will of its own and Land Rovers that were themselves armoured replaced it in 1979.

There was also a 'violent man' cage designed by one of the instructors. On 24 October 1977 police and bailiffs went to a council flat in Worthington House, Myddleton Passage, Islington, to evict Stuart Brickell from his first-floor flat. When a local superintendent and a sergeant approached they were attacked by Brickell who had armed himself with a stiletto knife, a machete and a cut-throat razor. In the ensuing mêlée the superintendent suffered a fractured skull. The sergeant was stabbed in the stomach and sustained a slash to his head.

Brickell threatened anyone who approached him. A specialist team and negotiators were sent for. At about 7 o'clock in the evening Brickell went into a small bedroom and this provided an opportunity to keep him confined to one place. By 9 o'clock the bedroom door had been secured with pieces of timber, barbed wire and furniture, and the officers settled down for another siege.

*Alex Moir*
The superintendent in charge asked us what we could do in view of the man's ability with the machete. We said that we would have to disable him in some way, but a commander told us that under no circumstances was Brickell to be harmed and that it may be necessary for police officers to go into the room to disarm him. I must say I did not fancy this and suggested that if we had a metal mesh screen then we could prevent him from swinging the machete. I also explained that we would need a long tool to pin his arm to the wall – a 'snake stick' with a 'V'-shaped head similar to those used when dealing with venomous snakes. After about four hours the commander came back and said that if I was prepared to go to Merton Garage the staff there would make this for us. Ron [Parrish] and myself were dispatched in the van to build the device.

Back at Myddleton Passage, negotiations continued and Constable
Ian Chadburn made a rather disturbing discovery:

In the main bedroom there was a tin trunk with a strong smell of
gas around it. Inside was a sealed and heavily taped plastic bag and
through one opening of the bag was a gas [stove] electric lighter.
What had happened was that he had made a crude gas bomb that
was operated by the gas lighter when the trunk was opened.
Fortunately, the gas had leaked out.

In the early hours of 29 October Brickell tried to hack his way
through the barricade covering the door but he was successfully
fended off. The mesh screen arrived later the same day. It consisted of
a number of sections that formed the cage when joined together.

*Ron Parrish*
One section of the cage was securely fixed to the doorframe. Alex
had also designed some medieval-looking long 'prods' which could
keep the man at a safe distance should he decide to attack again.
Those guarding the room could relax a bit more after that.

By the morning of 2 November Brickell was tired and there was
growing concern about his health. He had refused to accept food or
water from the start of the siege, fearing that it could be drugged, and
his worsening condition meant that the 'Play it Long' strategy was no
longer tenable. The siege had to end. The fully assembled cage would
not work if there were any obstructions to its progress within the
room and so the first step was to use the new tools to hook on to and
then pull out anything likely to get in the way. With the area clear it
was then possible to move on to the next stage.

*Bert Harris*
Alex was controlling the operation from the front and I was slightly
behind him with one of the long poles shaped with a 'V' at the end.
Members of the SPG were behind us, pushing the whole cage into
the room a piece at a time. After two pieces were through the door

the man, from a standing jump, nearly came over the top of the cage with his machete flying all over the place and nearly cleaving Alex's skull. I managed to push him back and at the same time the cage was pushed into the room, forcing him against the wall. I pinned the arm that was holding the machete against the wall and Alex then went inside the cage and disarmed him. I thought it was a very satisfying operation and I for one thought the cage was an extremely good idea.

Brickell was charged with causing grievous bodily harm to two officers at the start of the siege and on 26 February 1979 at the Old Bailey he was sentenced to five years in prison. Although the cage was taken to a number of other incidents, it was never used operationally again and developments in the use of riot shields eventually rendered it obsolete.

## INTERNATIONAL TERRORISM

The troubles in the Middle East spilled over on to the streets of London when the former premier of North Yemen was shot and killed as he sat in a car outside the Royal Lancaster Hotel in April 1977. His wife and a North Yemeni diplomat were also killed. In December two Syrian diplomats died when their car exploded, and the London representative of the Palestine Liberation Organisation was murdered in Mayfair in January 1978. In July a former Iraqi prime minister was killed outside the Intercontinental Hotel, and on 20 August aircrew belonging to El Al were attacked when their coach stopped outside the Europa Hotel in Duke Street, Mayfair. The terrorists used a sub-machine gun and grenades, and responsibility was later claimed by the Popular Front for the Liberation of Palestine. An air hostess was killed and a terrorist died when his grenade exploded prematurely, an event referred to as 'scoring an own goal'. In addition to the deaths, nine other people were injured. Gruesome photographs showing the aftermath appeared in most of the newspapers the next day. The response of the Metropolitan Police was to introduce temporary security measures where it could.

*Ian Chadburn*
For a time, Firearms Unit officers in uniform met the coach and the
airline crew at Heathrow. We boarded the coach and then acted as
bodyguards to the aircrew as the coach drove into London.

Other measures included the posting of divisional authorised
officers to a number of buildings that were not usually protected but
were thought to be potential targets. This was more obvious than the
escorting of a coach and one newspaper, the *Daily Mirror*, published a
photograph of a Metropolitan officer standing on the steps of a
building he was temporarily guarding. The officer was in 'shirt sleeve
order'; that is to say he was not wearing a uniform jacket. His revolver
could be plainly seen in its holster slung alongside his right thigh, and
the overall impression was not helped by the officer's relaxed pose, his
right hand casually hooked on to his right hip.

When the old Webley revolver was not being carried in a pocket it
was in a canvas holster with a top flap that completely covered the gun,
but the new Smith and Wesson revolver came with an ordinary leather
holster. Since May 1976 the force instructions had therefore required,
for the first time, that 'the holstered handgun will be carried out of
sight'.[1] At a policy committee meeting on 20 September 1978 chaired
by Sir David McNee, now Commissioner, there was a discussion about
the standard of dress of officers carrying firearms. Officers were 'causing
embarrassment' by letting themselves be photographed carrying guns,
and a few days later the instructors received an order from the ACD,
now John Gerard. They were to tell officers when they attended for
training that: 'The Commissioner wishes it to be known that it is still
the policy of this force to maintain an unarmed traditional image and
the unnecessary display of firearms is contrary to this policy.'

A few months later pictures of armed police appeared once again on
the front page of nearly every newspaper.

## HIGHBURY

In the autumn of 1978 two Glasgow-born criminals, Gary Miller and
Robert Morris, moved to London. Being unemployed, they lived off

their social security handouts and supplemented this money by robbing small shops at gunpoint. They took up residence in a derelict building that had been taken over by squatters in Blackstock Road, an Edwardian building above a disused fire station near Highbury police station. On 10 December in the late evening they tried their usual method of getting money in Mountgrove Road, not far from their squat. After entering an off-licence, one of them fired a shotgun into a wall while the other grabbed £100 in cash from the till. Both then ran off and the police were called. Sergeant Christopher Garner was unarmed when he saw the two trying to hide in a shop doorway and the pair were chased back to their squat where they disappeared. A specialist team was called and another siege began.

The sergeant had wisely decided not to venture into the total darkness of the squat, but the two could have run straight through the building and out the other side. Nevertheless, it was decided that it would be better to wait until daylight before attempting to enter the flats. Since February, the teams had been experimenting with conducting armed searches in combination with dog handlers and their dogs, and the routines had by now become quite well established. By 10 o'clock in the morning a plan to use a dog had been devised but, as the officers were preparing at Highbury police station, news reached them that a local detective chief inspector had decided all the planning was a waste of time. Accompanied by a reluctant inspector, he had walked from Highbury police station and kicked open the front door of the squat. Seeing the jumble of debris inside, he changed his mind about going in and walked back to Highbury police station, leaving the inspector behind. When the officers asked whether anyone intended to say anything to the detective chief inspector they were told: 'That's just him. We've found it's best just to ignore him.'

### Ian Chadburn

Two of us ran from the station to the front street door of the squat where we found the inspector in uniform standing by the door. The dog was put in at the same time and the inspector was 'gently' moved out of the way. The dog came back out and we withdrew

back to the police station, leaving armed officers covering the front
door from across the street.

The results of using the dog were inconclusive. Some movement
was detected on an upper floor but there was no way of knowing
whether it was the two men who were being sought. The incident
commander therefore called a conference of every senior officer
present, including the negotiators. When a white flag suddenly
appeared in a top-floor window the only officers left in a position to
see it were a Firearms Unit sergeant and a constable.

*Ian Chadburn*
It was quite eerie because it was all very quiet and in the distance
we could hear the noise of traffic. I had just taken over the loud-
hailer position when a white flag was waved out of one of the top
windows. I asked the guy waving the flag if they wanted to pack the
thing in and he shouted that they did. I told them to move slowly
down to the front door and wait. Before they reached the door we
discussed what to do with them and we decided to get them to lie
face down in the open where everyone could see them.

The two robbers were made to lie spread-eagled in the middle of
the road, a process that received massive television coverage that
day. They later admitted another six armed robberies and on 9
March 1979 at the Old Bailey they were both sentenced to seven
years in prison.

The siege had an unexpected side effect and again it was a picture
in a newspaper that acted as the catalyst. On 12 December 1978 the
*Daily Mirror* had published a photograph of a police dog handler
crouching with his dog behind a low wall at the Highbury siege. The
officer had a revolver in his right hand, but this time it was not the
fact that the gun was seen that caused the controversy. It was that the
officer was a dog handler. Within weeks, all divisional dog handlers
who were also authorised shots had their firearms authorisations
withdrawn by their senior officers who argued that an officer cannot
possibly handle a dog and a gun at the same time.

## DOMESTIC TERRORISM

The Balcombe Street siege had been the first major operation in London involving the arrest of Irish Republican terrorists. The next, on 11 December 1979, would take place under very different circumstances. A convicted member of the PIRA, Brian Keenan, was thought to have taken over control of operations in England in early 1973 and to have been the organiser behind the group arrested at Balcombe Street. After his arrest in Belfast in 1979 he had been flown to London to be charged with conspiracy to cause explosions and firearms offences. He was still being held in Brixton prison awaiting trial when the Anti-Terrorist branch uncovered a plot to use a helicopter that would land within the grounds of the prison to free him. So began 'Operation Otis'.

Surveillance and intelligence led police to Robert Campbell, who had himself escaped from prison in Northern Ireland in 1972 while serving an eleven-year sentence for armed robbery. He had been recaptured eleven months later and was subsequently released after serving the remainder of his sentence. Also thought to be involved were Robert Storey, Richard Glenholmes, and two women, Margaret Parratt and Jacqueline O'Malley. The Anti-Terrorist branch sought the assistance of the Firearms Unit when the men were traced to a top-floor flat at 38 Holland Park in west London. The ACC, Gilbert Kelland, later wrote:

I chaired a conference of senior detectives and we agreed that a unit of senior IRA members had assembled to release Keenan from Brixton prison and possibly also plan some diversionary bombing attacks. The risk of loss of life or serious injury was too great to allow these terrorist suspects to remain at liberty. An operational plan was prepared for coordinated police raids to take place on addresses which had been identified during the inquiry in London, Liverpool, Manchester, the West Midlands and Hampshire.[2]

The Firearms Unit was made responsible for dealing with the Holland Park flat and eight instructors (two teams) were directed to report back to Old Street at midnight.

*Ron Parrish*

We were then taken to Hendon to receive a briefing. I don't think I've ever seen so many at a briefing before. After that we travelled in convoy to Holland Park, arriving at about 3.30 in the morning, and we placed a sniper team to cover the rear of the building. We were told that lights had been seen in the building and it was thought that someone had been moving about. Knowing what we were likely to be up against, this was not good news. We made our way up the stairs (three flights) trying not to make a noise – not easy with about two dozen of us negotiating a narrow passage – and we eventually got to the landing. Our plan had already been formulated. Somehow we had managed to obtain a front door key to the flat and 'Robbie' [Robbins] was to open the door. We would then make a fast entry. In all the previous operations I had been on I had had no problem in dealing with what we had, but on this occasion I was almost convinced that once we went through the front door they would be waiting for us.

*Bert Harris*

Ron and I were to go in first, followed by the others working in pairs to the rooms they had been allocated. Ron and I worked out that the best thing to do was go in fast and as low as possible under any possibility that they had a shotgun or other weapons waiting for us.

*Ron Parrish*

The main group went to the left to the bedroom area, and Bert and I went to the right to the lounge. I hit the door and in one sweep I turned the light on, convinced, I'm afraid, that someone was waiting for us. I don't think my eyes have revolved in their sockets so quickly before or since. Bert and I covered and cleared that quite large lounge very quickly.

*Ian Chadburn*

Colin [Bulley] and I were to take one of the bedrooms and we were to be the second-to-last pair in through the front door. We could hear talking and the occasional laughter inside 'our' room and believe me the adrenaline was running high. Robbie gave the word and in we went. Inside the room were two guys in one bed and another guy on the floor at the foot of the bed. They appeared struck down with fear, what with Colin and I screaming at them: 'Armed police – don't move.'

All three men – Storey, Glenholmes and Campbell – were found in the flat, as was a fourth, later identified as Gerard Tuite, who was wanted in connection with a series of bombing attacks in London a year earlier. Anti-Terrorist branch officers formally arrested them and police found two loaded Browning self-loading pistols, 196 rounds of ammunition, a plan of Brixton prison and a list of country houses that were being considered as possible refuges. The four were charged with conspiracy to effect the escape of Keenan and with possessing firearms and ammunition. The two women were also charged, as indeed was Keenan himself, but Tuite escaped from Brixton prison in December 1980. Two London criminals, Alfred Moody and Stanley Thompson, were already planning to escape by tunnelling through the cell walls with tools supplied to them by Moody's brother during visits. To reach the outside they had to pass through a cell with an outside wall and it happened to be Tuite's.

The trial of the rest went ahead at the Old Bailey in March 1981, but the jury could not agree in the case of Storey and he was found not guilty at a re-trial in April. The others were convicted and Keenan was sentenced to three years' imprisonment to be added to the eighteen years he had by now received for the conspiracy to cause explosions and firearms offences. Campbell and Glenholmes were each given sentences of five years for conspiracy to effect the escape and ten years for the firearms offences. The two women were given suspended sentences and a fine of £1,000 each. Storey returned to Northern Ireland, but he was soon arrested again, this time after a shooting incident. He was in possession of an Armalite rifle and was sentenced to fifteen years in prison.

Before being arrested in Holland Park, Tuite had lived with his girlfriend in Trafalgar Road in Greenwich under the name of David

Coyne. In August 1980 a new tenant was redecorating the flat and pulled up a loose floorboard. He called the police when he found an Armalite rifle, shotguns, explosives and bomb-making equipment. In March 1982 Tuite was arrested in Drogheda in the Irish Republic. In the first case of an Irish citizen being tried in Ireland for an offence committed in England, he was convicted at Dublin's Special Criminal Court in July 1982 of possessing bomb-making equipment at the Trafalgar Road flat. Charges of conspiracy to cause explosions were adjourned with no pronouncement being made and he was sentenced to ten years in prison.

## GREENFIELD ROAD

The Firearms Unit returned to more routine matters when, on 7 January 1980, an Italian waiter, Carmello Pinelli, broke into a house in Greenfield Road in Tottenham to try to persuade Georgina Philipides to continue their relationship after she had thrown him out of the house. To emphasise his devotion, he armed himself with a revolver. When neighbours heard Pinelli breaking in through an upstairs bedroom window they called the police. Mrs Philipides ran from the house when police arrived and Pinelli then fired at the unarmed officers outside, fortunately without effect. Still in the house in an upstairs room was Mrs Philipides' diabetic son, but he was successfully talked down a ladder by a local inspector while the gunman's attention was distracted at the front.

A specialist team and negotiators were sent for and the siege ended peacefully after nine hours when two Firearms Unit officers using ladders gained access to the first floor of the house and arrested Pinelli. In March 1980 he pleaded guilty at the Old Bailey to firearms offences and was sentenced to seven years in prison.

The ending of the siege was widely reported, not least by the *Daily Express*, which also produced a photograph of the two officers at the top of a ladder, about to enter the Greenfield Road house. Over the photograph and alongside the headline 'Climb of the Siege Brigade' was the legend 'The Most Dramatic Pictures are in the *Daily Express*'. Dramatic it may have been, but genuine it was not. Bob Wells, one of the two officers concerned, could be seen at the top of the ladder and, in the same photograph, approaching the ladder on foot in the street. The photograph had been fabricated. It would prove to be only the first of a number of deliberately altered pictures purporting to show the Firearms Unit's officers in action that would appear in various newspapers in the years to come.

By the end of the 1970s the Firearms Unit in London had earned an international reputation as a training organisation and as Britain's only full-time operational unit. The arrangements made for both its spheres of responsibility had proved effective and, despite an initial hiccup over the provision of rifle training, in need of very little alteration. The only area still to be validated was the interface between the police and the army in the event of an incident that was beyond the ability of the police to resolve. The eventuality had been foreseen and, since Balcombe Street, there had been considerable planning and joint exercises. Formal procedures were in place between the Home Office and the MoD for the army to supply 'Military Aid to the Civil Power' (MACP) in the case of terrorist hostage-taking incidents. All of that preparation was about to be put to the test.

*Chapter 7*

# VICTORY AND DISASTER

## THE IRANIAN EMBASSY

A t about 11.25 on the morning of 30 April 1980, six terrorists burst into the Iranian Embassy, a five-storey building overlooking Hyde Park in central London at 16 Princes Gate, Kensington. They were armed with Polish wz63 sub-machine guns, handguns and grenades, and they quickly overpowered the officer on duty from the Diplomatic Protection Group (DPG), Constable Trevor Lock, although they did not consider it necessary to search him. After all, the British police did not carry guns! In a defining example of the power of the Dixon image, Constable Lock was able to keep his revolver on his hip, hidden under his uniform jacket, for the next six days.

The DPG had been formed in 1974 to protect diplomatic premises in central London, a role undertaken until then by the local divisions. The contingency plan now swung into action as the Anti-Terrorist branch, technical support, two specialist teams and negotiators were sent for.

*Alex Moir*

When we arrived we found the DPG officers stationed around the embassy. Some were out on the street about 20 yards from the front and some were in the gardens to the rear, out in the open, without any cover. We suggested that perhaps they needed to be a little further back and we located several vantage-points for them in other buildings and in the grounds in the rear of the embassy. We were directed to set up our operations room in the London School of Needlework in Queensgate. Inside we were shown the room that had been allocated to us but DPG officers were also there and other departments were arriving as well. They all seemed to be coming into this small room and nobody was getting anywhere. The use of electricity was increasing by the second and, as the electric meter was coin operated, it was evident that things would have to change. We found a suitable house two doors from the embassy and so we were moved into that. The house was ideally situated as we could set up our own control room and operate from there. We supplied two officers to the main control room and that kept us updated.

*Ron Parrish*
Shortly after our arrival 'Robbie' [Robbins] briefed us and told us to get ready as we may have to go in if any hostages were shot or in immediate danger of being shot. There were about nine of us and you can imagine the looks we gave each other. When the SAS eventually assaulted the embassy, I think they used over sixty personnel.

The temporary operations room for the teams was in the ground floor of 18 Princes Gate. District rifle officers had arrived by 3 o'clock in the afternoon and they were soon deployed in pairs at the back of the embassy at 52 and 64 Kensington House North.

Inside the embassy the terrorists had taken twenty-six hostages. They claimed to belong to the 'Mohadeen Anafar Martyr' (Group of the Martyr), part of a movement fighting for local autonomy for Arabistan, a small oil-rich part of Iran at the northern end of the Persian Gulf, bordering Iraq. They demanded the release of ninety-one Arab prisoners in Iran by noon the next day and that the Arab ambassadors from Algeria, Jordan and Iraq be brought to the embassy to mediate on their behalf. They threatened that if their demands were not met, they would blow up the building. Nevertheless, Frieda Monzafarian, a press officer at the embassy, was in such a state of terror that they decided to release her. At 4.20 in the afternoon she walked out of the front door but she was not in a fit state to give any information about what was happening inside the building.

The Cabinet Office Briefing Room, known by an extension of its acronym as COBRA, was set up under the chairmanship of the Home

Secretary, William Whitelaw. Its role was to deal with any 'political' dimension that might arise. All firearms training was cancelled and the Firearms Unit prepared itself for a long stay.

*Alex Moir*
As we had only two teams there, messages were sent back to Old Street for the other two teams to be made available to relieve us that evening at 8 o'clock. From then on we ran a twelve-hour shift system changing over at 8 a.m. and 8 p.m. We had teams upstairs and downstairs to exit on to the front or the back and we gave cover to the negotiators when they went forward or when food or telephones were being taken forward to the embassy.

That evening, the government of Iran announced that it had no intention of releasing the ninety-one prisoners. In the early hours of the following morning the first members of the SAS arrived.

*Bert Harris*
At the top of the house we were in you could go through a flat to get on to the roof of the embassy. We were responsible for guarding the roof and you could move quite freely up there over little iron bridges.

*Alex Moir*
Our teams found a way on to the roof and this allowed the technical support people to insert microphones down the chimneys. When the SAS arrived, they were taken to the roof so that they could see for themselves the various means of access.

During the morning of the second day the condition of another hostage, Chris Cramer, deteriorated and at 11.30 the terrorists let him leave. He staggered out into the street and for the first time the police got reliable information on what was happening inside the building. The noon deadline was extended first to 2 o'clock in the afternoon and then to 5 o'clock. This deadline also passed. At 9.30 in the evening Constable Lock started acting as a go-between, appearing at a window and passing on to the negotiators what the terrorists inside

were telling him to say. As night fell, members of the SAS carried out
another reconnaissance. They were planning for an assault that would
be codenamed 'Operation Nimrod'.

By the third day the terrorists had become increasingly disillusioned
at the lack of action, but they were not the only ones who had little
information about what was happening. Even the police officers at the
scene had little idea of the direction that the siege was taking and
sometimes the information they did get was wrong, as Inspector, later
Chief Inspector, John Warner and Constable John Nunn discovered.

*John Warner*
The information we got was very thin. Hardly any of us had much
idea of the whole picture, only that we might have to go in at some
time to do a rescue. For much of the time our shifts were boring,
mainly because of the lack of any real information. I think we
sometimes got more from the TV news when we got home than we
did from official sources.

*John Nunn*
The information was coming in but not much of it was being passed
on to us. We had to keep going out to see what was happening and
I remember that the technical people with the cameras trained on
the back of the building kept reporting movement. This went on
for about three or four days. We had to go out to see what the
movement was and saw nothing. It transpired that they had their
cameras pointed at the wrong building – they were watching us.

During the morning of the fourth day Constable Lock and another
hostage, Mustapha Karkouti, were forced to a window at gunpoint and
told to explain to the police outside that the terrorists were losing
patience and that the situation was growing serious. In particular, the
terrorists wanted the Arab ambassadors brought in to mediate, just as
they had requested from the start. The strain on Mustapha Karkouti
was too much and he later collapsed.

Inside the embassy some of the hostages did their best to persuade
the hostage-takers that their best option was to get publicity and then

to surrender before there was any loss of life. This seemed to have some effect because in the late afternoon the terrorists released a press statement. After demanding the attendance of the ambassadors they went on to say: 'The reason for us coming to Britain to carry out this operation is because of the pressure and oppression which is practised by the Iranian government in Arabistan and to convey our voice to the outside world through your country. Once again, we apologise to the people and the government for this inconvenience.'

The police, after getting the agreement of COBRA, passed on the statement to the news media with a request that it be broadcast as widely as possible. At 8 o'clock that evening the terrorists released Mrs Hiyech Sanei Kanji, a secretary. At 9.15, after hearing the statement broadcast, the terrorists released another hostage, Ali Ghanzafar. To the police it now seemed that the siege was going to end peacefully, but when the terrorists began to write anti-Ayatollah Khomeini slogans on the inside walls of the embassy, Abbas Lavasani, a press attaché, flew into a rage. He confronted the terrorists, saying that he was ready to be martyred. It seemed as though he was going to be shot there and then, but Mustapha Karkouti knocked him to the ground and, with the help of Constable Lock, the situation was temporarily defused. However, the atmosphere had changed inside the embassy.

On 4 May, the fifth day of the siege, the terrorists clearly believed that the transmission of their statement meant they would now see the Arab ambassadors and they became increasingly frustrated by the lack of response. They believed that the police were deliberately stalling. Nevertheless, they were also concerned about the deteriorating condition of Mustapha Karkouti and at just after 8 o'clock in the evening they released him. That night the SAS spent three hours clambering over the roof of the building.

At about 11 o'clock the next morning Constable Lock was told to tell the officers outside that unless an assurance was given that the Arab ambassadors were involved, one hostage would be shot within 30 minutes. This message was passed on but the police could do little. Any decision on whether to involve ambassadors, assuming that they were willing to come, was a matter for COBRA. At just before 1 o'clock in the afternoon the Firearms Unit's officers heard the sound of three shots being fired inside the embassy and the terrorists claimed to have shot a hostage. Then at 6.02 in the evening there was the sound of another shot. At 6.42 three more shots were heard and a few moments later a bundle was pushed out of the door of the embassy. The bundle was Abbas Lavasani. Members of the Anti-Terrorist branch collected the body on a stretcher while officers of the Firearms Unit provided cover, as Constable Peter McDonald later explained in a television interview:

Two CID officers, I think from the Anti-Terrorist squad, came forward with a stretcher to recover the body. . . . [We] went out to give them cover because they were unarmed and they were in civilian clothes obviously. Your eyes were everywhere. You couldn't look everywhere but you tried to look everywhere. . . . It was one of those situations where there was no opportunity to take cover. If you had worried about taking cover, like getting [to] the wall which was outside the embassy, it would have taken too long and we couldn't have been very effective from there. So it just had to be one of those situations where you took the bit between the teeth and did it.[1]

Sir David McNee later wrote:

At 5 p.m. on 5 May, the commander of the SAS reported that his troops were at ten minutes readiness for a full assault. . . . When the body of the dead hostage, Lavasani, was recovered from the front door of the embassy shortly before 7 p.m., examination showed that his death had occurred some hours previously. This seemed to suggest that the first three shots heard shortly after noon had killed him and that the later shots heard at 6.42 had possibly killed one or more others. As threats had been made to kill a further hostage at 7.15 p.m., we concluded that there was a high probability that at least two hostages had been killed and that the terrorists were ready to kill the remainder. Urgent action was required and I sought immediate discussion with the Home Secretary. . . . He authorised the commitment of the SAS.[2]

A further hostage had not been killed, however, and it has never been explained why the shots were fired before the body was pushed out of the door. Nevertheless, a short time later, Firearms Unit officers were told to take up their positions around the building.

*Tony Gray*
At the end when we thought it was going to happen, an SAS officer and his signaller came into our room. They hadn't eaten for a while and so I got them something to eat. I remember we kept saying, 'Come on, Willie; come on, Willie; give us the okay.' I suddenly saw soldiers come out on to the roof and start doing the recce for the ropes and that was my first indication that it was on.

*Ron Parrish*
After many false starts the code words 'Bushranger ready to go' were given over the radio and the SAS assault on the embassy started. At this time, Bert [Harris] and I were occupying the first-floor balcony at the rear of no. 18. Our brief was to assist the SAS and if any of the terrorists got past the SAS cordon we were to take targets of opportunity. When the front of no. 16 was blown out, all hell let loose. Apart from the noise of gunfire and shouting, slates rained down from the roof just missing us and a glass dome which had been on top of no. 18 crashed in, sending glass everywhere.

I was watching the outer cordon of the SAS in the garden and we heard this popping sound. We thought firing was coming from the garden but it was the SAS throwing smoke-pots across the lawns to cover the assault at the rear. When the hostages were brought out into the rear yard, Bert and I assisted the SAS to cover them while they were initially searched and escorted away. One of the terrorists had infiltrated the hostages but he was soon identified and removed.

Jack Parkes, one of the Firearms Unit's officers at the front of the embassy, said in a television interview shortly after he retired:

My immediate reaction when the bomb went off was that the terrorists had actually blown the building up. I did know that they [the SAS] were going to blow the front of the building in order to make an entry but it seemed such a violent explosion that I thought the terrorists had beaten them to it.[3]

The size of the explosion surprised some members of the SAS too, and it is certainly true that not everything went according to plan. One soldier became so entangled in his abseil rope that he could not move and was suspended just above the windows of one of the rooms that were now on fire.

*Tony Gray*
I saw the soldier in the flames. He was almost opposite me and I remember the two things that went through my mind. The first was that I should try to shoot the rope. It sounds silly now and whether I could have hit the rope or not I don't know. Then I thought that if I fired a shot everyone would start to shoot and so I decided to concentrate on the windows around him because it was my job to deal with them. I remember shouting 'Cut the rope; cut the rope.' He wouldn't have heard me but I was so concerned that a terrorist would come to one of the windows and he was very vulnerable. He eventually freed himself, dropped down on to a balcony and went in.

*John Nunn*
The SAS timing was wrong because the explosion went off at the front before the blokes were ready to go in through the windows at the back and they had to get down very quickly. Then you could hear the sound of footsteps on the floorboards in the embassy because there were many empty rooms. You could hear running backwards and forwards and then a burst of shots. Then another lot of running and then another burst of shots. We were convinced that everybody in there had shot everybody.

They were not the only people watching as events unfolded in front of them. So too were millions of viewers glued to their TV sets.

All of the major television networks cancelled their scheduled programmes and switched to cover the assault as it was happening. However, once the initial assault was over, there was only the outside of the front of the embassy to look at with smoke and then flames coming from it. What was happening inside was left to the imagination. In fact, nineteen hostages were rescued and five of the six gunmen were killed.

The *Daily Express*'s headlines 'Victory' and 'SAS bring 19 hostages out alive' were typical of the media reaction the next day. The feeling of elation was all-pervading and *The Times* editorial summed up the opinion of many:

> The technique on which the British police have relied up to now for dealing with sieges of this sort has been that of patiently talking the gunmen into submission. Such tactics have been used with success in previous sieges at Balcombe Street and Spaghetti House. They are the right ones to employ so long as there seems a reasonable chance of securing the release of the hostages unharmed. But the moment that any hostages are shot by their captors, as they were in this case, the time has passed for the methods of patient persuasion.

As is now known, Ali Akbar Samadzadeh, a temporary employee at the embassy, was shot dead when one of the terrorists opened fire into the group of hostages after the assault had started. Two others were injured at the same time, and for some of the officers assigned to the incident this left a sense of failure. In particular Constable Lock and the negotiators felt that they should have been able to resolve the siege without loss of life. Constable Lock had nothing to reproach himself for. His actions at the siege were little short of magnificent. He was later awarded the George Medal and the freedom of the City of London. Lock also received a special mention in a resolution passed in the House of Commons. That the negotiators should feel as they did was equally unwarranted. The earlier success of 'Play it Long' had raised false expectations. It had worked when criminals and terrorists unexpectedly found themselves surrounded by armed police, but at

Princes Gate the terrorists were exactly where they wanted to be and the hostages had been taken deliberately. Given the incendiary mixture of personalities inside the embassy, the result was almost inevitable.

The surviving terrorist, Fawzi Nejad, was sentenced to life imprisonment at the Old Bailey on 22 January 1981.


## FACILITIES

The instructions on the police use of firearms in London were updated in July 1980, although the circumstances under which a firearm could be used were still virtually identical to those published in 1955.[4] However, there was to be a change in the way authorised officers were distributed throughout the force. Commanders were to be allowed to set their own figure for the number that they thought they needed.

The effect of introducing such a policy could hardly be described as unexpected. A survey of all divisions and branches in 1979 had identified a need for 4,601 authorised officers. The Metropolitan Police policy committee had agreed and this became the target figure, but by the end of 1979 the actual number trained had still only reached 3,820. In April 1980 a new survey had been conducted to see if the 1979 figure was still accurate. The result was horrifying – commanders had assessed their new requirement at 6,039.

The problem was finding places where all these additional officers could be trained. The indoor range at Holborn police station had by now reopened after its closure in 1972, but the range at City Road was still having a new ventilation system installed at a cost of £133,000. A divisional club range at Marylebone police station had been completely refitted and a new police station to be built in Croydon had a range included as a part of its design. Another indoor range was being planned near Heathrow airport but this was not due until the autumn of 1983. Two other indoor ranges, in Greenwich and Stoke Newington, were likely to remain unusable for the foreseeable future. As a result, Purfleet, RAF Uxbridge and Lippitts Hill were bearing the brunt of the training programme.

*Ron Parrish*

Over a period of time we learned much about the requirement for ranges to effectively carry out the necessary training for different departments. The existing ranges at Purfleet and Lippitts Hill were refurbished, especially at Purfleet where the bulk of reclassification and practices were carried out. The firing points were prone to flooding and so special wooden, slatted platforms were installed at the 7- and 25-yard firing points.

*Alex Moir*

The range at Lippitts Hill had a grass surface and an open roof originally. When it rained the grass very quickly turned into a quagmire. Finally, the surface was relaid with bitumen chippings and a roof was installed with parts of it open to the elements to prevent the atmosphere being contaminated with lead pollution. A new turning target system operated by compressed air was installed and areas were concreted over to accommodate vehicles for protection officer training.

Work on the 50-metre range at Lippitts Hill, and the building of three new 25-metre ranges alongside it, had been completed in June 1980. The four-day basic courses were then extended to five days as had been recommended in 1975. In October use of RAF Uxbridge ceased. Its workload was transferred to Lippitts Hill, but operational commanders now inundated the Firearms Unit with requests for more of their officers to be trained using the wording of the new instruction as their justification. All that the instructors could do was explain that they were using all the facilities available to train officers as fast as they could.

## OPERATIONS AND THE USE OF CS

Responsibility for war planning and home defence was transferred from D11 to another branch in July 1981. From then on it was only responsible for firearms training and providing specialist teams, although it gained a responsibility for security at major events. The first was the wedding of His Royal Highness Prince Charles to Diana Spencer. For some months beforehand, two of the Unit's officers repeatedly walked the routes to be taken by the couple from Buckingham Palace to the Metropolitan Police boundary with the City of London police at the Royal Courts of Justice in the Strand and from the Palace to Waterloo station. They examined every building from ground floor to roof and identified the best locations from which D11 and the district rifle officers could provide counter-sniper cover. On 29 July, the big day, eighteen counter-sniper teams backed up by six SPG response vehicles covered the first of these routes and then moved to fifteen positions on the second route when the couple left for their honeymoon. Such counter-sniper cover would become a standard feature at ceremonial events in London.

Also in July, the Home Office announced that it intended to make CS and baton rounds available to police for dealing with incidents of serious public disorder. The decision was the result of a riot in Brixton the previous April during which 299 police officers had been injured, twenty-eight premises burned and another 117 damaged and looted. For the first time in England, petrol bombs had been thrown at police, and there were similar cases of rioting in the Toxteth area of Liverpool a few months later. No one noticed that it was almost exactly ten years since an assurance had been given that the police would never use CS to deal with riots. Never is a long time in police work.

The CS was fired from a battery-operated launcher and the canister burst in the air, spreading CS pellets over an area of about 15 metres. The baton rounds were fired from a discharger (designated Type L67) and the rounds were similar to those used by the Royal Ulster Constabulary and the army. The Firearms Unit's instructors were made responsible for training officers to use this equipment and, together with the district rifle officers, had to provide operational response should it be needed in London. The police now had the means to break up a large crowd that was setting fire to cars or buildings, and no longer would officers be expected to remain a static target at which petrol bombs and bricks could be thrown with impunity – or so it was thought.

## PROTECTION TRAINING

In November 1981 the one-week bodyguard course was extended to three weeks, the result of four D11 officers qualifying as bodyguard instructors with the SAS. As well as shooting and the opportunity to practise various protection techniques in the event of an attack, the courses now included input from experts on improvised explosive devices, first aid, self-defence and, for the first time, physical fitness training. The commander in charge of Special Branch was doubtful of the need for the courses, arguing that there had never been a case of a Special Branch officer using a firearm in the entire history of his branch. Providence was about to step in again and soon it would no longer be possible to make such a claim.

The Queen's Police Officer, Commander Mike Trestrail, was one of the earliest attendees at the three-week course. Unlike his counterpart in Special Branch, so keen was he that his officers underwent the training that he asked if he could help by returning as a guest speaker on future courses to explain the many idiosyncrasies involved in the protection of royalty – an offer that was accepted. Eventually the course would be duplicated by the other National Centres and adopted by the ACPO JSC as the recommended training for any officer who was about to do close protection.

## THE JUNE 1982 REVIEW

By 1982 complaints from commanders that insufficient officers were being trained resulted in the force Inspectorate being called in to mediate. The Inspector recommended that surveys be conducted annually to determine the level of operational need and that a report should then set out what was required in order to meet that need. The Firearms Unit doubted whether such a report would make much difference but it used the results of the 1980 survey to produce a review.

The June 1982 review pointed out that the instructors did not consider the level of training in London to be adequate. What was seriously lacking, the review explained, was:

Fieldcraft areas in which to train and practise tactics and Lippitts Hill is the only place where these can be built. . . . A field-craft village . . . is required. Building fascias are lightweight and pre-fabricated and do not require foundations and are not expensive, comparatively speaking. A suitable small training village can be built next to and around the present ranges. . . . A lightweight road system and eventually a drive-in vehicular range needs to be built . . . next to the 50-metre range. . . . The most pressing need is for a road system that will accommodate the bodyguard course and plans should be put in hand immediately.[5]

The review is a clear indication of just how much development there had been during the previous decade and a half. Although the additional ranges were still needed, the main emphasis was now on police officers being given the opportunity to practise, under realistic conditions, what their actions should be in different situations.

The instructors' scepticism proved to be well founded, however. The review was ignored. The instructors themselves now went looking for unused industrial sites that could be taken into temporary use. One of those they located was in part of an old hospital and the Firearms Unit asked for permission to use it. 'Police Plan Gun Training at Hospital' was the resulting headline in Socialist Workers Party's *News Line* in August 1982. Readers were told:

Paramilitary armed police plan to use a partially closed London hospital for secret training sessions. Scotland Yard's hush-hush D11 squad want to take over part of St Olave's Hospital in Bermondsey. . . . Harry Barker, Divisional Officer of the public service workers union NUPE, said 'I am appalled to hear there is even the suggestion of the use of the building for a frightening form of police training'.

The instructors decided that it would probably be best to look elsewhere.

## INTERNATIONAL TERRORISM

Even as the June 1982 review paper was being prepared, three members of Abu Nidal (Father of Struggle), a Palestinian terrorist group, were looking for a suitable target in London. Hussein Said, Marwan Al-Banna and Nauoff Rosan settled on Shlomo Argov, the Israeli ambassador to London. On 3 June 1982 at about 11 o'clock in the evening Hussein Said, armed with a Polish wz63 sub-machine gun, shot the ambassador as he was getting into his car outside the Dorchester Hotel where he had been attending a formal dinner. The ambassador's Special Branch protection officer, Detective Constable Colin Simpson, gave chase as the terrorist ran into South Street. The terrorist turned and fired at the officer who also fired one shot. The gunman was hit in the neck and a shot from the terrorist's gun ricocheted off the rear window of a parked car. The sub-machine gun then seems to have jammed and Said was arrested. Gilbert Kelland later wrote:

> It must be unique for the Commissioner and the Assistant Commissioner (Crime) both to be present at the scene of a terrorist attack. . . . Sir David McNee and I had also been guests at this dinner and were still inside the hotel when the Arab assassin . . . shot the ambassador in the head. . . . I was in the foyer of the hotel when the news was broken to me by the personal assistant to an executive of the company hosting the dinner. Her actual words, a typical example of British understatement, were, 'Excuse me Mr Kelland but I think you ought to know that the Israeli Ambassador has been shot outside.'[6]

A hotel security officer had seen a yellow Fiat 127 speed off after the shooting and the Force Control Room circulated the registration number of the car. Two unarmed officers, Constables Blake and Richard, saw the car and stopped it. Inside were Al-Banna and Rosan with another wz63 sub-machine gun. Both were arrested.

The ambassador survived but suffered irreversible brain damage. The would-be assassin fully recovered and with his two confederates stood trial at the Old Bailey in February 1983 charged with attempting to murder the ambassador and Constable Simpson and with firearms offences. All three pleaded not guilty but the jury convicted them of all the offences except that of attempting to murder Constable Simpson. Rosan was sentenced to thirty-five years' imprisonment and both Said and Al-Banna were sentenced to thirty years. Israel used the attempt on the ambassador's life as an excuse to attack the Palestine Liberation Organisation and, three days after the shooting, Israeli troops poured into Lebanon.

## MORE SHOTS FIRED IN KENSINGTON

In London in August 1982, the same month as the *News Line*'s hospital story, David Martin escaped following a break-in at an office by shooting at an unarmed police officer and wounding him in the groin. On 15 September Detective Constable Peter Finch was one of several armed officers waiting at one of Martin's possible hiding places, and when a figure dressed in female clothing appeared it took a few moments for them to realise that it was a man and that he had a gun. Constable Finch struggled with Martin who was arrested, but only after he had been shot in the neck when he produced yet another gun from inside his clothing.

Martin was charged with attempted murder, armed robbery and several burglaries, but on Christmas Eve 1982 he escaped from Marlborough Street Magistrates Court and an operation was mounted to find him. Posters bearing his photograph were produced with the warning that: 'This man is very dangerous. Be on your guard. He will not hesitate to shoot. Do not take any chances.' Firearms were issued and part of the team formed to conduct the operation included Constable Finch because he was able to identify the wanted man.

One of the possible leads was Martin's girlfriend, Susan Stephens. She was placed under surveillance and on 14 January 1983 at about 6 o'clock in the evening she was seen in the back of a Mini being driven by Lester Purdy. Someone was also in the front passenger seat.

Constable Finch was directed to see if he could identify the passenger and when the Mini was stopped by traffic in Pembroke Road near Earls Court in Kensington, Finch got out of his car. Remembering his previous encounter with Martin, he drew his revolver and held it straight down by the side of his leg so as not to let anyone see it. He then walked up to the passenger door of the Mini and saw what he believed was the side profile of Martin. He had started to back away when he saw the driver turn his head and appear to look at him. The driver said something to the front passenger who then turned around and reached toward the rear seat.

Constable Finch thought that the passenger was reaching for a gun. He fired two shots and hit the rear tyre (he would later say that hitting the tyre was unintentional) after which he fired two pairs of shots at the passenger. He then moved to the driver's side of the vehicle and, seeing the passenger emerging from the driver's door, hit the figure with his now empty revolver. When the shooting started Detective Constable John Deane rushed up to the back of the Mini. He believed that the male passenger must be Martin and fired five shots through the rear window. Detective Constable John Jardine also saw what was happening and went to the offside of the Mini where he saw the driver's door open and a man lying half out of the car. This officer also believed that the man must be Martin and, as he was making groping movements down his body, that he was again trying to reach a gun hidden in his clothing. Jardine fired two shots at the figure.

The front seat passenger was not David Martin. He was Stephen Waldorf, a freelance film director, and he had been hit by five of the shots. Five days later Detective Constables Jardine and Finch were charged with attempted murder and wounding with intent to cause grievous bodily harm. Nine months later, on 19 October 1983 at the Old Bailey, both officers were found not guilty and acquitted. Stephen Waldorf recovered and received substantial compensation, reported to be £120,000. He would also become something of a celebrity when, over the coming years, he would periodically relive his experiences for the benefit of television documentaries and newspaper articles.

For the Metropolitan Police the whole episode was a disaster that would result in the force no longer being afforded recognition of the 'special organisation and circumstances' that it had enjoyed since 1965, although at the time no one knew that this had actually ever existed.

*Chapter 8*

# NEW RULES AND
# A CONVENTION

## NATIONAL DEVELOPMENTS

The public outcry after the shooting of Stephen Waldorf was such that something had to be seen to be done and so, on 22 March 1983, the Home Office wrote to every chief constable in England and Wales.[1] Included with the letter were new 'Guidelines on the Issue and Use of Firearms by Police' and chief officers were told that copies would be placed in the libraries of the House of Commons and the House of Lords 'in the next few days'. This was another way of saying that they would be made public, that they were not negotiable, and that forces had to change whatever their internal instructions were to match this definitive new national version.

The level of authority required before firearms could be issued was standardised across the board at ACPO rank (commander in London and assistant chief constable in other forces), although if a delay could result in loss of life or serious injury, a chief superintendent or superintendent could authorise issue. The exception was that a standing authority could be given when firearms were issued regularly for protection duty. From now on, firearms could be used 'only as a last resort where conventional methods have been tried and failed, or must, from the nature of the circumstances obtaining, be unlikely to succeed if tried'.

The term 'authorised firearms officer' (AFO) became the official national means of identifying an officer trained in the use of firearms. The Waldorf incident was the main agenda item at a meeting of the ACPO JSC on 5 May. Geoffrey Dear, now the ACD, later Sir Geoffrey Dear and one of Her Majesty's Inspectors of Constabulary, was asked to chair a national working party: 'To examine and recommend means of improving the selection and training of police officers as authorised firearms officers, with particular reference to temperament and stress.'

The working party's report, to become known as the Dear Report, was finalised in November. It recommended that all officers selected for defensive weapon training undergo early psychological written testing. It was also suggested that the duration of the basic course be increased to ten days and the subsequent refresher training should be four times each year for two consecutive days on each occasion (a total of eight days).[2]

On 24 December *The Times* told its readers:

> Changes in the training and assessment of police officers who carry firearms are to be discussed by Mr Leon Brittan, the Home Secretary, with the Commissioner of the Metropolitan Police, Sir Kenneth Newman [Commissioner 1982–7] in the wake of the Stephen Waldorf case. . . . The changes . . . would increase initial training from one to two weeks, lengthen additional later training, assess reactions to stress and give better tactical instruction.

By now, an ACPO 'Manual of Guidance on Police Use of Firearms' covering police operations, equipment and training had been produced by the NWGFI with the new Home Office guidelines as its first chapter. The Chief Constables' Council unanimously supported the Dear Report but this did not make its recommendations any the more binding than had been the case with the 1965 Interim Report. However, the existence of the latter had not become public knowledge and this was not true of the Dear Report. So when the Metropolitan Police policy committee met in March 1984 to discuss the report, the expectation was that all the proposals would be adopted. Instead, before making any decision the policy committee asked for another report explaining how the proposals should be implemented.

There had already been indications that the Commissioner would not overly welcome the Dear Report. On 23 October 1983 the *Daily Mail* had told its readers: 'The head of Scotland Yard's crack "Blue

Berets" . . . is calling for a major boost in firearms training for the capital's police after the Waldorf affair. . . . The Commissioner's dilemma is that . . . while he sympathises with the marksman's needs, he is committed to freeing more officers for duty on the streets.'

Sir Kenneth Newman had far more than that on his mind. Since 1869 London's geographical coverage by the Metropolitan Police had been divided into four districts. In 1970 the districts had been renamed 'areas' with each of the divisions being renamed 'districts'. Sub-divisions in their turn had become 'divisions'. Plans were now afoot to divide London up into eight areas each with its own divisions.[3] This would remove 'districts' as a level of command, leaving a flatter command structure in line with what was seen at the time as being good business management. Two of the stated aims of the reorganisation were to 'reduce the size and power of [the] force headquarters' and for divisions to be recognised as 'the fundamental unit in the organisational structure'. Each division was to be self-sufficient, and only if it was demonstrably unworkable for a policing function to be carried out by each division individually would consideration be given to it being performed by the area headquarters. Each area headquarters was also to be self-sufficient, and any function performed at New Scotland Yard would only continue if it could not be carried out at area or divisional level.

The old departmental lettering was also to be replaced. What was left of 'A' and 'B' departments, together with the eight new areas, would come under a new Territorial Operations department (TO). The parts that were left of the former 'C' department would come under a new Specialist Operations department (SO) and all training would come under a department to be called Personnel and Training (PT). This was not just a case of changing all of the force stationery. A reorganisation on this scale was going to be both disruptive and expensive. Anything, therefore, that was not directly related to the force reorganisation was assigned a low priority, which had consequences for the Firearms Unit that were to go far beyond just the lack of interest now shown in the Dear Report.

In May 1984 the policy committee considered proposals that divided the Dear Report's recommendations into two phases for 'implementation'. At the time the force was still providing three days' training a year for its authorised officers. Psychological testing, the increase in the length of initial training and one extra refresher day were all included in phase one. The doubling to eight days, with the additional facilities and instructional staff required, were all made part of phase two. Phase one was agreed but it had to be completed within existing budgets. No additional financial resources were to be allocated and a decision on phase two was deferred to a later, unspecified, date.

Nevertheless, on 21 June *The Times* told its readers:

Scotland Yard plans to spend several million pounds on new facilities for firearms training, including a mock up of a street where a policeman's judgement of when to fire can be tested, it was disclosed yesterday. The street would be an advanced version of the type developed in the United States and used by the FBI where officers are confronted with electronically operated threats as they move along a 35-yard two-dimensional street frontage. The Scotland Yard version is planned to be larger and more realistic, with moving vehicles and doors opening on to rooms and new scenes of the street. . . . Mr Geoffrey Dear, Assistant Commissioner responsible for training, told a press conference that the first phase of the changes would be implemented within 12 months. They include longer training periods and psychological testing for officers chosen to use guns. . . . Mr Dear said the mock up street was being devised because 'high realism' was needed to test men in making decisions about shooting.

## SUB-MACHINE GUNS

The attempted assassination of the Israeli ambassador, almost in front of the Commissioner and the ACC, dramatically changed the prevailing attitude at senior level that an attack on a diplomat or politician being given personal protection in London was highly unlikely. VIP protection training assumed a new importance and by

February 1984 the five-shot Model 36 revolver had been replaced by
the six-shot Smith and Wesson Model 64 revolver in departments
such as Special Branch and royalty protection. The Model 64 was
heavier than the Model 36 and therefore absorbed more of the recoil
but, like the Model 36, it only had a short barrel. It was easy to
conceal, but when faced with a terrorist with a machine-gun its value
was limited.

Then, early in 1984, planning started for a major economic
conference to be held in London in June, and the decision was taken
to train a small number of protection officers in the use of the Heckler
and Koch MP5K 9mm sub-machine gun. This was a shortened version
of the MP5 already available to the Firearms Unit but with the
advantage that it was more accurate than a handgun and could be
readily concealed under a coat.

When the news broke on 2 April the *Daily Mail* reported:

British policemen are to carry automatic sub-machine guns for the
first time after training by the SAS. . . . It was forced on Home
Secretary Leon Brittan after an ultimatum from American security
chiefs over a visit to London in June by President Reagan. The
President's advisers wanted to bring their own heavily-armed
security men to accompany him everywhere during his stay for a
three-day economic summit. Mr Brittan refused, despite fierce
arguments. But he finally agreed instead that a 12-man team from
the Metropolitan Police would be trained to use the 9mm Heckler
and Koch MP5K sub-machine gun.

The Home Office denied that the proposed measure was because of
security for President Reagan specifically and the officers were not to
be trained by the SAS, as the Prime Minister, Margaret Thatcher,
made clear in the House of Commons. Members were told: 'The
officers to whom these weapons will be issued will be trained to high
standards by the Metropolitan Police force firearms training specialists
in techniques appropriate to the role of the police. They will not be
trained by the military.'

On 4 April an outraged *Daily Mirror* reported:

Our so-called unarmed police force is now to be issued with SAS-style sub-machine guns. The slippery slope towards a semi-military constabulary becomes steeper. . . . The reason our police are not armed to the teeth is not because of an eccentricity peculiar to this island. It is because by conviction and experience we believe that arming the police adds to the dangers to innocent people rather than reduces them.

With irrefutable logic the article continued with the observation that:

An unarmed policemen would not have been able, by mistake, to pump bullets into Stephen Waldorf. . . . The protection we give to the Queen ought to be enough for Mr Reagan. If it isn't, then we would prefer to see him stay at home rather than have machine-guns on our streets.

The *Daily Mirror* would presumably have been mortified had it known that Her Majesty would soon agree that 'back-up teams engaged on royalty protection may be issued with these weapons'.

On 5 April the matter came up again in the House of Commons. James Callaghan asked:

In giving permission to the Metropolitan Police to acquire sub-machine guns, have the government considered the impact of this serious further step in arming the police on the relationship between the police and the public and on the very nature of the police service? . . . If the Metropolitan Police are armed with sub-machine guns that could change the character of the force and sacrifice a long-term beneficial system of policing to a short-term need.

The Prime Minister replied:

The right honourable gentleman may recollect, as it is within public knowledge, that as long ago as 1976 the Labour Administration approved the acquisition by the Metropolitan

Police of a small number of conventional sub-machine guns for use in a terrorist emergency. A cause which I feel sure that the right honourable gentleman and the then Home Secretary had very much in mind when they approved that purchase.

There is some doubt about whether it really was 'within public knowledge' but the Prime Minister clearly believed that Mr Callaghan had been involved in the granting of approval for the purchase of the MP5s by the Firearms Unit. On 7 April *The Times* reported:

Mr Roy Jenkins yesterday explained and defended his decision as Home Secretary in 1976 to authorise the purchase of sub-machine guns by the Metropolitan Police and his decision not to consult Mr James Callaghan who was the Prime Minister. He said that his advisers thought that the police should have [the weapons] under stringent control in case a 'burst-in' response was needed when hostages' lives were at risk.

The first MP5K course for eight officers started at Lippitts Hill on 14 May. The officers nominated for instruction had already completed the full bodyguard course and of the eight, six were successful in the MP5K training. The second course, also for eight officers and with a similar pass rate, started on 21 May. The training for a handful of protection officers in the use of the weapon has continued ever since.

## THE MURDER OF CONSTABLE YVONNE FLETCHER

Meanwhile, there had been a political demonstration on 17 April 1984 outside the Libyan People's Bureau in St James's Square, Westminster, central London. Those opposed to the regime of Colonel Gadaffi were formed up behind barriers on the opposite side of the road to the bureau while pro-Gadaffi demonstrators were allowed to assemble on the same side of the road as the bureau itself. At just after 10 o'clock in the morning, as the two groups shouted slogans at each other, there was sub-machine gunfire from the first floor of the bureau. Several of the anti-Gadaffi demonstrators were hit, as was Constable Yvonne Fletcher. As officers rushed to her aid the square was cleared and armed officers from the DPG surrounded the bureau. All of the victims were taken to Westminster Hospital where Constable Fletcher died.

Negotiators, technical support and specialist teams were all sent for. The officer in charge of the Firearms Unit's response was Superintendent Peter Harris:

> Everyone reported to Old Street and we had sixteen officers with their equipment available by just after 11 o'clock. We were told to report to Cannon Row police station but we couldn't get authority to go to the scene. I had to go to New Scotland Yard to find someone in authority and it was not until 12.45 that the team arrived in St James's Square. Ron Parrish then assisted the DPG in setting up the inner cordon control and two officers went around the bureau to formulate an assault plan should one be needed. When it became apparent that no hostages were involved, team members were deployed in support of the DPG to strengthen the inner cordon.

The delay was the result of internal politics. Senior DPG officers had wanted guarantees that they would retain primacy of command at the scene before they would allow Firearms Unit officers to attend.

Not only were there no hostages in the bureau, there were no demands and no deadline – only claims to diplomatic immunity.[4] The Firearms Unit showed parties of SAS around the building almost every day and night but it became increasingly obvious that they would not be used. The real hostages were the British subjects living thousands of miles away in Libya. COBRA was set up and the serious negotiations were at a diplomatic level rather than in St James's Square. All that was left for the police to do was to arrange the manner in which the bureau's occupants left the country.

*John Warner*
I was at the meetings when the method of the 'surrender' of the Libyans was discussed. There were Home Office officials, senior

officers and so on there and many were of the opinion that as the
Libyans wanted an 'out', everything was okay. I had to stress to
those who thought everything was going swimmingly that the
Libyans could easily use their 'surrender' to stage an incident that
would be in full view of the media. Luckily, David Veness [then a
Detective Chief Superintendent, later Sir David Veness, Assistant
Commissioner, Specialist Operations department], was also in on
the discussion and he supported this view most strongly. Because
D11 had so often worked with David I think he appreciated the
problems better than most.

The main concern was that the Libyans would leave the bureau as a
body, chanting slogans and concealing in their midst someone with a
firearm. After ten days, on 27 April, the thirty occupants left the
building in groups of five, spaced two paces apart and in single file.
Each group was led to a reception area that had been created in Duke
of York Street (out of sight of the bureau), at which the Firearms Unit
provided the firearms cover. One of the officers there was Constable
Dave Tilley:

> I was one of the only two that were to be allowed to 'cover' their exit
> and we had to be inspected by a neutral official. We were only allowed
> to have shotguns and they had to be held in the 'high port' position.
> At our insistence, we were permitted to have an armoured Land
> Rover parked next to us to use in an emergency. We cheated and had
> four more of the team hiding in the back with full kit just in case.

Police officers were not allowed to touch anyone leaving the
bureau.[5] As a compromise, the 'diplomats' agreed to carry their
personal possessions in clear plastic bags so that the contents could be
inspected. Each person was then scanned using a hand-held metal
detector. Their 'diplomatic baggage' was the last item to leave the
bureau and it was loaded, unsearched,[6] into a van and driven away.
Coaches took the Libyans to Sunningdale where they were
questioned. They were then taken to Heathrow for a flight back to
Libya and their 'diplomatic baggage' went with them.

If good can be said to have come from such a tragedy, it was the Police Memorial Trust. Created by Michael Winner, a film producer, the trust decided that there should be a memorial plaque erected to indicate where police officers had been killed on duty. Ten months after the shooting Margaret Thatcher unveiled the trust's first plaque at the spot where Constable Fletcher fell. The incident would come to public attention again in April 1996. *Murder in St James's*, a *Dispatches* television documentary made for Channel 4, claimed to have uncovered 'dramatic new evidence on one of Britain's great unsolved murders' that 'explodes the accepted version of her killing. It reveals that she was shot not from the Libyan Embassy [*sic*] as we have all believed but from a very different direction.'

Conspiracy theories had started even before the siege was over. Dr Iain West, the pathologist who carried out the post-mortem on Constable Fletcher, later explained that:

> One of the initial allegations was that she had been shot by Israeli agents on the roof who were trying to foment trouble between Britain and Libya. . . . I had been up to St James's Square while the siege was still on and had a good look at the building from behind a police armoured Land Rover. In the Forensic Science Laboratory . . . we used an inclinometer and worked out the maximum angle. It indicated that the shot had come from the first floor of the building or, a lesser possibility, from the second floor. In any event, the shot could not have come from street level or from the roof.[7]

By convention, the angle at which a bullet strikes an object is described in terms of the angle between the bullet's track and the plane of the surface it hits. Dr West had described the track of the bullet that killed the officer as being at an angle of 60 to 70 degrees to the horizontal plane of her body. This was because her body had been horizontal at the time of his examination, but Constable Fletcher had been standing with her arms folded when she had been hit. In this position, the angle of the track to the ground would have been 20 to 30 degrees (photographs suggest the angle was closer to 20 than 30). The bullet had entered the officer's back at a point 10 inches below her right shoulder, 5½ inches to the right of her spine, and had exited her body into the elbow of her folded left arm.

The main contributor to the *Dispatches* programme was a former army officer and gunshot-injury expert who, although this was not mentioned, was no stranger to conspiracy theories. As an army doctor in 1973 he had examined the prisoner in Spandau prison known to most people as Hitler's deputy, Rudolf Hess. He had said nothing at the time but, after leaving the army, he created a sensation when he wrote a book in which he claimed 'the medical evidence is absolute' that the man was not the real Hess.

When asked to account for the injuries sustained by Constable Fletcher, the doctor used a medical skeleton that was suspended vertically to illustrate the bullet's track as passing down through her body at an angle of 60 to 70 degrees to the ground. To emphasise the point, computer animation showed the bullet entering the top of the officer's right shoulder and exiting at her left hip. Based on this hopelessly inaccurate reconstruction, the doctor was able to demonstrate that for Constable Fletcher to have been hit from the Libyan People's Bureau she must have been leaning backwards at an impossible angle. When interviewed again, this time in St James's Square, he indicated the buildings from which he believed the shot must have come. It was at this moment that expert medical opinion placing Constable Fletcher's killer in a neighbouring, much taller building became firmly embedded in conspiracy-theory lore.

When combined with speculation as to method and motive, this 'dramatic new evidence' was said to show that rogue elements within the CIA and the British Security Service had arranged for the officer's assassination. The parallels with other 'second gunman' conspiracy theories were many and today there are several versions on the Internet, all based around the same central theme. The distress that these cause to the officer's parents can be imagined.

On 17 April 2004 at 10.45 in the morning, twenty years after Constable Fletcher's death, a memorial service was held in St James's Square outside the Libyan People's Bureau. The officer's murder remains unsolved.

## SHOTS FIRED IN TOTTENHAM

In the House of Commons two months after the murder, Labour's Gerald Kaufman asked the Home Secretary if he would make a statement on the shooting of two men at a north London post office in Seven Sisters Road, Tottenham. Alfred Ficken and Daniel Carey had planned a robbery there but police were alerted when a member of staff realised that she was being followed. During the night of 13 June 1984 the two robbers broke into the post office and waited. Two armed Flying Squad detective sergeants accompanied the post-mistress, Marjorie Simmons, into the building when she opened it up in the morning and were surprised when the two robbers suddenly appeared. Both officers fired when they thought that the robbers were going for guns in a bag, but when the bag was opened no weapons were found.

Leon Brittan explained the circumstances. After contributions from several other speakers, Mr Kaufman said, 'On 23 December 1983, the Secretary of State said that what had occurred in the Waldorf shooting plainly indicated the need for change, and that it was essential that such change should now take place. That is what he said six months ago. Has that change taken place?'

Choosing his words carefully Mr Brittan replied, 'I am happy to repeat answers that the right honourable gentleman seems to have been unable to take on board. . . . I have said that the changes in arrangements for selection and training are taking place.' Mr Kaufman interjected 'Six months later', to which Mr Brittan replied, 'That is not correct. If the right honourable gentleman had taken the trouble to look at the statement and had seen the nature of the changes that I have outlined, he would realise that they involve a continuous process and that it is not a one-off thing. From the moment that the statement was made that process commenced. The right honourable gentleman could not be in any serious doubt about that.'

Ficken recovered and was sentenced to eight years in prison, later reduced to five years on appeal. Carey was confined to a wheelchair because of his injuries and was not prosecuted. Both men took a claim for damages to the High Court in London but this was dismissed in July 1989.

## FIREARMS TRAINING

The process of introducing the changes, or at least a few of them, had indeed 'commenced' in London. In July 1984 the basic course was extended to two weeks. At the same time, trials started of seven different psychological written tests, but by September it was realised that they were not producing any valid results.[8] A new package of tests was assembled but by December these too were ruled out. The project, at least as far as the Metropolitan Police was concerned, was then wound up, but not all forces did the same and in 1992 the Home Office would commission a study to find out why.

Researchers visited three forces that still used the tests. Their report identified that: 'There are a number of controversial issues associated with personality testing. Although the purpose of testing is to produce objective measures, the construction of tests and the interpretation of test results both have their subjective aspects. More importantly, it has not been demonstrated that scores on personality tests are actually predictive of behaviour in specific situations.'[9] The report was critical of the way the tests were being conducted and most of the forces still using them to select their authorised officers ceased to do so.

The first meeting of a new working group was held at 3 o'clock in the afternoon of 30 August 1984. The Deputy Assistant Commissioner (Training) chaired it and its remit was to advise on the feasibility of implementing phase two of the Dear Report's recommendations. The group heard that the number of authorised officers had by now reached 4,851 and a separate working group was created to examine ways in which this figure could be reduced. To improve the basic and other initial courses a provisional estimate of £750,000 was placed on the cost of developing the facilities at Lippitts Hill.

By the next meeting on 13 December the cost of buying another site and developing it to accommodate the increased refresher training was variously estimated at between £3 million and £10 million, and the provision was formally included in the force's building plan. However, further consideration of any proposals that involved expenditure effectively ceased when, a few days later and despite the announcement at the press conference the previous June, the chairman was told that the policy committee had agreed that in future the majority of funds would be spent on police stations. Only a very small proportion of the budget, if any, was likely to be available for any kind of training.

As a result, the date to which decisions on phase two had been deferred would never come, and although the 'advanced version' of the FBI's 'realistic mock up street' was built in 1985, it did not quite live up to its advance billing. The instructors had to construct it themselves on a grass strip alongside the 50-metre range at Lippitts Hill.

*Alex Moir*
The material used for our first attempt was only junk timber that was lying around. We obtained a car from a local scrap dealer who was contracted to remove abandoned vehicles from various police car pounds and we designed some wooden partitions that were painted to look like walls. We tried to incorporate moving targets and wax ammunition based on the old 'incident rooms' at Old Street. However, the targets usually jammed or the wood would swell up due to the damp conditions when they were placed outdoors. We tried to waterproof the places where the targets were but this was then a give-away to the students. We couldn't keep up production of home-made wax rounds and so the students used blue plastic training ammunition instead. This created its own problems because they were more expensive than the wax rounds which had cost just the price of the wax, the sterin [wax hardener] and the primer.

The 'street' was a 25-metre gravel path and the only thing about the vehicle that moved was the low-loader that delivered it. The Commissioner, in his annual report for 1984, was rather more forthcoming than the Home Secretary had been six months earlier. He explained, with disarming simplicity, that: 'In common with all training departments, the desired progress will necessarily be retarded by the constraints of finance.'

## Chapter 9

# A MORE SENSIBLE CARTRIDGE

### HIGH PROFILE OPERATIONS

Two operations in 1985 brought the Firearms Unit in London to national prominence once again. In August 1984 there had been a robbery in Petts Wood on the outskirts of south-east London during which a police dog had been shot and killed. One of the robbers was identified as Toni Baldessare, a serial armed robber with a long criminal record, and by 24 January 1985 he had been traced to an attic flat in Gleneldon Road, Streatham. In the early hours of the morning members of the Firearms Unit took up positions and a Flying Squad detective inspector telephoned him to invite him to give himself up. Instead, Baldessare invited the police to 'come in and get him'.

*John Warner*
It was a difficult flat to enter. There was only one door in and immediately there was then a steep stairway leading upwards. Once it was found that he was by himself, we decided that he was already as good as arrested and so we sat it out.

*Tony Gray*
I was on a listening device that had been put in. We heard him [Baldessare] on a telephone talking to a woman. He was saying that there was no way out and that he was not going to go to prison again. She said something like: 'Well you've got to do what you've got to do, whatever that might be.'

Negotiations continued throughout the next day and at 11 o'clock that night there was the sound of a shot from inside the flat. One of those to hear it was Sergeant, later Inspector, Peter Sidebotham:

We were in the room directly underneath his flat and the negotiators were on the ground floor below us. There was a shot and when we heard his heels drumming on the floor we realised that he had shot himself. No one would believe us and when the chief negotiator came to speak to us, all we could hear at that time was the telephone ringing. It was the negotiators trying to make contact. The commander was at home in bed and he ordered that no one was to enter the flat until he and others arrived at 9 a.m. The next day a ladder was put up against the outside wall and a hole drilled so that a probe could be put through.

*Colin Bulley*

A couple of shots were heard during the siege but he was only practising and in fact, he shot the head off a statue. At the end, a shot was again heard from the flat and a probe showed him on his back with what looked like a bullet wound to the centre of his chest. With [Sergeant] Dave Chambers keeping a watch on him, Alex Moir and my team smashed our way through the party wall from next door. My team then searched the flat and we had a dog and handler with us as it was suggested that Baldessare was only shamming. The dog entered the room where Baldessare was and from its actions we concluded that he was in fact dead. The proceeds of a robbery, many thousands of pounds, were found smouldering in the kitchen sink. We found that he had prepared for a police entry. He had placed weaponry in various places throughout the flat so that he would not have to reload.

On 21 March an inquest jury in Southwark heard that Baldessare had wanted to die in a shootout with officers but had been frustrated by the police tactics. The verdict was that Baldessare had killed himself.

In the early hours of the next day there was another high-profile operation. In October 1983 James Baigrie had escaped from Saughton prison near Edinburgh where he was serving a life sentence for murder. On 20 March 1985 Baigrie was traced to a flat in Philbeach Gardens near Earls Court, but when unarmed officers searched it at 6 o'clock in the morning it was empty. As he left the flat, a detective constable saw a white transit van parked by the side of the road and he opened one of its back doors to be confronted by the wanted man pointing a sawn-off double-barrelled shotgun at him.

Surrounding streets were blocked off and negotiations with Baigrie started using the public address system on one of the Firearms Unit's armoured Land Rovers, but that afternoon Baigrie agreed to discussions being made less public by accepting a field telephone.

### Colin Bulley

Baigrie refused to allow anyone to come right up to the van. As the van contained various tools, he suggested that he would hold out a bucket on a broom handle in order that the telephone could be placed in it. As team leader, I felt that it was my job to make the delivery.

The process made front-page news the next day. Baigrie had a good view of what was taking place around him and, unlike Baldessare, he had an abundance of places that he could easily run to, all of which had to be covered by armed officers and dogs.

### Tony Gray

There were several suggestions as to how we could get him out. One was that we could throw a blanket over the whole van and take it to a police station. The attitude was one of he is not going anywhere and we are not going anywhere – except that west London was coming to a standstill.

During the evening of the second day Baigrie broke into the front cab area of the van and this gave him another option: that of just driving the vehicle away. Although the road was blocked, the vehicle could still be moved and this would have offered yet more places to run to, although Baigrie had let it be known that he was contemplating suicide.

### Colin Bulley

There was no reason to go in shooting just to 'rescue' someone who was threatening to commit suicide. However, certain very senior officers were getting more than a little cheesed off at having the area at a standstill with so many police officers tied up. A plan was therefore drawn up whereby ferrets [CS rounds fired from a shotgun] would be fired in through the rear windows of the van and grappling hooks could then be attached to the van's rear doors. An armoured Land Rover would yank the doors open and we would arrest Baigrie. When the go-ahead was given, Bob Wells [by now a chief superintendent and the officer commanding D11] did the countdown and on the 'go', three others and myself went to the van and chocked the wheels to prevent it moving when the grappling hooks were attached.

The officers had been ordered to delay their action to give the news media time to get their cameras into position and the operation started at 1.40 in the morning of 22 March. Two CS rounds were fired into the back of the van and the public address system on the Land Rover was then used to call on Baigrie to give himself up. About 20 seconds later a muffled shot was heard and two officers attached the grappling hooks to the back doors. When the Land Rover reversed and the doors were pulled open it was discovered that Baigrie had indeed committed suicide rather than go back to prison.

### SHOTS FIRED IN BRIXTON

Six months later, on 26 September 1985, officers from Hertfordshire police went to 69D Stamford Street, Southwark, in south-east London, to speak to Michael Groce in connection with a robbery. Groce had earlier had an argument with his girlfriend and had discharged a sawn-off shotgun into a wardrobe. When the detectives arrived, Groce made off. Initially there was confusion about what had happened. A rumour circulated widely afterwards that Groce had fired at the officers.

Unknown to the officers who were looking for him, Groce appeared at Lambeth Magistrates Court the next day on an unrelated matter. He gave his home address as his mother's house at 22 Normandy Road in Brixton, and when this piece of information came to light it was decided to raid the place.

A local inspector, Douglas Lovelock, was placed in charge, although he suggested that a specialist team be asked to perform the operation instead. His chief inspector agreed, but other senior officers rejected the idea. On 28 September Lovelock and six other divisional authorised officers were briefed at Brixton police station at 6 o'clock in the morning. The operation started an hour later. The front door was forced open and Inspector Lovelock led the officers in. He kicked open a partly open door to a room with its lights on and as he began to enter he saw a figure rushing at him from his left. As he turned he fired, hitting Dorothy 'Cherry' Groce. The shot caused irreversible damage to her spinal cord resulting in paralysis from the chest down. Michael Groce was not there.

There followed two nights of rioting in the area around Brixton. Buildings and cars were burned and looted, and there were more than 200 arrests. Inspector Lovelock was charged with 'unlawfully and maliciously wounding Mrs Dorothy Groce' and his trial opened at the Old Bailey on 5 January 1987. His defence was that the gun had accidentally fired when he tensed. On 15 January he was found not guilty. The *Daily Mirror* reported with some sadness that: 'Britain used to be the envy of the world because our police weren't armed. We could still be the envy of all if our officers who are armed have the best weapons and psychological training, the coolest approach and the surest aim.' It was very different from twenty years earlier when the same newspaper had reported that: 'All Britain's policemen are taught to handle small arms expertly.'

## THE TOTTENHAM RIOT AND THE MURDER OF CONSTABLE KEITH BLAKELOCK

On 5 October, a week after the Brixton riots, police went to Thorpe Road, Tottenham, at about 6 o'clock in the evening to search Cynthia Jarrett's home after her son had been arrested. Tragically, during the search Mrs Jarrett collapsed and died. The next day, at just before 2 o'clock in the afternoon, about 100 people congregated outside

Metropolitan officers with a combination of .455 Webley revolvers and pistols, *c.* 1913. (*Author*)

Metropolitan officer with a .455 Webley pistol, *c.* 1921. (*Author*)

A rare photograph of officers armed with Webley revolvers at a roadblock in the snow, *c.* 1932.

This Metropolitan officer outside 10 Downing Street in 1939 was armed with a .32 Webley pistol although few people would have known it. *(Getty Images)*

Metropolitan officers outside 10 Downing Street in 2005. (*Getty Images*)

**Firing by Sense of Direction** (See figs. 5 and 6)

20. Assume the 'READY' position. Gripping the butt as firmly as possible, FOREFINGER ON THE TRIGGER, raise the pistol QUICKLY in front of the centre of the body, keeping the arm slightly bent. The height to which the

21. Fire TWO shots in quick succession and return to the 'READY'. Repeat this until the exercise is completed. Then return to the READY position, forefinger pointing along the trigger guard.

pistol is raised depends on the range of the target. At point blank range (under 10 yards) the pistol need not be raised above the waist (see figure 5). At over 10 yards it will be necessary to raise the arm higher (see figure 6).

22. The unload procedure must be carried out as instructed in para. 16.

23. At the end of every practice and BEFORE leaving the firing point the chambers of every revolver must be examined as in para. 4 by the officer in charge.

'Sense of direction' shooting according to the Metropolitan Police Shooting League in 1957. (*Author*)

The scene after three police officers were killed in Braybrook Street in 1966. (*Mirrorpix*)

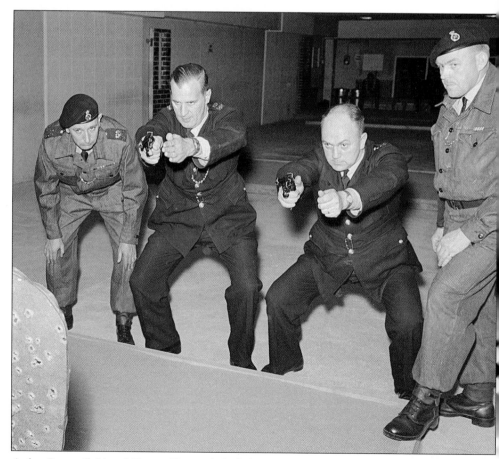

Arthur Batten (left) and George Hepworth (right) giving 'sense of direction' shooting instruction on a basic defensive weapons course in 1967. (*Mirrorpix*)

Ken Colby giving 'aimed shooting' instruction on a basic defensive weapons course in 1967. *(Getty Images)*

Bob Gould, the first Metropolitan Police Chief Firearms Instructor, demonstrating two-handed shooting in 1968. *(Getty Images)*

Training with the armoured shield in 1977. (*Author*)

The 'violent man' cage used in 1977 is tested on Bob Wells. (*Author*)

Officers letting themselves be photographed carrying .38 Smith & Wesson revolvers were 'causing embarrassment' in August 1978. (*Mirrorpix*)

The author (centre) and Ian Chadburn (left) find the inspector outside the door of the squat in Blackstock Road in December 1978.

Two officers on the inner cordon during the assault on the Iranian Embassy in April 1980. Jack Parkes is on the left. (*Empics*)

The Police Memorial Trust's first plaque on the spot where Yvonne Fletcher was killed outside the Libyan People's Bureau in April 1984. (*Mirrorpix*)

Hostage rescue training in 1985. (*Author*)

Prisoner reception training in 1985. (*Author*)

Colin Bulley delivers a handset from an armoured Land Rover during the van siege in March 1985. (*Mirrorpix*)

The 'realistic mock-up street' in use at Lippitts Hill in 1986. (*Author*)

The 'streets' at the Metropolitan Police firearms and public order training centre in 2004. (*Author*)

Surrounded by the news media in 1986, Dave Chambers (centre) is one of the first officers to carry an MP5 sub-machine gun on patrol. (*Mirrorpix*)

Metropolitan ARV officers training with MP5 single-shot carbines. (*Metropolitan Police*)

An intrepid cameraman (left) records police abseil training for a television company in 1993. (*Author*)

Specialist team training in 1999. (*Author*)

Officers rehearse boarding a ship from an RIB in 1999. (*Author*)

In April 2003 Sir John Stevens is the first Commissioner to be photographed gun in hand. (*Empics*)

Hostage rescue training in 2004. (*Author*)

The remains of the bus in Tavistock Square after the suicide bombing in July 2005. (*Getty Images*)

Armed City of London officers outside Liverpool Street station in July 2005. (*Empics*)

Armed Metropolitan officers outside the Houses of Parliament in July 2005. (*Empics*)

Armed West Yorkshire officers in November 2005. The officer on the left is also carrying a Taser o
his body armour. (*Empics*)

Tottenham police station carrying placards accusing the police of murdering Mrs Jarrett. The abuse from the crowd included threats to kill police officers and their families in revenge. At 6.49 p.m. there was a call to a large group of black youths throwing stones just outside the Broadwater Farm estate in Tottenham. Four minutes later there was another call to the same road, this time to the effect that police were 'urgently required'. The police personnel carrier sent to investigate drove into a storm of bricks and petrol-bombs and the bodywork of the vehicle was attacked by youths carrying machetes. The Tottenham Riot had begun.

All available police resources were mobilised. Just before 8 o'clock in the evening police realised that they were being shot at. One officer reported a bullet hole in his riot shield and another, who had been taken to hospital, was found to have a gunshot injury. The official report then records that:

Deputy Assistant Commissioner Richards . . . obtained authority from the Commissioner at 9.45 p.m. for the use of baton rounds and/or CS gas as a last resort should all else fail. In the event, by the time that the specially equipped team of officers from the Force's Firearms Branch (D11) arrived at Griffin Road from Tottenham at about 10.20 p.m., the severity of the attack had lessened considerably. . . . The baton round trained officers were not, in fact, called to take action.[1]

The officer in charge of the baton-round trained officers was Superintendent Peter Harris and he remembers the situation slightly differently:

At just after 9 o'clock I went to the scene. There were at least three burning vehicles immediately in front of the shields, a large number of missiles were being thrown at, and over, the front shields and many officers were injured. Persons repeatedly ran up to the front line of shields and assaulted officers with missiles before retreating down Griffin Road where they re-armed and attacked again. I told DAC Richards by radio that my advice was to use baton rounds.

However, the officer commanding the shield serials, a chief superintendent, told me that he did not consider the use of baton rounds to be necessary and he refused to facilitate their deployment. His attitude was that of complete surprise at my presence and of horror that the use of baton rounds was even contemplated.

The extremely violent attacks continued with bricks and petrol-bombs being thrown directly at police. I was told that my officers were nearby and I told [an officer] to bring them to Griffin Road. I then telephoned DAC Richards who directed that I deploy the baton gunners forthwith. I told him that I couldn't do so without the cooperation of the chief superintendent and DAC Richards then directed that I get the chief superintendent to the telephone immediately. The chief superintendent told DAC Richards that his officers, though under heavy attack, would continue to hold their line. He questioned the morality of the use of baton rounds and expressed his own fears for his conscience were he involved in the first use of baton rounds in this country. He expressed the view that the Metropolitan Police had managed for 150 years without using them and that we should not resort to their use now. As a result, the DAC rescinded the order to deploy the baton guns. I withdrew my officers – to the utter dismay of the officers under attack.

When the Home Office had given authority for the police to have baton rounds just over four years earlier it had not been fully appreciated that some senior officers would actually prefer that their officers be a target for petrol bombs and bricks. The alternative was too far outside their experience. It would not be for the first use of baton rounds that the Tottenham Riot would be remembered.

A short distance away all was quiet but a fire had broken out in one of the shops on a first-floor deck of Tangmere House, a pyramid-shaped block of flats that formed the centrepiece of the estate. While discussions were taking place over the use of baton rounds in Griffin Road, a party of just twelve police officers was sent in from Gloucester Road to support the fire brigade in dealing with the blaze. One of the officers was Constable Keith Blakelock. As the firefighters started their work, they and the police were attacked by a gang of youths. The officers and the fire brigade withdrew, but as they reached the ground floor they were attacked again and Constable Blacklock was hacked to death.

Fuel was poured on the already acrimonious debriefing sessions after the event when the local council leader and future Labour MP for the area, Bernie Grant, said with evident satisfaction that the police had received 'a bloody good hiding'. In June 1986 a major police internal study into the riots in Brixton and Tottenham made seventy-one recommendations covering everything from the purchase of twenty-four additional armoured Land Rovers to greatly improved training for senior officers.

Detective Chief Superintendent Graham Melvin led the investigation into the death of Constable Blakelock. At the Old Bailey in 1987 Winston Silcott, Engin Raghip and Mark Braithwaite were convicted of murder. However, in December 1991 they were granted unconditional bail and then acquitted by the Court of Appeal. It was alleged that the interview notes relating to Silcott had not been written at the time that they were said to have been. DCS Melvin was suspended from duty in January 1992 and both he and his former deputy, Detective Inspector Maxwell Dingle who had retired by now, were charged with conspiring to pervert the course of justice. On 26 June 1994 at the Old Bailey both men were acquitted. The murder of Constable Blakelock remains unsolved.

## SHOTS FIRED IN NORTHOLT

Christmas is traditionally the time of goodwill, but to the police it is also the period when already unstable family relationships finally break down. So it was in London in December 1985 with Errol Walker and his wife Marlene. Walker was well known to the police. In April 1982 he had been arrested for armed robbery and had then become what was later described as 'the first black supergrass'. After admitting twenty-six other robberies and informing on his associates, he was sentenced to five years in prison. In September 1982 he married his girlfriend, Marlene.

Their relationship foundered after Walker's early release and Marlene, together with their daughter Patricia, aged four, moved out in November 1985. They went to live at 62 Poynter Court, Gallery Gardens, Northolt, with Marlene's step-sister, Jacqueline Charles, who had a daughter called Karlene, also aged four. On Christmas Eve Walker arrived at Poynter Court and persuaded Marlene to return to the family home where he sexually assaulted her and then prevented her from leaving. On Christmas Day Walker demanded that Marlene collect Patricia and return. As a pretext for getting away she agreed, but when she arrived at Poynter Court at about 11 o'clock she called the police from a neighbouring flat.

When Walker realised he had been tricked he went to Poynter Court and found Jacqueline and the two children alone. The local duty officer, an inspector, arrived with two other officers just in time to see Walker forcing his way into no. 62 through the kitchen window. By the time the police officers reached the outside of the third-floor flat, Walker had grabbed Jacqueline and threatened to kill her unless Marlene was brought to him immediately. When the officers tried to negotiate with him he carried out his threat and pushed Jacqueline out of the kitchen window. She died of multiple stab wounds on her way to hospital.

From outside the kitchen window the officers managed to persuade Walker to hand out his daughter, Patricia, but he refused to part with Karlene who now became the object of his threats. Negotiators were sent for and at just before midday authority was given for the issue of firearms. The first armed officers from the local division arrived at just after 12.30 in the afternoon and a specialist team was also sent for.

*John Warner*

I went straight to the scene from home in civvies and I was the first D11 representative there. The suspect was black and at the time the whole [force] was on tenterhooks not to cause another riot. When the team arrived there was already a local AFO on the balcony not far from the flat concerned. It was simple to put in containment but the suspect went into the rear room of the flat, out of sight. Of course at that moment, the team having just arrived, we were not set up for an entry but it worried us greatly that we did not know what was going on. Luckily, the suspect came back into the kitchen with the child so, although the child was at risk, at least we could see them both. Bearing in mind that the team had taken a little while to get to the scene, senior officers and trained negotiators soon arrived. From that moment onward, any suggestion that we should intervene to rescue the child was not even considered. For all practical purposes, the negotiators took over the running of the incident.

The negotiators left the local officers talking to Walker who continued to demand that his wife be brought to him; the negotiators agreed. Marlene was sent forward alone and Walker left the flat, grabbed her by the throat and tried to drag her inside. She managed to resist him and even tried to hang on to him so that police could grab him, but no such move was permitted.

After her escape Walker wanted Marlene sent forward again. His attacks on Karlene included hacking at the child's right hand with a knife (severing several tendons), slashing at her arms and legs (leaving a deep gash in her right arm) and dangling her out of a third-storey window. Blood dripped on to an officer who was standing underneath ready to try to catch her. Walker also tied the child tightly to a chair using flex around her neck, repeatedly hit her on her head until she passed out, suffocated her to the point of unconsciousness by holding a plastic carrier bag over her head and threatened to cut off her right hand. Many officers present felt nothing but utter disbelief that the police service seemed incapable of protecting a small child.

Karlene's injuries were left untreated overnight. On the second day Walker continued with his demand that Marlene be exchanged for the child. This was accompanied by more threats, including one of electrocuting the girl by means of wires attached to a plug in an electrical socket. The negotiators insisted that this was nothing to worry about since the fuses would probably blow before any serious harm was done and they kept the senior Firearms Unit officer present out of any further discussion.

*Peter Harris*

The negotiators and the commander were so against the use of D11 officers to end the siege that they told me nothing and pretended that we were not even there – to the extent that I was not even invited to their 'command' meetings.

Walker demanded that the officers with firearms be removed from outside the flat, and when this was agreed he demanded that they leave the vicinity entirely. The negotiators suggested that it would be a way of showing good faith if all of the officers with firearms were formed up platoon fashion outside the front in the car park. Walker could then see them all being marched away. After strong objections a compromise was reached.

*John Warner*

The team was ordered to back off; sledgehammers and other equipment were banned from the balcony and the armed officers were moved out of sight. We were then not in a position to cater for any of the possible contingencies.

As morning turned into afternoon Walker became increasingly confident that the police were going to do nothing, but he took the opportunity to improve his barricades in case there was a change of mind. Tables, doors, mattresses, an ironing board, boxes and anything else movable was placed in the kitchen, hall and bathroom to make a forced entry more difficult. The kitchen window was now securely closed and barricaded. Most of the Firearms Unit's officers remained out of sight at the staircase end of the balcony but three others were in a flat next door to no. 62. This flat's letterbox gave a view of the entire length of the balcony, but the officers inside had been unable to move since being told to keep out of sight.

*Tony Gray*

We were put into this room at the far end of the balcony but once we were in there we were trapped. Anyway, this guy came out on to the balcony and came right up to our door and looked through the letterbox. Literally, I was 4 inches from him on the other side of the door. I said that if he came out again I would just open the door and grab him.

At 3.48 in the afternoon Walker appeared in the doorway of no. 62 and looked furtively up and down the balcony. Seeing no one, he ran, hunched over, towards the staircase end of the balcony with a large kitchen knife tied to his left hand.

*Tony Gray*
We opened the door and he got spooked. We chased him but unbeknown to me at that time he was carrying a riot shield [left behind by local officers when the balcony had been given up]. He threw the riot shield at me and I sort of fended it off. The interesting thing is that I cannot remember it. I've no memory of it at all. I've seen it on video but I can't remember it happening. I was so focused on catching him. Anyway, he got back into the flat and slammed the door.

After bolting the front door Walker screamed 'She dies, She dies', and believing that he meant to carry out his threat, the officers alerted the other team members who, in view of the negotiators' evident antipathy towards their continued presence, thought that the chances of their being used were remote. They hurriedly collected their equipment and raced from the other end of the balcony. While one officer tried to break down the front door with a sledgehammer, the remainder of the team went for the two windows, those of the kitchen and the bathroom.

*Tony Gray*
I remember telling [an officer] to get the stun grenades. He smashed the window [of the bathroom] and threw the stun grenade in and I was literally going in the window when the thing went off. All the glass came back past me. I was the first one in but by then [an officer] had got in the other way and had already shot him [Walker].

The kitchen was full of smoke from another distraction device. It was also an obstacle course and the first officers in expected to be stabbed by Walker at any moment. One officer managed to get to the living room door and in the darkened room he could see Walker lying on the sofa with the child held across his chest. He was still screaming 'She dies, she dies', and the officer could barely work out where the bodies of Walker and his hostage met. Walker plunged the knife into the little girl and, at the same time, the officer fired 'sense of direction' at Walker's shoulder and then at his head. When the curtains were opened it was found that the knife was still in the child and she was carried to a waiting ambulance.

Before the dust had even settled there was a barrage of criticism in the media, although, ironically, most it was directed at the way the assault had been carried out. An article in *The Times* on 31 December, co-written by a former Essex police firearms instructor, asked whether the operational commander had detailed two officers with sledgehammers to break down the door and why the officers had climbed rather than rolled through the window. The article went on to explain that only three forces had shown innovation in their training and that, not surprisingly perhaps, one of the three was Essex. Even at the best regulated of sieges, commanders have more pressing matters to consider than sledgehammer allocation, and rolling through windows only works in films.

In the midst of the furore a small card arrived at Old Street from Karlene's grandparents. It read: 'A special thank you message. To all at D11. We just wanted to thank you all very much for giving us back Karlene. This card cannot tell you how grateful we are. Thank you again. PS. Karlene is doing fine.'

Walker recovered from his injuries and in December 1986 at the Old Bailey he was convicted of the murder of Jacqueline Charles and of attempting to murder her daughter. He was sentenced to life imprisonment. The internal police recriminations following the siege continued for many months. The lesson had been learned as long ago as the Spaghetti House siege that negotiators should act only as a go-between and never exercise a command function. A hostage-taker should never come to believe that a negotiator could personally meet any demands. This was ignored at Northolt, and if the reason was indeed to avoid the possibility of another riot no matter what, then it would explain the need constantly to play down the little girl's plight. There was no riot, despite the ending. One outcome was the recognition that, irrespective of intended roles, for some officers the habit of command can be irresistible. The negotiators had mainly been superintendents, and from then on more officers of a much lower rank were trained in the role.

## INTERNATIONAL TERRORISM

The day after the end of the Northolt siege, on 27 December 1985, three Arab terrorists using Kalashnikov rifles opened fire at Schwechat airport in Vienna killing two people and injuring another forty-seven. At the same time, four more opened fire at Leonardo da Vinci airport in Rome killing thirteen and injuring seventy-six. In response, the British Army was again assigned to Heathrow and, on 9 January 1986, members of the Firearms Unit also returned, this time carrying 9mm Heckler and Koch MP5 sub-machine guns.

The MP5's single-shot capability when aimed and fired from the shoulder using handgun ammunition provided a highly accurate alternative to a handgun, allowing officers to deal with threats at a greater distance and with greater precision. It had none of the disadvantages associated with the power of a rifle or the spread of a shotgun. One of the first officers to patrol with an MP5 was Sergeant Dave Chambers:

> I was there on the first day and I remember being briefed by a senior officer. I recall being assured that this was to be a low-profile exercise and that there may be a 'little press interest'. As soon as we entered the terminal there was a stampede of photographers who were fighting with each other to get their pictures. I realised how people must feel when they have the press hordes following them and it was only by escaping to airside [the runway and aircraft stands to which the public do not have access] that we could get

away from them. As for the passengers, they generally felt that it was long overdue and accepted the armed presence.

The officers patrolled with airport police but, as had been the case in 1970, such a commitment could not be sustained for very long. In due course training in the use of the MP5 was given to some of the officers stationed at Heathrow.

*Tony Gray*
When we handed over, the plan was that for the first day the instructors from the courses would carry the MP5 accompanied by one of the trained officers from the security section. It was not so much from a tactical point of view but it was thought that we could deal with problems if there were any. One of the suggestions had been that carrying the MP5 overtly at the airport would deter the travelling public from coming and asking questions. Although there were two of us, every single person that came to ask questions came to me and I had to refer them to the bloke I was with. This went on all day and only two people mentioned the MP5. One was quite obviously a squaddie who asked a few questions about whether it was single shot or fully auto and so on. He told us that it was good to see us, and the other was an old bloke who came up to me and said that it was about time that we had some decent security at the airport.

Although identical in appearance to the automatic version, the weapon carried by Heathrow officers could only be fired using its single-shot capability and it was referred to as an MP5 A2 9mm carbine. Nevertheless, deployment of the weapon was not without its critics. A chief superintendent and a sergeant from Gatwick airport in Sussex visited both Vienna and Rome and, in a reproach aimed at the Metropolitan Police, reported that: 'A suitable handgun used by trained officers can match an automatic weapon used by terrorists in the context of a crowded airport concourse.' If another weapon was needed, 'pump-action shotguns should be considered because of the limited penetrating power'.

In the February 1986 edition of *Police*, the chairman of the Police Federation was quoted as saying:

It is totally absurd . . . to attempt to reassure the public by pointing out that the automatic weapons carried by these police officers may only be fired by them using the single shot operation and that they must be fired from the shoulder. Presumably officers will be required to warn terrorist suspects, who may not speak a word of English, that they are police officers; that they are armed; and that they will fire. To put the entire responsibility for out-shooting terrorists on the police, and at the same time to withdraw the special army units at Heathrow, looks to me like a weakening, not a strengthening, of airport security.

The federation's chairman must have known that the soldiers would be pulled out eventually and the 'entire responsibility for out-shooting terrorists' had already rested on the police officers armed with handguns at Heathrow for more than a decade. Furthermore, the prospect of officers being required to initiate conversation with terrorists who were in the act of shooting passengers was just as unlikely after the introduction of the MP5 as before, but there was much more.

The same edition of *Police* carried an article by a former army officer that included the observation:

The weapon chosen for their new image patrolmen at Heathrow was thoroughly unsuitable even if one does accept the need for overt para-militaries. As a fully automatic weapon of 9mm calibre [it] was a bad choice, but if we are to take seriously statements that it is to be fired only from the shoulder and solely as a semi-automatic (i.e. one shot per trigger pull) it is an extraordinary choice. Why not have a purpose built semi-automatic carbine firing a more sensible cartridge in the first place?

The article went on to explain that the police could only use 9mm round-nose bullets in the MP5, that these were 'statistically ineffective man stoppers', and that their use 'may well be illegal in Britain'. Several newspapers also ran the story, giving readers the impression that the introduction of this weapon was all very much contrary to the considered opinion of the experts.

It is likely that the idea of the MP5 being fired from the shoulder was hard to 'take seriously' because it was still popularly believed at the time that a sub-machine gun should be held and fired at waist level. The origins of this long-outdated practice can be traced back to the introduction of the Thompson and then the Sten sub-machine gun during the Second World War. New trainees were taught that: 'The [Sten] can be carried in any convenient position, but when expecting to meet the enemy it should be held at the waist. From this position it can be instantly cocked and fired.'[2] Today, the practice of shoulder-mounting is considered unremarkable – action films and news reports frequently show police and even military forces conducting operations with weapons already up in the aiming position.

The criticism was more difficult to reconcile with the facts when it came to the ammunition. Where the idea came from that round-nose bullets were 'illegal' is a mystery, and it was not true to say that they were the only type that could be used in the MP5. The Metropolitan Police was by now using a bullet configuration of jacketed soft-point (JSP) in its self-loading and automatic weapons. The 'purpose built carbine' was never identified but a few months later the 'more sensible cartridge' was revealed in another article in *Police*. In a list of 'effective bullets for police use', and described as being 'the main contender in the frangible category', was the Glaser safety slug with the same former army officer making the claim that such bullets 'comply with the Hague Convention and cannot be described as "dum dums"'. It should have been self-evident that they didn't and that they could.[3]

The Glaser consists of a number of tiny lead balls compressed together. On impact, it expands into its constituent pellets and, as each pellet follows its own path, the result is greater internal damage than would be the case with almost any other handgun bullet. The Home Office exercised control over the ammunition issued by police forces and in this it took account of the 'rules of war' applicable to the British armed forces. At The Hague conferences in 1899 and 1907 bullets 'which expand or flatten easily in the human body'[4] or which 'cause unnecessary suffering'[5] had been specifically prohibited, but it was not simply a matter of the Home Office applying the restrictions directly to the police.

The declarations made in The Hague were the product of an age that had seen the British Army in India make use of bullets from one of its arsenals in a small town just north-east of Calcutta. The .303 calibre rifle bullet of the early 1890s appeared to lack the stopping power necessary for use against the tribesmen of the Northwest Frontier. At the arsenal at Dum Dum the tips of the bullets were therefore ground away to expose the soft lead inside – in effect, thereby converting them into jacketed soft-point bullets – and this seemed to solve the problem. In 1897 a hollow-pointed .303 calibre bullet was produced and issued to the British Army as a whole. This was expressly designed to expand. It was referred to as the 'Woolwich bullet' to distinguish it from its predecessor and the modifications made in India. Both were condemned (unfairly as far as the British were concerned[6]) in The Hague in 1899, but the 'Dum Dum' name caught the public imagination and it has been synonymous with expanding bullets ever since.

The Hague agreements were 'only binding for the Contracting Powers in the case of a war between two or more of them' and they did not apply to a country's internal police forces. The Home Office therefore applied the spirit of the agreements to the police and the Glaser was considered unacceptable when viewed alongside the alternatives.

An international agreement on police ammunition would be drawn up in 1990 in the unlikely setting of Havana, Cuba, and this required that governments 'prohibit the use [by police forces] of those firearms and ammunition that cause unwarranted injury or present an unwarranted risk'.[7] Whether an injury or risk is unwarranted is a matter of opinion, and in 1998 in the House of Lords the Home Office would explain its position on the use of JSP ammunition:

Authorised police firearms officers may use soft-point ammunition operationally. In accordance with our obligations under the Hague Convention of 1899, the armed forces would not use such ammunition in wartime. The convention does not apply to police use of firearms. The circumstances in which the police are, on rare occasions, required to use firearms are different from those found in wartime. Police use of soft-point ammunition reflects the need for them to have ammunition which is effective in quickly incapacitating someone who is presenting an immediate threat to life and who cannot be dealt with in any other way. [8]

A retired lieutenant-colonel decided to enter the fray by pointing out that it would be quite safe for police officers to carry the MP5 as long as they observed certain rules. The most important of these was that, as a young officer during the Second World War, he had made sure his soldiers carried rifles and sub-machine guns without mishap by using the simple expedient of not issuing ammunition. Another expert suggested that, from photographs he had seen, police officers would not be able to fire their MP5s because they were wearing gloves. This was answered the following week when yet another expert explained that the MP5 had been designed to accommodate a glove-wearing user.

Another Sandhurst graduate wrote to the Firearms Unit direct, suggesting that the problem was not with the MP5 but with the idea that an officer could actually decide to use one without first obtaining permission. His solution was to mount an MP5 on tracks that would run the entire length of an airport terminal ceiling. The weapon would have a camera fitted instead of sights and its movement would be controlled by two police officers, each with a joystick, in a control room monitoring events. Both officers would need to agree that it was necessary to shoot since, if only one of the officers pushed the firing button on their respective joystick, the mechanism would not operate. The suggestion was not pursued.

The introduction of the MP5 to Heathrow turned out to be the next major event to have an influence on police policy nationally. The mould in which police officers only carried handguns had been broken and the MP5 would go on to become standard issue in over 90 per cent of the police forces in the UK (including Sussex). Most of the forces that chose not to adopt it elected instead for the Steyr 9mm AUG and the introduction of a 9mm carbine would see the phasing out of shotguns other than for specialised purposes. It would also lead to the abandoning of policies requiring that handguns be carried out of sight.

## NATIONAL DEVELOPMENTS

In February 1986 the Home Office announced the setting up of a new working group. In August 1985 a boy aged five, John Shorthouse, had been accidentally shot and killed in Birmingham during a police raid on a house. As a result, a member of the West Midlands police, Constable Brian Chester, had been charged with manslaughter and later acquitted. The group's remit was to take this incident and the shooting of Mrs Groce the following month into account as a part of its deliberations. Its terms of reference were:

> To examine the policy and procedures relating to the issue to and use by the police of firearms in England and Wales with particular regard to the selection and training of police officers for firearms duties; the criteria for authorisation to issue firearms for particular operations; the relevant instructions and guidelines; the planning, briefing for and supervision of armed operations; and the choice of weapons and ammunition; and to make recommendations.

The Home Office provided the chairman. The group's report in December endorsed the recommendations in the Dear Report and added that the physical suitability of officers should be assessed by way of a range of fitness tests.[9] The group also recommended that firearms teams be given a more significant operational role, but added that this should be supplemented by an adequate distribution of authorised officers throughout a force area.

Most of the other recommendations did little more than confirm the *status quo*, but one suggestion from an outside organisation should be mentioned. The Association of County Councils proposed that: 'There should be research into the effectiveness of deploying officers on 24-hour patrols in traffic cars containing guns in locked boxes.' Today these would be called armed response vehicles. The group canvassed the opinions of all chief constables on the proposal. There was little support for it and the group decided that: 'We do not, therefore, see any reason to commend the practice to chief officers.'

# Chapter 10

# UNAUTHORISED
# AND UNORTHODOX

## INSTRUCTIONS

On 5 February 1987 in the House of Commons, Labour's Gwyneth Dunwoody asked the Home Secretary, Douglas Hurd, whether he had any proposals to increase the training available to authorised firearms users. He replied that he had accepted the conclusion of the Home Office Working Group on the Police Use of Firearms (December 1986) that the recommended length of initial and refresher training was sufficient. After a short further debate on police arming Mr Hurd concluded by saying:

> One of the reassuring things which I have found as Home Secretary is that [the police] want to adhere as closely as possible to the tradition of unarmed British policing. I entirely agree with them. Of course, there are occasions . . . when armed criminals or armed suspects are about and the police need to draw and protect themselves with firearms. The police and I are determined that those occasions should be kept to a minimum.

Some senior officers still had less than the minimum in mind. On 9 May at 10.24 in the evening police were called to Wieland Road, Northwood, in north-west London. Constable Cove arrived at about 10.35 to be told that a man at no. 35 had fired a shotgun. The officer looked towards the house and saw a man standing in the doorway with a shotgun in his hands. After telling the assembled onlookers to leave he took cover behind his police car. Constable Shorrocks arrived and Constable Cove left him behind the car keeping watch on the front of the house while he went into the house opposite no. 35. There he found Maureen Woods who explained that a man had shot her husband and that both were still in the house, as was Sandra Webster.

Meanwhile, Constable Shorrocks had begun to feel vulnerable and so he asked several onlookers whether any of them had a gun he could borrow. It turned out that one of them did. A neighbour had a Beretta 'over-and-under' double-barrelled twelve-bore shotgun used for clay pigeon shooting. The officer gratefully accepted it and then returned to his position behind the police car. He was rejoined a few moments later by Constable Cove and a sergeant arrived to set up a rendezvous point nearby.

The local inspector requested the assistance of the TSG (Territorial Support Group – the area headquarters-based successor to the Special Patrol Group) and the late senior duty officer, a superintendent. When the inspector arrived he found that TSG officers were already there. He saw Constable Shorrocks with the shotgun but he thought nothing of it, assuming that the gun was a police weapon and that it must have come from the TSG. The inspector sought permission for the issue of firearms and authority was given for the issue of one gun to one authorised officer. At 11.26 Mrs Webster left through the back door of the besieged house and made her way to the still unarmed officers at the rear. Shortly afterwards, the authorised officer arrived with his gun and the inspector sent him to the back of the house on the grounds that if Mrs Webster could leave that way then so could the gunman.

The incident was brought to a successful conclusion when the gunman gave up, but one particular question nagged away in the minds of senior officers afterwards – where did Constable Shorrocks get the shotgun? When the source was discovered his action was described as 'unauthorised and unorthodox' and there was talk of disciplinary proceedings, although the officer was qualified as an authorised firearms officer. He also had shotguns of his own at home and so he knew how to use one. Although this did not constitute any form of authority to commandeer a gun, it was difficult to identify a regulation that had been contravened and those on the ground countered by asking why only one gun had been authorised. They pointed out that since 1980 the force instructions had required that 'firearms should be issued to pairs of authorised officers [i.e. at least four] for incidents requiring an armed response'.[1]

*Bob Wells*
I remember being very annoyed on behalf of the PC from Northwood and feeling that the senior officers were worthier of opprobrium than he was. I complained that they must be aware of the urgency of such occasions and not leave their officers hung out to dry when they use their initiative, especially when the officer is more qualified than the senior officers themselves to make the decision.

In the end the incident was chalked up to experience but it was clear that something needed to be done. The force was therefore told that officers who were planning an armed operation or who were responding to an armed incident in future must always seek the advice of the Firearms Unit.[2]

## FACILITIES

In London, 'D' department became Personnel and Training department under the Assistant Commissioner Personnel and Training (ACPT) in January 1987. D11 became PT17 and by May the size of the Firearms Unit had grown to one chief superintendent, one superintendent, one chief inspector, six inspectors, fifteen sergeants and thirty-eight constables. The one extra refresher training day required under phase one of the changes made following the Dear Report had been introduced in September 1985 and the instructors had then been divided into six teams operating on a six-week cycle. For four weeks the instructors trained other officers. The fifth week was devoted to personal training and during the sixth week a team provided a 24-hour operational response.

There were now two national reports on recommended training levels, each publicly backed by the Home Secretary of the day. Work had by now started on refitting the indoor range in Greenwich and it would reopen in February 1988, but the acquisition of a site for the required tactical training had been removed from the force building plan. It was not possible to identify who had done this and the chairman of the phase two feasibility working group, which had been in a state of suspension after the shooting of Mrs Groce, felt that it would be pointless trying to get it restored.

He sought new suggestions from the group and two ideas were put forward. The first was to build a 'tactics house', consisting of a steel framework on which could be hung movable walls and doors, in one of the hangars at the public order training site at Hounslow. The second was for some roads and plywood buildings to be constructed at Lippitts Hill. Neither facility would allow for the full recommended increase in training but it was felt that this was the best that could be done.

The group's last meeting was held on 6 October 1987 at which it was agreed that 'the construction at Hounslow would go ahead, with Lippitts Hill to follow within the next five years', but the frustration felt at the lack of progress was evident when the group reported:

> The opinion has been expressed in financial circles that it would be cheaper to pay out compensation every four years for police tort than to carry out the development required to prevent it. In purely financial terms this is no doubt true. The moral implications of such a stance are, however, indefensible when dealing with the lives of [the] public and police officers. . . . Firing ranges appear as a practical and sensible investment in a building programme, as indeed they are, but all of the skills learned on those ranges are of no avail if the officer has no experience of how and when to use them.[3]

It was all for nothing. The 'construction at Hounslow' was never built and Lippitts Hill did not 'follow within the next five years'.

### FIREARMS TEAMS

The number of Metropolitan Police areas had increased from four to eight during 1985, each under the command of its own deputy assistant commissioner, and any DAC could authorise the use of a

specialist team. There was still only one team available each day and
it was common for two or more DACs to authorise the use of the
team at the same time.

The Firearms Unit therefore suggested that it be treated as a Level
1 response and that each area and each specialist operational branch
should have a Level 2 team of its own, to be used with the authority
of a commander. The expectation was that the Level 1 teams – the
instructors – would then only be used for incidents involving
criminals with 'exceptional firepower', terrorist incidents and hostage
situations. The Level 2 teams would deal with everything else.

On 20 December 1985 another working group on the police use of
firearms was created in London, this time chaired by Commander,
later Deputy Assistant Commissioner, A.W. Young. At the group's
first meeting the Firearms Unit's proposals were rejected. It was felt
that there would be insufficient work for so many teams to do and the
members suggested instead that the size of the Firearms Unit be
increased so that it could provide three Level 2 teams for use by all
concerned. The group's report was presented to a meeting of the
Metropolitan force's policy committee in March 1986 where the
recommendations were agreed with the arrangements to be reviewed
six months after implementation.[4]

*Dave Chambers*
Level 2 was a whole new ball game within the Unit. A brand new
type of course was written to accommodate the parameters under
which Level 2 teams would operate. For the first time, we were
training others in some of the skills that were always the 'personal
property' of D11. We were looking for the best eighteen constables.

The new officers joined on 1 June 1987 and were formed into
three teams, each under the command of an experienced Firearms
Unit sergeant.

*Bob Wells*
Level 2 officers were welcomed, and rather over-used, by the
divisional commanders. The sergeants who led the teams were

exposed to far more operations by their association with Level 2 than they had been with their Level 1 teams. I think they went on to a steep learning curve but they soon became very confident.

*Dave Chambers*
[The Level 2 teams] rapidly gained the respect of area officers of all ranks and were called upon on an ever-increasing basis. But they started with fairly rigid rules as to what they could and couldn't deal with and this quite quickly became unmanageable.

This was because the Metropolitan Police had unwittingly tied itself into a bureaucratic knot. While it was relatively easy to categorise an operation after it had taken place, it was much more difficult to do so beforehand. As a result, an operation that started within a Level 2 team's terms of reference could (and often did) alter as more information became available and it was too late to change teams. In addition, on twelve of the operations during the first six months it was necessary to use two Level 2 teams together. This led to a shortage of teams and the Level 1 team had to be used to make up the shortfall. This introduced a formidable procedural difficulty since a Level 1 team could not be authorised by a commander, a throwback inherited from the days of the DACA (ops). It would be 1990 before the tangle was unravelled.

Another unexpected difficulty arose over the phraseology used when the policy committee had agreed to the formation of the new teams – that the arrangements would be reviewed after six months. At the time the intention had been to review whether the number of teams was sufficient given that they had been reduced to three. However, it was interpreted by some of the provisioning departments to mean that the teams could actually be disbanded after six months and consequently all requests for kit met with the same response: if the teams disappeared, anything lavished on them would be wasted.

The officers themselves acquired some equipment and the Firearms Unit supplied items such as firearms and body armour, but it could do nothing about the larger requirements, including vehicles. The first suggestion was that the teams could use three very old police coaches. The Metropolitan Police now rarely used them, but each was originally intended as transport for a 'serial' of police officers – one inspector, two sergeants and twenty constables, the manpower of a postwar police mobile column. When these were rejected the Transport department offered three personnel carriers instead. Their previous users had worked all three into the ground and had just been supplied with new vehicles. By police budgeting rules these old vehicles should then have been sold, otherwise the size of the Metropolitan Police fleet would increase by three, for which there was no prior Home Office authority. On the understanding that the vehicles were only for the 'trial period of six months' the Firearms Unit accepted them, and the officers put up with the rusted bodywork and constant breakdowns with remarkably good humour.

Outside London, more forces were starting to create firearms teams of their own in response to the December 1986 Home Office report, although as yet there was still little need for them to be available full-time. In 1985 only Greater Manchester police, with sixty-five operations, and West Yorkshire, with fifty-eight, exceeded one operation a week. The forces of Cheshire, Cleveland, Derbyshire, Durham, Lincolnshire, North Yorkshire, Nottinghamshire, Warwickshire, West Mercia, Wiltshire, Dyfed Powys, Gwent, North Wales and South Wales did not reach double figures for the whole year. However, it would not be in London, Manchester or West Yorkshire that the next event to have a major influence would occur.

### THE HUNGERFORD MASSACRE

On 19 August 1987 Michael Ryan, armed with a 9mm Beretta pistol, a Kalashnikov assault rifle and an M1 .30 calibre carbine, drove to Savernake Forest in Wiltshire. He parked and walked up to a young woman, Sue Godfrey, who was just finishing a picnic with her two young children. He forced her to put the children into her car and then marched her into the forest where he shot and killed her. Sue Godfrey became the first victim of what was to become infamous as the Hungerford Massacre.

Ryan headed back towards Hungerford in Berkshire and after about 8 miles he stopped at Froxfield where he filled his car and a 5-litre can with petrol. He then went to the boot of his car, took out one of the rifles and fired it at Mrs Dean who was behind the service station's cash desk. He missed and when he sped off Mrs Dean telephoned the police. Ryan first went to his home at 4 South View in Hungerford and after dousing it in petrol, he set it alight. When he returned to his car he found that it would not start and in frustration he fired at it using the Kalashnikov. He then shot and killed two of his neighbours. After putting on his body armour, he went hunting. During the next hour or so he killed another thirteen people, including Constable Roger Brereton, an unarmed traffic officer, and wounded fifteen more before going to ground in the John O'Gaunt School building, thereby ending the carnage.

The new armoured Land Rovers purchased as a result of the 1986 study into the riots in Brixton and Tottenham had that day been delivered to the public order training site at Hounslow. Two of them were replacements for the armoured vehicles that the Firearms Unit in London had been using since 1979 and a team was at Hounslow practising with them. Two of the officers were Constable Bryan Galley and Inspector Clive Rawlings.

### Bryan Galley

Clive Rawlings came over and told us that we may be required for a job in Hungerford where a suspect had killed five people and was on the loose. Our first thought was, 'Where on earth is Hungerford?' [Hungerford is about 60 miles due west from Hounslow in an area covered by Thames Valley police.] The next was that this sounded a bit more serious than the run-of-the-mill jobs we'd had in the past few weeks. As we started to get our kit together we were told that it was the armoured Land Rovers that were required and not the team.

### Clive Rawlings

I had to phone a DAC at the Yard in the end and I told him that we were the standby team, that they were our vehicles and that I'd got a full team available. He said that he would phone me back and when he did he said for us to go.

*Bryan Galley*

Either just before or on our arrival we were told that the suspect was in possession of a 7.62mm rifle and that the Land Rovers were to be used to draw fire in an attempt to locate him. This was not a recognised tactic and we were not keen to be the first ones to try it out. Thankfully, shortly after our arrival, Ryan was located in the school.

At about 5.30 in the evening Ryan fired shots from inside the school, possibly at a police helicopter. He had finally been spotted, and it was like a cork popping from a bottle – suddenly all of the ambulances, police vehicles and terrified inhabitants could move about freely, except in the area near the school.

*Clive Rawlings*

It was chaos because the police station was under repair and they were working out of a Portakabin. Ryan was holed up and they had a bloke who had been shot in a house nearby and they couldn't get an ambulance up to him. We put a doctor and a local PC as a guide into an armoured Land Rover. When we got to the address we reversed the Land Rover over the privet hedge into the front garden, right up to the front door.

*Bryan Galley*

We found a family who were petrified and in a severe state of shock, hiding in the loft. The injured person was found near to the rear door with a head wound but still alive. The house was evacuated and the injured person was taken away in the armoured Land Rover. We remained in the house for a short time and from a first-floor window we witnessed a bizarre scene of negotiators moving up to the school to attempt face-to-face negotiations with this crazed madman. We must have been about 150 metres away and I remember feeling frustrated at our not having our 7.62mm rifle with us. Those officers' lives were very much at risk.

Despite attempts to persuade Ryan to give himself up, there was the sound of a muffled shot and at just after 7 o'clock in the evening he was found by a Thames Valley police firearms team. He had committed suicide and any chance of discovering the reason for his killing spree died with him.

Apart from the traumatic effect the incident had on many of those involved, there were two major consequences. The first was the introduction of a prohibition on civilian ownership of self-loading or pump-action rifles, other than those chambered for .22 calibre rim-fire.[5] The second was a document produced in July 1988 that was to become known as the McLachlan Report.[6] This examined the police response to the incident and made recommendations on a wide range of subjects, including the purchase of armoured vehicles by police forces, but the greatest amount of space was taken up with the merits of armed response vehicles. In 1977 as Chief Constable of Nottinghamshire, the report's author, had introduced ARVs into his force area and he was critical of the Home Office Working Group report in 1986 that did not 'see any reason to commend the practice to chief officers'. The McLachlan Report's impact did not immediately become apparent, but it was to change dramatically the way the police service nationally dealt with armed response.

## AIRPORT SECURITY

Commissioner Sir Kenneth Newman gave authority for officers at Heathrow airport to carry their sidearm openly when in shirtsleeve order in the summer in May 1987. At the time it was widely believed that the 1976 instructions that weapons should be carried out of sight had always existed and that this was a major break with 'tradition'. Nevertheless, the MP5 carbine could not be hidden under a police uniform, and it was therefore no longer deemed necessary to hide the fact that some other officers were armed too, particularly since similar authority had already been given to officers at Manchester and Birmingham airports.

As winter approached, officers at Heathrow asked that the authority be extended to cover all year round, whether they were in shirtsleeves or not. In November the new Commissioner, Sir Peter Imbert, agreed to the proposal, noting that: 'You will be aware of my views on the overt carrying of firearms. . . . Nonetheless, I do regard Heathrow airport, with its high level of risk, to be a special case, and authorise the carrying of firearms by officers of the security section at [Heathrow] overtly all the year round whilst engaged on security duties.'

## SHOTS FIRED IN WOOLWICH

'Operation Turkey', which took place in November 1987, was the result of the Flying Squad in London receiving information that Anthony Ash had stolen a BMW car. Ash had a string of convictions dating back to 1955 and to the Flying Squad the stealing of the car meant that he and his associates, Ronald Easterbrook and Gary Wilson, were about to commit a robbery. Easterbrook had been released from prison in February 1986 after serving an eight-year sentence for conspiracy to rob and firearms offences. His convictions dated back to 1946 and included one for shooting at a police officer. Wilson also had a string of convictions that included robbery. On 23 November the three men met up and two of them, Easterbrook and Ash, drove off in a Mercedes while Wilson took the stolen BMW.

Two of those involved in the police operation were Inspector, later Chief Inspector, Dwight Atkinson, who had only joined the Firearms Unit earlier that month, and Constable Bill Rowlinson.

*Dwight Atkinson*
The problem was that we were unaware of where the robbery was going to take place. A surveillance team would have to follow them with the Unit's teams shadowing the surveillance team. Easterbrook and his accomplices set down the Mercedes (which was a clean car, i.e. correctly registered) in Sunbury Street, Woolwich. Sunbury Street was a quiet side street with a fairly large enclosed car park set off it and it was believed that their intention was to come back to this car after a robbery.

The surveillance team lost sight of the BMW and after Easterbrook and Ash had parked the Mercedes they too disappeared when they set off on foot.

*Dwight Atkinson*
It was agreed that the main Level 1 team and some Level 2 officers would deal with Easterbrook and his accomplices at whatever premises they attacked and I was sent to Sunbury Street. Although I was not aware of it at the time, and I had been authorised and trained to carry firearms since 1969, it was thought that this was a fairly safe place for me to be. A sergeant, who was running the tactics side of the operation, had been told not to let me get into trouble. My job with Sergeant Jim [name omitted] and Constables Bill Rowlinson and Graham [name omitted] was to sit and observe the Mercedes just in case Easterbrook and his accomplices returned to it.

I set up a small observation point in the doorway of a nearby block of flats and I sent Bill and Graham around the corner in the car to come in as and when required. As we listened to the radio communications between the surveillance team and our colleagues it became clear that the surveillance team were unaware of the suspects' whereabouts, although it was strongly believed that they were still in the area.

A short time later the stolen BMW was spotted. Wilson was driving, Ash was in the front passenger seat and Easterbrook was sitting in the back. The question now was – had they committed a robbery?

*Dwight Atkinson*
There was an urgent radio message stating that the BMW was heading back towards our location with its headlights on. It seemed more than likely that they had committed a robbery and that they were now heading back to the changeover vehicle.

It was a good guess. Ash had entered a Bejam freezer centre in Woolwich and grabbed a Securicor bag containing £10,411 while holding a loaded revolver to the head of a member of the shop's staff. Easterbrook, also armed with a loaded revolver, had stayed outside, ready to deal with any interference.

*Dwight Atkinson*
Several seconds later the BMW turned into Sunbury Street and drove straight into the car park, and Jim and I ran to the car park entrance. I didn't have a clue as to the whereabouts of Bill and Graham although I knew they had heard the radio messages and had probably seen the arrival of the BMW. As Jim and I reached the car park entrance I saw Ash getting out of the BMW with a large handgun in his hand. I drew my revolver and shouted to him to drop his gun. He said nothing but put his hands slightly up and started to change the gun into his other hand. I shouted again for him to drop the gun but I then suddenly saw a head and shoulders appearing from the rear door of the BMW. It was Easterbrook who appeared to be lying across the rear car seat, just showing out of the door opening. There was a gun in his hand and he immediately started shooting at us. I was also aware that Ash had run to the front of the BMW.

I was half protected by the car park surrounding wall but I suddenly felt a sharp pain in my left leg below the knee. I returned two shots at Easterbrook who was still firing and then I became aware of other officers now taking up position and shooting at the BMW. The pain in my leg was intense and, knowing that there were sufficient officers now to deal with Easterbrook and his accomplices, I dragged myself out of the line of fire to a safe position by a parked car in Sunbury Street. I looked at my leg and saw blood overflowing the top of my boot. I found out later that I had been shot straight through the front of my leg with the round exiting through my calf.

*Bill Rowlinson*
All I was aware of was Tony Ash crouched down by the front of the car, dressed in a pale raincoat and with a Webley pistol in his left hand. I was pointing my Smith and Wesson Model 10 revolver at

the rear passenger compartment of the car, where Easterbrook was. Ash was looking directly at Graham and me. I started to swing my weapon round to point at him as he was bringing his pistol up to shoot me. Everything just seemed to slow down, like being involved in a car crash. I remember thinking 'Oh Christ! This is it.' Then I saw him fall, just like a puppet with the strings cut. I realised Graham must have fired, but I don't remember hearing any shots.

I looked to where Easterbrook was. I could see the silver Smith and Wesson .357 magnum in his extended right hand. He appeared to be twisted around, leaning back out of the rear offside door. I saw a huge plume of fire coming from the 6-inch barrel, straight at where Dwight Atkinson was, right by the end of the wall. It seemed to go on forever, in slow motion. I was aware of a number of gunshots, then I heard someone shout 'I'm hit', off to my right. I thought 'Oh shit', and while all this was happening I was bringing my weapon back from where Ash was lying; back on to the rear of the car.

I brought my pistol up on to the crouched figure of Easterbrook and fired a pair of shots right at him. I saw the rear window smash as my shots hit. I then saw two more holes appear on the near side of the rear window as Graham also fired at Easterbrook. It sounded as if a minor war was being fought but it must have all been over in less than 5 seconds.

Then it all went very quiet, so I left the cover of the garage wall and moved to my left. I pointed my weapon at the near-side rear window where I could see Easterbrook crouched down in the seat. I didn't realise at the time but he was desperately trying to reload his weapon, but because his spare rounds were in his left jean pocket he was having difficulty. He was wearing tight jeans and is right handed. I shouted at the top of my voice: 'Armed Police, show me your hands, now.' I don't think that I was the only one shouting. He seemed to pause, and then very slowly, he left the car with his hands up. He looked extremely unhappy!

*Dwight Atkinson*
The sergeant, who was with the main team, arrived and saw me crouched behind the parked car. His eyes said it all. Look at the

new inspector – when trouble starts, he hides behind a car. He shouted that he wanted me to follow him as one may have got away. I just looked at him and told him that I had been shot. I think the blood drained quicker from his face than it was doing from my leg. He was meant to keep me safe and there I was on the ground with a hole in my leg.

The sergeant would later remark that never again would he make a promise that his inspector was not prepared to keep.

Ash died of his injuries. Easterbrook recovered and even tried to use explosives to blow his way out of the van taking him to and from prison during his trial at the Old Bailey. He claimed that he and his associates were the victims of a government 'shoot-to-kill' policy, but on 30 November 1988 he was sentenced to four terms of life imprisonment. His tariff, the minimum period he would have to serve, was later set at twelve years six months. Wilson was sentenced to seven years. Inspector Atkinson recovered and returned to duty to take over his own Level 1 team. He was the first member of the Firearms Unit in London to be shot. He would not be the last.

## Chapter 11

# MORE WORKING PARTIES

### NATIONAL DEVELOPMENTS

On 16 March 1988 in the House of Commons Sir Eldon Griffiths asked the Home Secretary whether he had 'established common physical standards for firearms' officers in all English forces'. Douglas Hurd replied: 'The Home Office Working Group on Police use of Firearms [December 1986] made 36 recommendations . . . all of which we support. . . . [An] ACPO working group is considering how best to develop a range of physical fitness and medical standards to meet the requirements of each category of firearms specialism.'

The 'ACPO working group' was actually the NWGFI. Initially it had no idea of the difficult waters into which the police service had just dipped a toe. It had not been possible to assign the work to the group's equivalent in the field of police physical training because no such group existed. The only fitness testing done at all was for new recruits and every force had a different test.

The group produced a draft national test in May 1990 but this was rejected. Physical training instructors (PTIs) in individual forces all had their own ideas on what constituted a suitable test and although they could not agree on what that was, they had no intention of allowing one to be imposed on them, particularly by firearms instructors. The only proposal that all forces could agree on was that 'suitable arrangements' for fitness testing should be made within each force and this became the eventual recommendation of the ACPO JSC.

In the years to come it would be realised that the need to ensure a test could withstand a legal challenge that it was irrelevant or discriminatory would take up almost as much in the way of resources as the testing process itself. Although the Firearms Unit had a test for its own members, within the Metropolitan Police it would be another eight years before applicants for firearms training had to fulfil a number of pre-course criteria that included a job-related fitness test, designed in the end by the University of Loughborough.[1]

While attempts to implement this recommendation followed their tortuous course there were other matters on the agenda. During 1985 the police staff associations had expressed concern over the effect that a shooting incident had on the police officers involved. The degree of reaction varied from mild shock to severe post traumatic stress disorder (PTSD) and the ACPO Working Party on Police Stress asked the Home Office to fund a study.

A number of officers volunteered to take part and the resulting report in 1986 gave a disturbing insight into how ill-prepared the police service was to manage the aftermath of a shooting incident.[2] Cases were found of senior officers seeming to distance themselves from their staff until they were certain that the shooting had been carried out in an acceptable manner and would not reflect badly on the force. There were also examples of perceptual distortion. In one incident two officers did not hear the shots they fired, and in another case an officer hardly registered the sound of his own gun firing but that of his colleague seemed so loud that it was ringing in his ears for hours afterwards.

The ACPO JSC asked the Metropolitan Police to draw up proposals for national consideration. By January 1989 a draft had been prepared dealing with assistance for the officer and the officer's family, the investigation, the opportunity for legal advice and the provision of psychological support. Suspension from duty, it was proposed, should only be considered in exceptional cases. The usual course should be for an officer to be temporarily employed in a non-operational post and resume armed duty as soon as it became clear that no criminal or disciplinary matters were being considered. This draft was circulated to all members of the ACPO JSC and the proposals were accepted, although it would be September 1991 before they became the first official national guidance.

Another matter to attract national attention was hostage rescue. On 28 September 1987 a prison officer, Jackie Stuart, had been taken hostage at Peterhead jail in Scotland. The prisoners threatened his life and, although the inmates did not have firearms, after five days the SAS was asked to end the siege. The resulting unarmed operation was successful, but there was considerable unease in ministerial circles about breaking the principle that the SAS should only be used for terrorist hostage-taking incidents. There was also disquiet within the SAS. To fail against a group of unarmed prisoners was unthinkable.

The MoD therefore made it clear that in future, unless the incident was within the limited remit of the SAS, responsibility for hostage rescue rested with the police. The Home Office then came up with the idea that since the Metropolitan Police already had such a capability, it could provide the national response, although it was nearly a year before the rumours were picked up in the media. On 26 October 1988 the *Daily Mail* told its readers: 'An elite SAS-style police unit is being set up to combat prison rioting and hostage-taking. . . . Scotland Yard anti-terrorist teams, firearms officers from the specialist PT17 Support Group and explosives experts have already started training.'

They hadn't, at least not in the way suggested by the article, and the matter was finally settled when the Home Office wrote to all chief constables on 27 April 1989. Forces were told that the MoD had agreed to the SAS being used in 'exceptionally difficult non-terrorist hostage-taking incidents, in which the use of helicopters or explosives is essential in order to bring about the hostage's release'. However, police forces would have to deal with all other hostage-taking incidents themselves. This was probably because there was no agreement on how a national police team would be funded and the concession over use of helicopters and explosives was intended to reduce the level of training that each force would now have to undertake. As will be seen, the Home Office letter would get a very mixed reception.

## OPERATIONS

The additional firearms teams in London removed the need for divisional authorised officers to be used for anything other than immediate armed response and the occasional protection duty. The number of operations carried out by the Firearms Unit increased from 127 in 1986 to 382 in 1988, with over 214 suspects being arrested, including three in the act of robbing a Security Express vehicle in Hoxton in April. On 12 May a team caught another three red-handed as they robbed a National Westminster Bank in Thames Ditton, although at least one person seems to have been unimpressed. One of the officers involved was Constable Terry Webster:

> Luckily enough it was my old ground and I knew the area like the back of my hand. I was in the back of a vehicle and we sat across the road from the Nat West Bank that was situated at the side of a triangular green. The suspects were seen to enter and the intention was to arrest them as they left to make their getaway. We drove down the short driveway as two of the robbers were leaving and they approached the offside of our car. I got out and challenged them and the one nearest to me, without breaking his stride, just went down on his knees and put his hands in the air. The second one legged it but I wasn't too worried as I knew that he was running straight into more officers in another vehicle that was around the corner. An old lady then approached the bank and, after being told what had happened, said, 'Does this mean the bank isn't open then?'

On 24 May 1988 a team arrested three men in the act of robbing a Securicor vehicle in Kingsbury. The operation was the result of three weeks of patient waiting before the robbers made their move, but the officers were unable to prevent one of the gang shooting a security guard in the foot. On the same day, another team arrested four robbers in the act of robbing a post office in Sidcup. The cash, two .44 calibre revolvers and a .45 calibre revolver were all recovered.

Many operations had a tragic story behind them. One started with Lorraine Tann breaking up from her boyfriend, Tim Steadman, and starting a relationship with Derrick Rose. Steadman could not take the rejection and so on 31 July he armed himself and went to the Tann family home in Brockhill Crescent, Brockley, in south London.

After bursting into the house through the back door in the early hours of the morning, he found Lorraine together with her mother and sister. Derrick Rose was also in the house with two of his sister's children. Steadman shot him in the head. Police were called and the three women managed to escape, but the children were left in the house. There was another complication, as Constables Dave Tilley and Pete Bradley remember.

*Dave Tilley*
We arrived after a callout from home within 40 minutes to find television crews filming our every move. There was a national television programme showing live coverage of police work in London, Melbourne and New York. As we pulled up the children wandered out into the street and were scooped up.

*Pete Bradley*
It was Police International Weekend and we were getting changed in the street being filmed by the various cameramen. They were moved on but one of them gave an old lady £250 for the use of her bedroom that overlooked the subject premises.

*Dave Tilley*
A shot rang out and we formed up and sent a dog in. I was at the front watching the dog through the crack in the door. A man was lying on the floor with a serious head injury and after I got the dog called out we entered. The suspect [Steadman] was dead in the bath (the shot we heard), but the man on the floor was still alive.

*Pete Bradley*
Dave could see that the casualty was still breathing. He called the dog out and we then made an entry. The casualty was placed on a ballistic blanket and removed from the premises. The subject, found dead in the bath, had died from a .410 shotgun blast and when searched at hospital, another firearm was found in the waistband of his trousers. The casualty survived a number of hours before passing away.

There is a well-known military maxim that goes 'No plan survives first contact with the enemy'. The same can be said of police operations, as was illustrated in September 1988.

*Dave Tilley*
This team kept taking out Securicor vehicles by shooting the guard in the leg and then stealing the hole-in-the-wall refills. We were on it for two or three months and it ended up with me in the front of a Flying Squad car with a Squad driver. Terry Webster was sitting behind him and a DS was sitting behind me. When the attack went in we were parked in a side street and we flew down this little road after being told over our radios that the villains were on the pavement.

It was after 11.30 at night and it was dark. As we hurtled down towards where the robbery was taking place the Securicor van drove into our road from the opposite direction. Although we weren't aware of it, the Squad were being told over their radios that the van had been hijacked. As we approached the van I turned to our driver to say that we'd never get through the gap just as he swerved and rammed it head on. I flew forward and hit the windscreen. Terry got out and ran towards the High Street but I couldn't get out on my side because there was too much damage. I crawled across the seat, got out on the driver's side and ran after Terry.

When we got there the road was empty. None of our blokes were there and we flagged down a passing CID car. This took us after the getaway car that was being chased towards a railway line. We joined the search of the railway arches and track, and I heard [an officer] shouting at someone to stand still. We found him high on the embankment covering a suspect down by the track. As we were handing him over we were told that a dog had picked up a scent at our crash site. This caused some confusion because we still didn't know the van had been hijacked. Terry and I got a car to take us back to the scene and we found our DS, who had chased a suspect from the van and been shot at. The driver of the van had run into a house and taken the family hostage, but when he realised we had all run off, he escaped through the back of the house, over a fence and on to the railway line.

A dog handler took us round the back and showed us some shotgun shells by the fence. We climbed over and started a search. The dog was first, followed by me, then Terry and then the dog handler. It was pitch black but we decided not to use our torches as we worked our way slowly after the dog. After some distance the dog started to growl and the handler whispered that it was a contact. Terry and I decided to turn on our torches and there, about 5 yards from us, was our man, raising a sawn-off shotgun at us. The dog leapt on him, as did we all. He was duly arrested and an ambulance was called for him as he had a broken ankle and some dog bites. Our driver then came over and handed me my [Browning self-loading pistol] magazine. It had fallen out as I crawled from our crashed car. I had done the whole operation unarmed but we caught the whole gang.

## CHANGE OF WEAPONS

June 1988 saw the end of a twelve-month project to identify a suitable sniper rifle to replace the Enfield Enforcer in London. The chosen weapon was the Steyr SSG-P rifle in 7.62mm NATO (.308 Win) and this would remain in use until 2003 when it would be replaced by the Accuracy International AWP in the same calibre. (The fully suppressed (silenced) version and the Super Magnum in .338 calibre would also be made available then.) In August 1988 it was agreed that all royalty protection officers would be issued with the Browning 9mm self-loading pistol, although they had been asking for the weapon for some time. The move had been resisted, but when His Royal Highness Prince Charles paid a visit to the Firearms Unit he asked why it was obstructing the introduction of the Browning for his officers. Training started shortly afterwards.

The resistance to the weapon change had been because trials were being conducted to find a replacement for the Browning. By December a weapon had been selected for trial by the specialist teams, and since June 1990 the 9mm self-loading pistol used by the

Metropolitan Police has been the Glock Model 17. At the same time, since the Cold War was now over, the Webley and Scott revolvers that had been kept since 1974 were sold. Over 740, most in almost brand-new condition, were part-exchanged to be resold, according to a representative from the company concerned, to a police force in Africa.

In a triumph of caption over content, on 17 January 1991 the *Daily Mirror*, under the heading 'Royal Cops Given a 17-Shot Super Gun', told readers that: 'Royal bodyguards are carrying a slick new gun – which packs more firepower, the *Mirror* can reveal today. The lightweight, self-loading Glock pistol is replacing the much heavier, older-style Browning introduced by Scotland Yard 15 years ago after the attempt to kidnap Princess Anne.'

### ABSEIL

Ever since 1979 the force's specialist teams had been trained in abseil, and since 1986 the Firearms Unit had even had its own qualified instructors, but acquiring the skill was mainly seen as a team- and confidence-building exercise. Then came 'Operation Oxford' on 5 April 1989. A drug dealer in Hackney in north London was continuing his activities even though he knew police were watching him because he thought that his flat was impenetrable. Although there was no mention of firearms, a Firearms Unit team was asked if it could help.

*Pete Bradley*
We were told the premises were in a block of flats on about the fourth floor. The front door was heavily barricaded and had a wire cage protecting it, which led the planners to believe that it would take too long to use as an entry point. The only rehearsals we could do were on a fire brigade tower but the lads were keen. The reality was that we turned up at the tower block late at night and when it became obvious that we would be doing a substantial drop in the dark the atmosphere suddenly became very quiet and serious. We reached the roof and tied off four lines for two teams of four.

*Dwight Atkinson*

We hung around on the roof for some time and then finally got the go ahead. We threw the drop-bags over with the ropes and they landed with a hell of a thud on the ground. Luckily, one of them just missed a parked car. Anyway, we went over the edge of the roof and we were on to the balcony in no time. The guy inside was with a female and they had the surprise of their lives. Needless to say there was very little struggle as the guy was still trying to assess where we had come from. We let the Drug Squad in and left them to it.

This operation was followed in 1990 by a rather unusual request. The Metropolitan Police dog section wanted to change its usual display of dogs chasing various criminals at the Royal Tournament at Earls Court, and seven volunteers asked to be trained in how to abseil with their dogs from the roof into the arena. Constables Pete Bradley and Dick O'Grady provided the training, and in July the performances went off without a hitch, but the operational application was so limited that it was not taken any further. However, in 1993 eighteen members of the Unit would equal the UK record for the highest building abseil using the 695.5-foot tower at Dartford power station.

## SHOTS FIRED IN HARROW

By the end of 1988 the Firearms Unit's teams were supporting the Flying Squad in dealing with a series of armed attacks on bank premises and security vehicles in north and west London. The campaign was codenamed 'Operation Char'. Flying Squad officers tried to identify patterns and, as the robberies continued, they found that they could predict a probable getaway vehicle from among the dozens stolen every day. They could also predict the probable false registration number it would be given.

On 1 March 1989 there was another robbery, this time in Perivale. At 10 o'clock in the morning three guards in a Securicor security van found themselves under attack from two vehicles that had steel roof-supporting joists (RSJs) fitted to them for use as battering rams.

Getting the guards out of the vehicle took longer than planned and when police sirens were heard, one of the robbers fired his Luger pistol in frustration and the three ran off to their first getaway vehicle. Unarmed uniformed officers in a marked police car arrived and managed to block this vehicle in, whereupon the robbers threatened them at gunpoint. While one robber remained with the officers, the other two got a second getaway vehicle ready. After warning the officers not to follow them and then firing at the police car, the robbers made off. It had all the hallmarks of another 'Char' robbery and catching those responsible became a priority.

The problem was finding a 'Char' vehicle after it had been fitted with its false number plates and parked ready for the next robbery but before it could be used. Every uniformed patrol officer in north-west London was briefed on what to look for, and searches were carried out every night duty for several weeks. Finally, during the late evening of 12 April, a stolen red Ford Sierra was found in a small car park in Rayners Lane in north London. Over the next few hours more stolen vehicles, all matching the 'Char' characteristics, were found in the surrounding streets.

Early the next morning, officers from the Flying Squad and several teams from the Firearms Unit were positioned in hastily found observation points and in cars to keep watch on the stolen vehicles. Although it seemed likely that a robbery was going to take place, the police still had no idea of when or where. In fact, the robbers had selected a post office near where the first vehicle had been found and which, on that day, had £76,000 ready to pay out in pensions.

The gang consisted of James Farrel, Terrence Dewsnap and John Gorman. Farrel was a serial armed robber with convictions dating back to 1959. He had only been released from prison in October the previous year after serving ten years of an eighteen-year sentence. In 1980 Dewsnap had been sentenced to eight years in prison, reduced on appeal to six years. Gorman had a string of convictions going back to 1951, including unlawful possession of firearms and armed robbery. Armed with a sawn-off shotgun, a Colt Service revolver and a 9mm Luger pistol, the gang intended to smash open the rear doors of the post office and attack the staff.

As the officers watched, the three robbers arrived, made their final preparations and then used a van fitted with an RSJ to ram what they thought were the rear doors of the post office. Despite all their hard work, they rammed the wrong door and all they achieved was access to some flats. Realising their mistake, they sped away in the Ford Sierra with Firearms Unit and Flying Squad officers not far behind them. The vehicle chase through the suburban streets of Rayners Lane and Harrow ended at Thackeray Close where the robbers abandoned their vehicle.

*Terry Webster*
The suspects ran across a grassed area at the back of some flats at the end of Thackeray Close and then up and over a footbridge over the railway line towards Twyford Road. Pete [Sidebotham] and I ran up the steps of the bridge telling the Squad lads to stay back. As we did so, shooting started from the other side of the bridge.

Two other Firearms Unit officers had chased the robbers as they ran down the alleyway on the other side of the footbridge and then out into Twyford Road where they had parked yet another stolen vehicle, a blue Ford Granada. As the two officers came out of the alley both Farrel and Dewsnap opened fire. One officer returned fire at Farrel who fell to the ground. The officer was then hit and, as he too fell to the ground, he fired one or two more shots. While on the ground he managed to get into a sitting position and fire at Dewsnap. The other officer also fired and Dewsnap fell. Gorman by this time was crouched behind the Granada by the front wheel arch. The Luger pistol dropped by Dewsnap was within reach but he left it alone.

*Terry Webster*
Arriving at the other side, I saw an officer standing in a front garden with one male [Farrel] lying on his back on the footpath in front of him. Another officer was to the right, sitting on the kerbside shouting at a man [Gorman] who was standing at the far side of what turned out to be a getaway car. I couldn't see his right hand and so I challenged him and at the same time I moved to

cover the officer sitting on the kerb. As I went towards him I could see another man [Dewsnap] on the ground next to the one who was standing. Pete [Sidebotham] came from my right and [Gorman] was secured.

Afterwards we went to a local police station for a debrief and then we paid the wounded officer a visit in hospital before going back to Old Street where Bob Wells thanked us and gave us a drink before telling us to go home. Strangely enough, we didn't go for a drink afterwards. Instead, we all made our own way home. I remember on the tube looking at other people reading [the London *Evening Standard*] and thinking that I was involved in the shooting that they were all reading about.

The wounded officer recovered and was later awarded the Queen's Gallantry Medal. His colleague received a Queen's Commendation. Both Farrel and Dewsnap died of their injuries, and at the Old Bailey on 15 January 1990 Gorman pleaded guilty to attempted robbery, having a firearm with intent to commit an indictable offence and wounding with intent. His guilty plea was accepted and a charge of attempting to murder a police officer was not proceeded with. He went back to prison, sentenced to another thirteen years.

## Chapter 12

# INDECISION

### THE ROACH REPORT

When Paul Condon (later Sir Paul Condon, Commissioner of the Metropolitan Police 1993–2000, and then Lord Condon) took over as the new ACPT in September 1988, he reviewed the difficulties his department faced. These included its continuing inability to provide the recommended level of training for divisional authorised officers, and since no obvious solution sprang to mind, he set up a working party to: 'Examine the number, training and deployment of officers authorised to carry firearms and to make recommendations as to the employment of such officers in the force response to both spontaneous and pre-planned operations.'

The Working Party on the Metropolitan Police Use of Firearms was chaired by Commander, later Deputy Assistant Commissioner, Laurence 'Larry' Roach, and as its starting point it was given a copy of the McLachlan Report. This was soon followed by another report resulting from an incident that had occurred in March 1988.

At just after midnight on Tuesday 8 March a message had been sent to all cars in the Metropolitan Police area that the driver of a red Ford Orion was believed to have been involved in two incidents earlier that night in which a firearm had been used. A few minutes later the crew of a traffic car spotted the Orion being driven south along the M11 motorway towards London. The officers were unarmed, as was the crew of another car that soon joined the first. As they prepared to stop the Orion at Woodford they received a message that it was believed the driver had a sawn-off shotgun. The officers sought advice and were told to 'use your own discretion'. They stopped the vehicle and arrested the driver, after which they made very clear their views on the lack of armed support.

Chief Superintendent P.D. Wiglesworth from the traffic office at New Scotland Yard set up a working party to highlight the failings in the system and the resulting document, to become known as the Wiglesworth Report, was finalised in January 1989.[1] It gave a number of options for change, the favoured one being that armed response vehicles should be created within each area's traffic unit.

News that the Metropolitan Police was considering introducing armed vehicles reached the outside world on 21 July 1989 when *Police Review* told its readers:

> The Metropolitan Police is considering a 24-hour rapid response force of armed police units in London. The idea being studied by a firearms policy working group would involve up to 200 officers covering the city's eight police districts [sic], although the Met says it is premature to speculate on whether the proposal will be adopted. . . . Scotland Yard says it is looking at what provincial forces are doing.

It was not until March 1990 that the working party's findings, known as the Roach Report, officially made a number of recommendations, one of which was that armed response vehicles replace all divisional authorised officers. The working party believed that 120 officers would be needed for a centrally based system. As *Police Review* had reported, it was thought that 200 would be required if each area had a system of its own and this was the working party's preferred option. Other recommendations included that the rifle officers be transferred into the Firearms Unit, that commander should be the highest rank necessary for any firearms-related authorisation and that four Specialist Firearms Officer (SFO) teams be created by merging the existing two levels of firearms team into one.[2]

The SFO initials were deliberately chosen so that they could not be turned into 'SWAT', a term frequently used by the US equivalent. In 1967 the Los Angeles Police Department had formed a unit to be trained in 'special weapons and tactics' and the SWAT acronym was born. In 1975 an American series, *S.W.A.T.*, appeared on British television. The image created by the violent (if somewhat improbable) story lines was in sharp contrast to that of George Dixon. By coincidence, the final episodes of *Dixon of Dock Green* were shown from March to May 1976 and the *S.W.A.T.* series ended in April the same year. Since this was the formative period for the first firearms teams in London, the use of the term 'SWAT' was carefully avoided and this has remained the case ever since.

Although the proposals soon became widely known, unarmed officers on divisions became increasingly critical of the time that the whole process was taking, and the Firearms Unit was asked to put out temporarily an immediate armed response using its own resources. From 17 August between the hours of 6 o'clock in the evening and 2 o'clock the following morning from Monday to Friday, half a Level 2 team patrolled north London while the other half patrolled south London. They were given the radio call signs 'Trojan North' and 'Trojan South'.

### THE MURDER OF CONSTABLE LAURENCE BROWN

Just over a week later, on 28 August, Mark Gaynor made a hoax emergency call to lure a police officer to Pownel Road in Hackney, north-east London. Constables Laurence Brown and Peter Townsend from City Road police station, both unarmed, responded, and when they arrived they split up to search the area. Constable Brown met up with Gaynor who grinned as he shot the officer in the chest at point-blank range with a stolen shotgun. The officer was dead on arrival at the London Hospital, Whitechapel.

Two unarmed officers arrested Gaynor after the shooting, but all he would say by way of explanation was: 'I blew your copper away because my girlfriend blew me away.' At Gaynor's trial at the Old Bailey in March 1991 the judge, Mr Justice Tucker, described him as 'a thoroughly dangerous man' and his actions as 'a most wicked, callous and cowardly act for which the jury have found you wholly responsible'. Gaynor was sentenced to life imprisonment with a recommendation that he serve at least twenty-five years. Shortly after his conviction he committed suicide in prison.

## DISSENT AT SENIOR LEVEL

Enticing a police officer into a trap so that he could be killed was something new outside Northern Ireland and there were rumours that the Police Federation had decided that it was time to call for all officers to be armed. Once again something had to be seen to be done and so on 1 October 1990 the Metropolitan Police's eight areas were each given authority to start their own temporary armed response vehicle system using divisional authorised officers. They were allowed to decide for themselves how this should be done and the result showed all the symptoms of having been introduced in haste.

For example, one commander suggested that the arrangements made for the security of the weapons in the car on his area be used as an example of good practice and the crew was asked to bring the vehicle to the Firearms Unit's headquarters at Old Street. On the appointed day the crew arrived and showed off an old metal ammunition box that had been bolted to the floor of the car's boot. It was pointed out that any weapons kept in it could not be reached in an emergency, but the crew explained that such a situation was not likely to arise. There were no guns in the box because it was locked and there was no key. The guns, in their holsters, were in a cardboard box on the back seat.

It was not until 26 October that the Commissioner's policy committee discussed the Roach Report and agreed that: 'The fundamental issue concerned the introduction of permanent armed response vehicles into the Metropolitan Police Service which was supported.' However, it did not agree that each area should have its own vehicles and concluded that: 'Such a mobile and immediate armed response would be better located as part of a central rather than an area structure.'

A few days later the policy committee decided that the Firearms Unit would have an operational wing consisting of a chief inspector, 5 inspectors, 11 sergeants and 110 constables. This would include 75 constables and 6 sergeants for armed response vehicles. A training wing would then consist of a chief inspector, 4 inspectors, 8 sergeants and 41 constables.

The policy committee did not accept the recommendation that the rifle officers should become a part of the Firearms Unit, a decision that provoked a chorus of protest from around the force. Chief superintendents in particular voiced their disapproval because the force reorganisation had created a mind-set in which the needs of 'the division' took priority over everything else. It was 'the fundamental unit in the organisational structure' and whenever divisional rifle officers (so renamed after the abolition of 'districts') attended training or were employed operationally they were not contributing to the achievement of local divisional objectives. However, this was not the cause of greatest dissent at senior level.

The next week's edition of *Police Review* on 9 November told its readers:

Armed response vehicles are to be introduced by the Metropolitan Police following the example set by several provincial forces. . . . The Met policy committee's decision to put the vehicles under central control is said to have angered some senior officers. . . . Centralisation appears to be a reversal of the policies introduced by Sir Kenneth Newman aimed at moving operational control away from Scotland Yard.

### HOSTAGE RESCUE

While those who disagreed with the decisions lobbied to get them changed, for the Firearms Unit it was business as usual. On 29 October 1990 *The Times* reported: 'Police were yesterday questioning a man aged 25 after a 19-hour siege at the home of sisters Dorothy and Carmen Gomez in Thornton Heath, south London.'

*Peter Sidebotham*
It was in a terraced house occupied by two elderly sisters, and a young drug addict had broken in and been disturbed. He was armed with a knife and one of the sisters had managed to escape and raise the alarm. The suspect and the remaining elderly sister were in an upstairs bedroom at the front of the house. TSG officers were outside

the bedroom door, and a team from the Unit was called and told to remain in case it was needed to rescue the hostage. We had a couple of officers in the front garden in case the suspect tried to climb out of the window, and a negotiator was negotiating through the bedroom door. The suspect would not allow any delivery through the door and so a ladder was placed up against the window for deliveries. I was against this as I felt we could eventually persuade the suspect to let us deliver via the door, but the negotiator won the day.

We managed to get a camera into the room so we could see everything that was going on and we sat and watched the poor wretched hostage forced to sit on the suspect's lap with a knife held to her throat. The suspect was terrified that if he left the hostage for a moment we would storm in through the door. The negotiator and I had been on the negotiators' course together and he was considered to be the top student. He certainly forgot all his training that day. Without any consultation with the officer in charge he arranged for a bucket to be used as a toilet. He left his position outside the door and, without telling anyone, climbed the ladder at the front of the house and delivered the bucket.

We then had to sit there and watch as the hostage used the bucket with the hostage-taker's knife to her throat. This was all too much for a young WPC who was sat in the room with the local superintendent. She burst into tears, rounded on the super-intendent and gave him a very emotional dressing down for his lack of action. Because of the small size of the house, everyone could see what was going on and it had a serious effect upon the morale of all involved. A psychologist was called but his only contribution was to tell us that the hostage would have serious psychological problems after the experience she was going through. We were eventually relieved late in the evening and I recall saying that if matters continued as they were, it would all end in tears. I could see the hostage-taker doing something silly.

*Dave Tilley*

When we got there, Pete told us that the door was barricaded and that one hostage was still being held. There was a ladder up against the left-hand side of the bow window (which was open) and we put a ladder up on the right-hand side. During the night it was decided that, as the woman needed medication, it should be stormed. The local commander refused to let us do it carrying weapons and said the TSG would do it using our ladders. We decided that the honour of the Unit was at stake and so two of us went up the left-hand ladder and [a sergeant] followed me using the right. I smashed the window and ran through it, cutting my hand, and the sergeant cut his head. We floored the suspect and held him down while the hostage was pulled into a corner and we waited for the TSG to get in through the door.

Windows were not usually the only access point and by now there were a growing number of ways of forcing an entry through locked doors. One of these was to use a 'Hatton Round', which consisted of a shotgun cartridge filled with a slug of compressed lead dust. This disintegrated when it hit a metal door lock or a hinge, but it was usually successful in removing the item that it was fired at. Authority for its use by police had been given in 1989, and it was first deployed in London in March 1991 in Kiver Road, Holloway.

*Clive Rawlings*
I think the guy was high on crack and that he was holding a young kiddie, his son, as hostage. We had the listening devices in but he was so far gone that he couldn't be negotiated with. He was threatening to set fire to the first-floor flat. He'd stuffed paper all around and the fire brigade were already on scene. We had two guys on the ladders ready to go in and we could smell inflammable fuel, petrol or something like that. I was outside the door with the scene commander and the blokes with the listening devices from technical support told us that he was striking matches. I said that I thought we ought to go in and what brings it to mind is that we used Hatton Rounds and I'm sure it was the first time they were used operationally. We got the go ahead, and with the Hatton Rounds going off he literally threw himself out the rear window and fell into the back garden, almost knocking [an officer] off a ladder. The child was rescued and it all went off fine.

## NATIONAL DEVELOPMENTS

The Regional Crime Squad was another group that often sought the assistance of the Firearms Unit. Its remit extended outside the Metropolitan Police area and in 1990 it was trying to deal with a series of armed robberies in south London, Surrey and Kent. After five weeks of surveillance, on 27 November team members were concealed in various vehicles and buildings surrounding the Woodhatch service station near Reigate in Surrey. Shortly after 10 o'clock in the morning a security vehicle pulled in, followed by a red Nissan pick-up truck. A tarpaulin on the back of the truck was suddenly thrown back and armed men jumped out. They grabbed the security guard and led her back to her vehicle.

As two of the men managed to get inside the security vehicle, another two went back to the pick-up truck. One of them was Kenneth Baker, a south London armed robber with a string of convictions, and as the officers moved in, he tried to shoot the driver of a police car that had pulled up alongside him. He was shot and he died of his injuries. The gang was armed with a sawn-off pump-action shotgun, two revolvers and two self-loading pistols.

*The Times*, under the heading 'Shooting of robber reopens debate on arming the police', reported:

At least half a dozen criminals have been killed by armed police in Britain during operations such as the one in which a robber was shot dead yesterday at Reigate, Surrey. Newspapers and television pictures regularly feature heavily armed, flack-jacketed officers protecting courts, watching over state occasions, or patrolling airport concourses. Given such images, questions over whether the British police should be regularly armed may seem academic. Yet the recent news that the Police Federation, representing 123,000 junior officers, may call for all officers to be armed [Constable Brown had been killed three months earlier] is likely to send a shudder of anxiety through the Home Office and senior ranks. In spite of the publicity surrounding the police use of firearms, very few officers are armed or qualified to use weapons. . . . Chief constables acknowledge evidence of an increasing use of guns by criminals but they advise that attitudes should not be swayed by isolated emotive incidents.

The problem was that, taken together, the 'emotive incidents' did not seem to be at all isolated to officers on the ground. In 1988 Constable Gavin Carlton had been shot and killed by armed robbers in the West Midlands and Constable Frank Mason had likewise been killed in Hertfordshire. In 1989 Constable Anthony Salt, also of the West Midlands police, had been beaten to death while on undercover duty and Inspector Ray Golding of Greater Manchester police had been shot and killed in an M62 service area. Then had come the death of Constable Brown in London. Another nine officers had been wounded by firearms during 1988, ten in 1989 and four in 1990.[3]

Criticism over policy as it related to the issue of firearms was best summed up on 9 November 1990 by an article in *Police Review* entitled 'Give Dixon the Bullet'. Dave Brady, a former Metropolitan officer, wrote:

The spectre of Dixon of Dock Green is constantly resurrected as a guideline for police attitudes and behaviour. The national press uses Dixon as an example in editorials whenever events reflect adversely on the service. . . . Dixon and countless [officers] before and since have died precisely because the public, the press and even the police service itself have resisted the arming of officers. We have inched a little closer towards armed response, but with typical British compromise. Permission has to be received from a very senior officer – of at least the level of a commander or assistant chief constable – before arms can be issued to street officers. . . . I joined the Met in 1955 . . . at a time when the Dixon influence still lingered. *The Blue Lamp* was still being shown at Hendon training school as part of our training. . . . Between 1970 and 1980 villains fired on me on six occasions. . . . Though an authorised shot, I was never armed when it really mattered.

The debate on police arming had been renewed and this time it would reach an intensity not seen for more that a century.

## ARMED RESPONSE

Female officers had not been allowed to carry a firearm in London until the late 1960s, and even then only if they were in plain clothes and their duty specifically required it. In November 1980 the policy committee allowed the training of women who wished to join the security section at Heathrow airport, and all of the restrictions were finally lifted in September 1985.[4]

The first armed response vehicle course started on 11 February 1991 and one of the first applicants was Constable, later Sergeant, Sandra Perry:

Was I on a mission? Was it the battle of the sexes, the last great male bastion finally overcome? Unfortunately not. Sometime during the summer of 1988 I was at Bethnal Green when the inspector asked whether 'any of you chaps want the next firearms course'. I asked whether that included the girls and he asked me whether I was 'some sort of female Rambo'. That stung, but a few weeks later the inspector called me into his office. He had considered the applications and felt that I was the best person to go on the course. I had not submitted an application and had no interest in firearms. I had never held a gun in my life but I felt unable to refuse. In November I attended Lippitts Hill where I spent two hard and stressful weeks on a basic firearms course. I left clutching a bullet mounted on a key ring that was awarded for the top student.

I returned to Bethnal Green where I spent the next two years in the CID, but by January 1991 I wanted to return to uniform. I was unsure of what to do until I saw an advert for the soon-to-be-formed armed response vehicles. I don't think I ever believed that I would really end up patrolling the streets of London with a gun, but I completed the application form. Six months later I walked in through the doors of Old Street.

On 1 July 1991 the cars and their three-person crews took to the streets with the firearms kept in two gun-safes, one for three revolvers and the other for two MP5 A2 9mm carbines. There were three response levels for the cars. 'Stage one' indicated that the officers should go to the vicinity of a call and monitor the local personal radio channel but they should not approach the incident. 'Stage two' required that the officers go to the scene and give a situation report to the Force Control Room. 'Stage three' was authority to deploy with firearms.

## ALL CHANGE

There was some confusion when the new cars answered the first calls, probably because the force had not yet been officially told of the decisions that had been made. Not until 3 July was it announced that divisional authorised officers would cease to have responsibility for armed duty from the end of October. From then on, each of the eight areas could keep twenty authorised officers based in their respective TSGs as a reserve, sixty in the case of the central area. In their place would be armed response vehicles, and the rifle officers would be allowed to join the Firearms Unit after all.[5]

The assimilation of new officers, which this time nearly doubled the size of the Firearms Unit, and the taking on of a role with no established precedent in London were not without difficulties. The person under whose immediate command all the operational teams and the new ARV crews now came was another new officer, Chief Inspector, later Superintendent, Norman Mackenzie:

Old Street was a truly dismal place from the outside and a closer inspection inside did nothing to change that view. I became aware immediately of a sense of mistrust internally towards this new breed of Firearms Unit officer. Being one of the latter there was a tendency for ARV officers to come to me with their various suggestions for changes. One of my earliest recollections was about the weapons – initially the Smith and Wesson revolvers were carried unloaded. This changed when a TV crew went out on an ARV. When the car was called to a robbery at a bank an ARV officer only had an empty weapon when he challenged a suspect, the rounds having fallen to the floor when the car was travelling at high speeds through London streets.

The filming was being done for London Weekend Television and the story appeared in several newspapers on 2 August.

There were also attempts to discredit the very idea of a centralised armed response vehicle system. Within weeks, a superintendent well known for his opposition happened to be in his police station when a call came in. He contacted the Force Control Room and directed that the ARV crew be told to remain at 'stage one'. He then authorised his own divisional officers to draw weapons from the station.

When the incident was over, the superintendent submitted a report to his area deputy assistant commissioner pointing out that it had been his own officers who had dealt with the call and that the armed response vehicle had not arrived. The DAC in turn wasted no time in regaling his senior colleagues with the story of how one of his divisions had been let down by the 'centralised system'. A few days later, buried in a mass of paperwork and computer printouts, the two lines were found recording the order for the armed response vehicle to remain at 'stage one'. When these were pointed out to the DAC concerned the matter was quietly dropped, but, on 2 October, the 'stage one' part of the response was abandoned. From then on the coded radio message 'Trojan Alpha' was used when the intention was that the officers go to the scene and 'Trojan Delta' meant that authority had been given for firearms to be removed from their gun-safe, the revolvers being carried loaded by now.

Although on the face of it matters were starting to settle down, there had in fact already been a substantial spanner stuck in the works. Out of the blue on 30 August an 'All Stations Message' had been sent out from New Scotland Yard. This informed the force that, although the decision had originally been taken that the divisional rifle officers would not join the Firearms Unit and this ruling had then been reversed (as announced the previous month), it had been decided to reverse the position again. Furthermore, divisional authorised officers would not cease to have responsibility for armed duty from the end of October 1991 after all. They were to carry on as if nothing had happened.

There was no explanation given for the new decision and members of the Firearms Unit were just as bewildered as everyone else, but for some there was now a chance to get away from the force's internal power struggles for a while.

## TURKS AND CAICOS

Since the 1970s Colombia had been home to some of the most violent drug trafficking organisations in the world. During the 1980s the Medellin cartel alone was reputedly sending as much as 30 tons of cocaine a month into the United States and the profits ran into billions of dollars. When the Colombian government threatened to extradite the drug traffickers to the US, their leadership fought back. The cartel was responsible for the assassination of dozens of government officials and the bribery of many more.

In the early 1990s several of the leading members of the Medellin cartel surrendered in return for lenient prison sentences. High on the list of those still wanted, however, was Robert Elesi Serry, brother-in-law of the cartel's leader, Pablo Escobar. In March 1991 Serry was arrested when, travelling on a false passport, he arrived on Grand Turk in the Turks and Caicos islands. Situated 575 miles south of Miami and with a resident population of less than 20,000, the islands had been a British Crown Colony since 1962.

Proceedings began for Serry's extradition to Florida, but on 8 October he disappeared after sawing through the bars of his cell. It was suspected that his guards had connived in the escape, but Grand Turk is only about 6 miles long by 3 miles wide which did not give him many places to go. Serry was prevented from leaving by the presence of a navy frigate and he was recaptured on 14 October.

Arrangements for Serry's extradition were agreed, but he had until 24 October to lodge an appeal and there were concerns that in the interim an attempt would be made to free him in a military-style rescue. Initially an approach was made to the MoD for aid but this was turned down on the grounds that it was a 'civil matter'. The Foreign & Commonwealth Office, for the first time, sought the operational assistance of the Firearms Unit in London. Inspector

Rawlings with Constable Jonathan 'Dino' Ferrari and four others left
for Grand Turk on 19 October.

*'Dino' Ferrari*
Our firearms and ammunition were signed in at Heathrow under
the supervision of the security section. On arrival at Miami we
decided that we would collect our personal belongings and then go
to customs to get our firearms. What shocked us was that all of the
firearms and equipment appeared on the carousel with our luggage.
One bag was half open with some loose 9mm rounds rolling out on
to the carousel, but no one batted an eyelid. How things have
changed since then.

*Clive Rawlings*
When we arrived on the island I asked for a vehicle to give us some
independence and mobility and they hired a small Jeep for us. Serry
had a cell on his own but the prison was a joke. There was just a
small compound, like a prison yard, with a couple of cells and a cell
passage. It seemed as though the other prisoners could come and go
at will. They weren't locked up in cells – they were out in the
compound cooking their food, playing cards and pumping iron. The
Deputy Commissioner of Police on the island was an ex-
Metropolitan Police chief superintendent and I think his original
request had been for the frigate to put some Royal Marines ashore.
They obviously said no but, although I don't know how far away
they were, we were told that if the wheel came off they could try
and get us some help.

There were two of us sitting outside the little cellblock, two
patrolling in the Jeep, and two with their heads down. That's how
we ran it for the five days – four hours on and two hours off. We got
towards the last evening and Serry's time to appeal was due to run
out at midnight. I thought that if anything was going to happen it
was going to be around that time and I wasn't happy with the
prison. I put it to the Deputy Commissioner that we had to get him
moved and so we got the police HQ designated as a prison. We
found a secure room with no windows and the six of us sat with him

overnight until we took him to the airport in the morning. From there he was flown to Miami by the DEA [US Drug Enforcement Administration] in a helicopter.

The DEA was so pleased to get their hands on Serry that the US Department of Justice officials involved personally congratulated the Home Secretary when he paid a visit to Washington a few days later.

## SHOTS FIRED IN ACTON

David Barfield had joined the Territorial Army at the age of eighteen. His mental health had then deteriorated, resulting in a charge of assault and criminal damage that was discontinued when he was admitted to a mental hospital. During the late afternoon of 11 November 1991 Barfield, now aged twenty-seven, put on his TA camouflage clothing and stood guard on the pavement outside the house where he was living with his parents at 17 Old Oak Road in Acton, west London. The duty social worker, a psychiatrist and the family doctor arrived, but when Barfield went inside and reappeared in the hallway with a sword, they decided that they should leave. At the doctor's surgery they completed the necessary paperwork for Barfield's re-admittance to a mental hospital and then called the police to back them up when they returned to Old Oak Road.

*Sandra Perry*
We were filling up with petrol when a call came over the main set requesting the attendance of TSG units to Old Oak Road. Darren [name omitted] had previously worked in that area and said that he had been to the address before. He called up on the main set and surprisingly he got us assigned. When we got there a doctor and social worker discussed the case close to our vehicle. We listened intently until the decision was taken that the TSG would make a forced entry with shields to allow the doctor to section the man. Simon [name omitted] put the car in gear and we moved slowly along beside the TSG. As the TSG officers approached the house the man reappeared on the doorstep and opened fire with a rifle.

There had never been any suggestion that the man had access to a firearm and as the shots rang out, the TSG officers ran for cover.

Darren and Simon armed with their revolvers and ran from the car. As the rear-seat officer, my job was to get the MP5s. I urgently pulled at the door of the gun-safe and the weapons slid free, but I watched as one of the double magazines disappeared into the cluttered footwell. The man was now in the street and he opened fire on our car. I hurriedly threw on my body armour and then grabbed the two MP5s and the one double magazine that was left. The man continued to fire in my direction as I ran down the street to join Simon behind a TSG carrier. Darren had taken up a position to the front of the house and had returned fire with his revolver as Barfield went back inside.

On reaching Simon, I told him that I thought I had been shot but I was not really aware of any obvious injury. Hurriedly we broke apart the double magazine and taking one magazine, I ran to join Darren at the front of the house. Simon began to make his way to the rear. Barfield reappeared and fired in our direction. Darren returned fire but I was unable to do so from my position. Barfield went back inside to reload and then reappeared pointing the rifle at us. I shouted 'Armed police!' and watched as he brought the weapon around to aim at me. Everything I had been taught in training now fell into place. My reactions were instinctive as I brought the MP5 up into the aim. There was a feeling of time slowing down as I waited to see who would fire first. I pulled the trigger for the first shot and was about to fire a second when a man ran up the path, bundling Barfield inside with him. Darren and I immediately followed them in, only to find Barfield still standing and ready to fight. We were quickly joined by a number of TSG officers and after a short struggle Barfield was handcuffed and secured on the floor. The other man, who it later transpired was his father, was also secured and escorted from the house. When we emptied Barfield's pockets we found a large number of cartridges – in excess of sixty – and as we opened his jacket it became apparent that he was bleeding from a stomach wound.

Darren and I then went and sat in a TSG carrier where I realised
that I was bleeding quite heavily from a head wound. Barfield and I
were taken to hospital where he was found to have a round lodged
in his liver. It was later confirmed that this round had been fired
from my MP5, but he made a good recovery. The gun turned out to
be an Enfield rifle that had been bored smooth to take shotgun
cartridges. I had a number of wounds to the scalp caused by pellets,
most of which were removed that night, although a few are still
embedded in my skull.

Barfield was charged with attempted murder and assault, but he was
found guilty of causing actual bodily harm and detained under the
provisions of mental health legislation. Constable Perry returned to
full duty with the Firearms Unit. However, an ARV could not be at
every call that came out over the radio, let alone be wherever there
was a police officer.

## THE MURDERS OF SERGEANT ALAN KING AND
## DETECTIVE CONSTABLE JIM MORRISON

As a teenager Nicholas Vernage had a string of convictions for
burglary, criminal damage, theft and assault. Then, in 1987, he had
been jailed for seven years for conspiracy to rob and aggravated
burglary, and while in prison he told a cellmate that he was going to
teach Lorna Bogle, a former girlfriend, a lesson for not visiting him.
Before his release in October 1991 he also told fellow inmates: 'Don't
worry. I'll be back. I'm going to kill a copper.'

On 21 November 1991 Vernage, now aged twenty-seven, stabbed
and killed Lorna Bogle outside her flat. Three days later he was
burgling a flat in Leytonstone, east London, when he killed Javaid
Iqbal, the owner, who had caught him in the act. On 28 November in
Walthamstow Sergeant Alan King was investigating a Cortina car, in
which Vernage kept some of the proceeds from his burglaries, when
the killer saw him through the window of a room he was in nearby.
Vernage went out into the street and stabbed the sergeant in the head
and chest. He then walked back into the building where he kicked

open the door of a room occupied by another man, Peter Grenfell. Vernage told Grenfell to help him push the sergeant's car, which was blocking the Cortina's exit, out of the way.

When the two went outside they saw Sergeant King in the road attempting to flag down a passing car. Vernage stabbed the sergeant again. The officer was taken to Whipps Cross Hospital where he died. The next day Constables Castrey and Jenkinson stopped Vernage and Grenfell in Thornton Heath. Vernage drew a knife from his back pocket and stabbed them. Fortunately they both survived.

Vernage showed no remorse when, just before Christmas 1992, he was found guilty of three murders and two attempted murders. He was sentenced to five terms of life imprisonment with a recommendation that he serve at least twenty-five years. Some of the family and friends of his victims were in court to hear the sentence and, in a final act of pure evil as he was being taken from the dock, Vernage turned towards them and shouted, 'Happy Christmas, by the way'. Grenfell was dealt with separately under the provisions of mental health legislation.

A month after the murder of Sergeant King, an off-duty officer, Detective Constable Jim Morrison, was in a public house in Covent Garden waiting for his wife to finish work when he spotted a handbag thief. Despite being threatened with a knife, the officer gave chase and was stabbed. He was taken to St Bartholomew's Hospital where he died two hours later. The murder of Constable Morrison remains unsolved. Both deaths further heated up the debate over the arming of police officers, a debate that had not had the chance to cool down after the murder of Constable Brown just over a year earlier.

## Chapter 13

# TO ENCOURAGE THE OTHERS

## NATIONAL DEVELOPMENTS

In 1992 the Home Office decided that it was time to have a close look at what forces were doing with armed response vehicles. After all, in 1986 a Home Office working group had rejected the idea, but there were now eighteen forces with an ARV system and the number was rapidly increasing. The resulting report in May found that: 'The ARV system was a sensible way of providing an immediate firearms response, that those working in it were competent and responsible officers, and that it provided reassurance to unarmed sub-divisional officers.'[1] However, it was in the area of authority to arm that the report examined the issue which would attract the most attention over the next few years. It was explained that:

> An officer of ACPO rank must give authority for the issue of any firearm. . . . However, the rules go on to say that, should such an officer not be quickly available, then others can give authority: a Superintendent or Chief Superintendent or, failing that . . . the force control room. Where their own or another's life is threatened the ARV officers themselves can take decisions to arm. . . . Although this hierarchy of responsibility and decision making looks logical on paper, rules can easily get blurred in the heat of the moment; emergencies do not wait conveniently for bureaucratic procedures to be followed. . . . One force reported that . . . when going to incidents, the crews 'arm up', but do not (except in an emergency) actually leave the vehicle until authority to do so has been received. Variation on the definition of 'arming' is reflected also in a suggestion from another force that such preparatory arming should be considered where crews are likely to be suddenly

confronted by armed suspects. This would not be defined as having authority to arm, but [as] 'authority to prepare'.

The report recommended that: 'Forces should examine more closely just how they are translating the concept of authority to arm into operational terms and try to achieve a greater degree of consistency of practice.'

Chief constables saw no reason for a 'consistency of practice' and they had already discovered a simple way of avoiding any national guidelines for ARVs – they only had to call their cars something else. There was nothing to say that a car containing firearms and authorised officers had to be called an armed response vehicle. Chief officers were therefore able to argue, with absolute sincerity, that their 'incident response cars' or 'containment response vehicles' were not ARVs, and that any differences in procedure were the result of not comparing like with like.

## SHOTS FIRED IN PENGE

On 24 February 1992 the Firearms Unit in London was notified that the teams and the instructors had been taken out of Personnel and Training and moved into Specialist Operations department. They were given the designation SO19, but there was no mention of ARVs when the move was announced and so theoretically these were left behind. This was corrected on 4 March.

On 23 June at just before 9.30 in the evening, Peter Swann telephoned New Scotland Yard to say that he had a shotgun and that he had hostages. Swann lived on the third floor of Queen Adelaide Court, Queen Adelaide Road, Penge, in south-east London. Two ARVs and a specialist team were sent on the authority of a commander of the area. Containment was quickly set up around the whole block and by 10 o'clock most of the paraphernalia associated with a siege was in place. Negotiators tried to talk to Swann but all he would do was issue threats and use obscenities to tell them what he thought of the police. He released a neighbour, Kelly Lumis, but after 45 minutes he shouted that he still had his wife as a hostage and that he was armed with a sawn-off shotgun (true) and an Uzi sub-machine gun (untrue). He also said that either the police would shoot him or he would shoot a police officer.

At just after 11 o'clock Swann stood on the balcony at the front of his flat and shouted: 'Hurry up. If you're not going to shoot me then I will come down and shoot you.' He then walked, sawn-off shotgun in hand, along the length of the balcony and down part of the staircase before turning around and going back to his flat.

The problem for the police was that during this walk Swann could have met someone who did not realise what was going on. At the same time, they could not evacuate the other flats while Swann was able to roam at will. The area that Swann had available had to be reduced, but this risked putting officers into a position where they had no choice but to shoot him. It was an impossible situation. Then Swann announced that the police had 10 minutes to get him or he would come down and get them. Negotiators tried their best to reason with him, but at 11.35 Swann again walked along the balcony and down the stairs. He met armed officers at the bottom, pointed the gun at them and was shot. Despite being rushed to hospital and being given emergency surgery, he died of his injuries.

An inquest jury at Croydon Coroners Court in September 1993 returned a verdict of lawful killing. However, it is far more likely that this was the first case in London of a person who was determined to end his life using a phenomenon referred to in the US as 'suicide by cop' or 'victim precipitated homicide'.

One of the earliest recognised examples had occurred in 1981 in Rochester, New York. William Griffin killed three people including his mother. He then walked to a nearby bank and took the nine staff hostage. During a 3½-hour siege he shot and wounded two police officers and six bystanders. He also told the bank manager to let the police outside know that if they did not enter and shoot him, he would 'start throwing out bodies'. The 'Stockholm syndrome' was no more apparent than it had been in other cases where hostages had been taken on purpose, and when a deadline was reached, Griffin shot and killed a female member of staff. He then deliberately stood in full view of the police outside and was shot and killed.

A common feature in such incidents is that the situation is entirely of the victim's own making. The presence of the police is somehow forced, as is the result. However, knowing of the phenomenon's existence does not make it any easier to deal with.

## ORGANISATIONAL CHANGES

The armed response to Penge had been achieved within a time-scale that could not have been matched by divisional authorised officers, but the Metropolitan Police was finding this new instant availability hard to come to terms with. For instance, on 3 July 1992 at about 10.30 in the morning a man was seen dressed in combat clothing and carrying a rifle in a wooded area near Bushey on the outskirts of north-west London. With the events in Hungerford still very much in mind, the chief inspector in the Force Control Room sent ARVs to the scene, together with the force helicopter, and gave authority for the officers to draw their weapons from the gun-safes in the cars.

This immediate granting of authority was not in line with the instructions for ARVs. If 'delay could result in loss of life or serious injury' then a chief superintendent or superintendent could give authority, and so telephone calls should first have been made to the nearest police station to where the incident was taking place to establish whether they could be contacted. Officers of these ranks were often no more 'immediately available' than they had been in 1965, but it was only in their confirmed absence that the Force Control Room could grant authority. As the Home Office review had reported, 'emergencies do not wait conveniently for bureaucratic procedures to be followed' and the Force Control Room would sometimes cut corners.

Sightings of the armed man were continually being reported, and it seemed as though he was moving on foot across the Metropolitan Police border into Hertfordshire. The Force Control Room contacted an assistant chief constable in Hertfordshire who granted authority for his own and for the Metropolitan Police ARV crews to carry firearms in his area. Since the person being sought could still be on the Metropolitan side of the border, the on-call ACPO officer, a commander, was then asked to endorse the authority granted by the chief inspector in the Force Control Room. He flatly refused to do so on the grounds that the proper procedure had not been followed and his refusal would 'act as an object lesson for the future'. The officers on the ground greeted the decision with disbelief, particularly after being told that they could now only carry firearms on the Hertfordshire side of the border. Fortunately, when the man was found it was discovered that he was merely living out a fantasy with a replica British Army SA80 assault rifle.

Another example of how some officers were unprepared for the reality of having ARVs available occurred a few months later. In 1992 there were 2,914 armed robberies in London, more than the total for each of the twenty-five years after the end of the Second World War added together, and one of them occurred on 16 October at 10.33 in the morning at a Lloyds Bank in Kilburn.[2] ARVs were sent and when the officers arrived they found that a shotgun had been fired. They also discovered that one of those responsible had run down an alley towards an area of undergrowth alongside a railway line.

It seemed unlikely that any of the robbers were still in the immediate vicinity, but when the local chief superintendent arrived he readily agreed that the ARV officers and some dog handlers should conduct an armed search of the undergrowth. However, the situation was now not one where 'delay could result in loss of life or serious injury' and so the chief superintendent could not give the authority for the officers to carry firearms. The on-call ACPO officer, a commander, was contacted and to the astonishment of everyone he refused the request on the grounds that the robber might not be there.

The circumstances under which firearms could be issued were unchanged from those drawn up in 1983 and these only required that there be 'reason to suppose' that firearms might be necessary, not that it be a proven fact. Nevertheless, in this instance the dog handlers and local unarmed officers were asked to search alone, but they were unwilling to do so without armed support. In the event, everyone withdrew, and whether the robber was actually still there will never be known.

Disagreements over whether or not firearms should be issued were nothing new. The difference now was that the firearms were already at the scene of an incident and all that was necessary was for the officers to step out of the cars with them. The expectations of the armed and unarmed officers alike had been irrevocably altered by the introduction of ARVs, but the highest-ranking Firearms Unit officers likely to be immediately available when an incident occurred were sergeants and they could not always persuade more senior officers of the need to act. In November 1992 the inspectors were taken off the teams and given responsibility for the ARVs as well. Most of them agreed that this move was long overdue, but even an inspector could do little when faced with an intransigent senior officer far removed from events.

The chief inspectors in the Force Control Room had become quite adept at identifying which senior officers were more likely than others to grant a firearms authority and, after finding out who was 'on call', they would sometimes not bother to ask the question if they thought they knew the probable answer. Rather than risk a negative response, they would leave it to the officers themselves to make the decision under the provisions that allowed ARV officers to arm themselves 'where their own or another's life is threatened'.

This only served to stir matters up even more, and the anti-centralisation lobby formed a small group to 'produce an implementation plan for the devolution of ARVs to areas' so that each area could devise and enforce its own rules. The plan[3] landed on the desk of the Assistant Commissioner Territorial Operations (ACTO) in October, but by then there were rumours that another force reorganisation was on the cards.

It had been obvious for some time that organising the force into eight self-sufficient areas had been a serious mistake, leading to a costly duplication of resources. In addition, areas increasingly saw themselves as independent entities, and the time had come for New Scotland Yard to re-establish its authority. On 17 May 1993 William Taylor, the Assistant Commissioner Specialist Operations (ACSO), directed that nothing more should be decided on the future of ARVs until the next force restructuring exercise was complete – and it was thought that this would take at least another year.

### MESSING ABOUT IN BOATS

November 1992 had seen the culmination of fifteen months of work by the Regional Crime Squad and HM Customs and Excise on an operation under the codename of 'Operation Emerge'. Information suggested that large quantities of drugs were being supplied to the UK from South America using a converted 300-ton, 115-foot oilrig support vessel, the *Fox Trot Five*. At a planning meeting in early November it was decided that, in order to deal with the ship, the Firearms Unit in London needed outside support. Essex police agreed to help, as did the MoD with the offer of Special Boat Service (SBS) vessels. One of those involved was Inspector Doug McConnachie:

> The operation was divided into a land operation and a waterborne operation. The *Fox Trot Five* could dock in London and unload into vehicles; moor up at a distant location for unloading; be met and unloaded into smaller boats as it went upriver or the load could be dumped overboard. The purpose of the waterborne operation was to secure the boat and the occupants, to intercept other boats, to prevent disposal of the cargo and to recover anything thrown overboard.

The operation required that the ship be tracked as it crossed the Atlantic and then monitored by a string of observation points as it entered the Thames estuary. Two potential landing points were identified, as was the probable destination of the cargo. Rehearsals were arranged with the SBS for 16 November when officers from the Metropolitan and the Essex police Firearms Units practised getting on to a moving ship.

*Doug McConnachie*
This took place in the Solent where we practised transferring from rigid inflatable boats [RIBs] on to a large tug, at various speeds and using various techniques. The training consisted of boarding the boat from the side and rear, while the instructors warned us of the

dangers of falling in and being drawn into the screws of the boat and being chopped up – all without the comfort of a safety rope. Preparations for the land operation were also well under way. The routes along the Thames were planned with a view to shadowing the ship up the river. There were also numerous static observation points along the river as identification was to be made primarily by the light configuration of the vessel.

On cue, the *Fox Trot Five* picked up its cargo at sea off the coast of Aruba, a small island in the Caribbean just north of Venezuela, and was monitored by military aircraft as it crossed the Atlantic. On 22 November there was a call to say that the operation was under way.

*Doug McConnachie*
One Sunday morning at about 11 o'clock the call came in to activate 'Operation Emerge' with the final assembly being at Greenwich section house. It involved a large number of SO19 personnel, at least three teams and ARV officers as support [drivers]. From this point the teams were split and we headed off to another holding point at an old Royal Engineers depot on the River Medway. There we met up with the SBS crews and a chief inspector from Essex. The SBS provided two boat commanders and drivers, and we had an inspector, two sergeants and seven constables for the two SBS RIBs. Essex had two sergeants and nine constables for two RIBs of their own.

Another ten team members from the Metropolitan Police and six from Essex made their way to locations north and south of the river so that they could follow the ship from the shore. They were in for a long wait. The speed of the vessel was much less than expected and the probable arrival time was put back from 5 o'clock in the afternoon to 7 o'clock in the evening and then to 11 o'clock at night. Even this proved optimistic: the officers did not take to the boats until 2 o'clock the next morning – not a good time to be out in an open boat in November.

*Doug McConnachie*

We remained concealed in the Medway until the *Fox Trot Five* had passed. We then slipped out and began to shadow it up the Thames. The river was quite busy with some fairly large boats and we were running without lights. It wasn't too long before our first mishap – one of the Essex boats broke down off Southend. We continued up the river and, although we were all wearing FRIS [fire-retardant immersion suits] and other warm clothing, we were frozen, particularly our hands. I was amazed how much water was splashing over us in fairly calm conditions. Fortunately we had taken along a few cases of [self-heating] hot-can meals which we activated and used to warm our hands. By the time one had cooled down, the next one was ready. For most of the time the target was not in sight as we were anything up to a mile behind to avoid any chance of being detected.

The shore teams joined in, but progress was painfully slow because of an unexpectedly high ebbing tide. It was not until 7.30 a.m. that the ship eventually moored at Woolwich where the cargo was unloaded and taken by van to Roth Street in south-east London. The duration of the operation had taken its toll on the police radios.

*Doug McConnachie*

Communications were virtually non-existent as the batteries were flat. We parked up among a collection of barges by the entrance to the royal docks for further updates but I believe we had one radio left with any power in the battery and that could only be used by climbing on top of a container on a barge. At about 9 o'clock the 'attack' was called. The SBS RIBs took off at full power and we caught the Woolwich ferry midstream with one SBS boat crossing its bow and the other its stern. We found the *Fox Trot Five* moored up to a pier and after we had boarded we conducted a full search but the boat was empty. The boat was secured and handed over for further searching.

At the same time, team members entered a warehouse in Roth Street and six arrests were made, but the operation had not passed unnoticed. The next day, photographs of the officers boarding the ship appeared in just about every newspaper. The coverage in the *Daily Express* was typical: under the headline 'The Coke Busters', readers were told:

> The trail started 5,000 miles away and ended in Britain's biggest ever cocaine haul on a grey Thames morning yesterday. Special Boat Squadron commandos stormed a smuggler's ship while armed police and customs men smashed down a warehouse door with a JCB. They found a ton of pure cocaine worth £160 million – drugs bound for smart-set dinner parties and council estate crack dens. Yesterday's triumph and a similar raid in March netted almost twice as much cocaine as in the whole of 1991.

'Operation Emerge' proved the need for the Firearms Unit to have a waterborne capability and training started using the RIBs belonging to the Metropolitan Police Thames division, but it would be eight years before another major operation became necessary on the river. On 7 November 2000 there was an attempted robbery at the Millennium Dome next to the River Thames at Greenwich in south-east London. The target was the exhibit housing the De Beers Millennium Diamonds – eleven rare blue diamonds totalling 118 carats and the flawless 203-carat, pear-shaped diamond, the Millennium Star, worth by itself over £200 million. The getaway vehicle was to be a speedboat.

Detectives from the Flying Squad had pieced together the intelligence that had been gathered during a surveillance operation codenamed 'Operation Magician' and when the gang struck, team members were ready and waiting. Some were hidden behind a secret wall that had been specially constructed for them inside the Dome. Others were dressed as cleaners with their weapons hidden inside black plastic bags and rubbish bins. Still more were in RIBs on the river.

At just after 9.30 in the morning a JCB digger crashed into the Dome as the speedboat moved into position nearby. Two of the gang went into the diamond exhibit while a third waited outside on guard.

All three were wearing gas-masks and body armour. As the two inside used a nail-gun and a sledgehammer to smash their way into the armoured-glass cabinets, team members moved in to arrest them. The pair had managed to punch a hole the size of a fist in the glass surrounding the Millennium Star but when confronted they threw themselves on the floor and gave up. Outside, the third man also gave up, as did the driver of the JCB. On the river, the RIBs moved in and secured the speedboat and its driver. Had the gang been successful, it would have committed the biggest robbery in history.[4]

## DOMESTIC TERRORISM

In April 1992 the Firearms Unit had been asked to assist the Anti-Terrorist branch when Glasgow-born James Canning, aged thirty-seven, and his mistress, Ethel Lamb, aged sixty, were discovered in Northolt in north-west London. They were known locally as 'The Odd Couple' but there was more to the pair than met the eye. Canning had a secret life as a PIRA quartermaster with a supply of weapons and explosives that he kept in Lamb's bungalow. While the Unit's specialist teams provided armed support to the surveillance it was noticed that the relationship between the two had started to deteriorate. This was probably because of Canning's trips back to Northern Ireland to collect money to pay the living expenses of other PIRA terrorists on the mainland, and he had a wife and family living in Crossmaglen.

Canning decided it was time to move the arms cache elsewhere and he was seen arguing with Lamb as he put the material, wrapped in plastic bin liners, into the boot of his car. He was followed to a lock-up garage not far from RAF Uxbridge where he unloaded the bags and then went on a pub-crawl. After downing several pints he made use of a public telephone and then drove on to the next pub a few hundred yards away where the process was repeated. It was not long before he was intoxicated. The surveillance commentary caused increasing amusement as it described his staggering from a pub, falling over, and on one occasion falling asleep at the wheel of his car when he stopped at a set of traffic lights.

The arrest of the couple was ordered, and when the pair returned to the bungalow after a night on the town they were confronted by several team members who had been hiding in the shadows in the front garden. Canning tried to reach for a loaded .357 calibre revolver in the waistband of his trousers but he was overpowered. A total of 88lb of Semtex and six Kalashnikov assault rifles were recovered from the garage, and in February 1993 at the Old Bailey, Canning was sentenced to thirty years in prison for conspiring to cause explosions and for possessing firearms and explosives. Lamb was sentenced to three years after being described in court as a 'pathetic creature' who had been 'abandoned' by her previous lover before falling under 'the fatal orbit of Canning'.

The removal of Canning and Lamb made only a slight dent in the activities of the PIRA. Two months after the arrests, Constable Sandy Kelly and Special Constable Glen Goodman, both unarmed, stopped a car in North Yorkshire. Unknown to the officers, the two occupants were Paul Magee and Michael O'Brien, both PIRA terrorists. Magee opened fire, killing Constable Goodman and severely wounding Constable Kelly. As they made off at high speed they fired at another police car containing Constables Mark Whitehouse and Susan Larkin. Both men were eventually caught and Magee was imprisoned for life for the murder of Constable Goodman and the attempted murder of the three other officers. O'Brien was sentenced to eighteen years for attempted murder.

Back in London, on 15 November 1992 a bomb made up of just over 1½ tons of home-made explosive was left near Canary Wharf tower in London's docklands, the second tallest building in Europe. The detonators malfunctioned and the device failed to explode, but on 28 January 1993 at 9.40 a.m., a bomb containing 2lb of Semtex exploded outside Harrods department store. Four people were injured. Then, on 3 February, passengers were evacuated 10 minutes before a Semtex bomb exploded on a passenger train.

The Anti-Terrorist branch released a video taken by a security camera covering the outside of Harrods showing the device being planted. This led to Jan Alexander Taylor, a former British Army corporal, and Patrick Hayes. Attention focused on a ground-floor flat belonging to Hayes at 54 Walford Road in Stoke Newington and on 2 March both men were seen entering the address. A plan was quickly put together that involved officers from the Firearms Unit entering through the front door, the front windows and the back door, all at the same time. As the entry began the officers came under fire. A handgun was pushed round an internal door and shots were fired in the direction of the front window. Fortunately they missed and the two terrorists were arrested.

They had been in the process of priming an explosive device. A large number of timer and power units, Semtex explosive, two AK47 assault rifles and two handguns were recovered. Two devices, ready to be placed at Monument and Bank underground stations, and a list of important figures, including the head of MI5, Stella Rimmington, were also found, as was more than £1,400 in cash hidden in a sofa. In a garage rented by Hayes there was a cache of more than half a ton of home-made explosive.

On 8 March Commissioner Sir Paul Condon telephoned Old Street to thank the officers concerned, saying:

> Please pass on my belated congratulations to all officers involved in the operation that resulted in the arrest of two men in Stoke Newington last week for terrorist offences. In conversations I have had with the Home Secretary, the restraint displayed by the SO19 officers was particularly remarked upon and they have attracted very favourable comments from many sources. We are all basking in their excellent work. I believe no other firearms team anywhere could have done the job so well.

In May 1994 at the Old Bailey Hayes was convicted of eleven terrorist offences and Taylor of eight. They were both sentenced to thirty years in prison.

## FIREARMS TRAINING

The instructors in London had started to export British police firearms training in the 1970s and this continued throughout the

1980s. The first foreign trip of the following decade took three officers to Brazil for three weeks in May 1992. The United Nations Conference on Environment and Development (UNCED), more generally referred to as the first 'Earth Summit', was due to be held in Rio de Janeiro in June, and the Brazilian Federal Police asked for some additional training as a part of its preparations. Unlike previous training assignments, this one was not quite as confidential as the officers had expected.

*Dave Tilley*
In Brasilia we were escorted to the Federal Police Training School where we were put in front of a televised press conference. After the interviews we were shown our accommodation – a brick Nissen hut with a glass wall at one end, an air brick wall at the other and no air conditioning. As the temperature was 40 degrees, there was some discussion and we were relocated to a nearby hotel. The range complex was outdoors and quite modern and an interpreter was provided as our Portuguese was not thought to be up to the task. We ran a three-week course teaching bodyguard skills and some hostage rescue techniques. The walking and vehicle anti-ambush procedures were reinforced with exercises on the campus. On the range we taught advanced shooting techniques with handguns and MP5s. The students used a wide range of weapons that depended on which area of Brazil they had come from. They were mostly Federal Police but the President's personal protection officer, a major in their Special Forces, attended too.

After two weeks the whole course relocated to Rio where the Earth Summit was to take place. Our hotel this time was the Copacabana Palace and the rooms we were given were to be for the Prime Minister [John Major] and his staff on their arrival. We fitted into the five-star-hotel clientele very well, although dressing in training blues, berets, and being picked up everyday by armed Federal Police in a 4x4 raised the odd eyebrow. The room combat and hostage rescue training took place at the Special Forces camp. Unfortunately, there was nowhere we could use as a range and so I used a clearing in the jungle. I got the students to construct a series of rooms from a large stock of car tyres and there were just enough of them to make waist height walls, but the live-fire required careful positioning of the hand drawn targets.

It was not just in Brazil that the instructors had to make do with what they could find for themselves. In London by the early 1990s the temporary sites used for tactical training were parts of the former Propellant and Explosives Research and Monitoring Establishment (PERME) and the now disused RSAF site, both in Enfield not far from Lippitts Hill. However, the major element that both sites lacked, apart from such obvious essentials as heating, lighting, toilets, briefing rooms, catering, privacy and any provision for first-aid treatment, was any degree of permanence. The instructors could be asked to leave with little or no notice.

In August 1992 a Firearms Unit report pointed out that the force still had no dedicated facility for tactics training.[5] This was followed by a second[6] in September but this also failed to provoke a reaction, and so another report[7] was produced in April 1993. This one found its way to a meeting being chaired by the ACSO, William Taylor, in May. The meeting was astonished to hear that in the five and a half years since it had been agreed that 'the construction at Hounslow would go ahead, with Lippitts Hill to follow within the next five years', very little had actually happened. The Metropolitan Police Property Services department (PSD) was directed to study the feasibility of purchasing the RSAF site, and it was also decided that there would be yet another examination of the current numbers of authorised officers to see where there could be reductions.

The working party set up in August 1984 to reduce the number had decided on a figure of 2,963 in March 1986 but this had soon been overtaken by events when the actual number fell to 2,701 in 1987 and to 2,568 in 1988. One reason for the decline was a continuing reaction to the prosecution of the officers involved in shootings in London and the West Midlands. Many had simply handed in their authorisations, and despite hundreds of new officers being trained every year, by the end of 1992 the number left on the list stood at 1,884. The ACSO announced the new reductions on 25 August 1993 with instructions that they were to be made as soon as possible and in any case by 30 September. Had the eight area DACs taken any notice, the number would have reduced to 1,718. By the end of 1993 the figure stood at 1,952 and in 1994 it would reach 2,013, the first increase since the shooting of Stephen Waldorf a decade earlier.

By August 1993 the prospect of the Metropolitan Police acquiring the RSAF site was looking increasingly unlikely. There were rumours that the price for the land alone was in the region of £20 million, and so in November the Firearms Unit produced yet another report seeking the provision of a purpose-built firearms training site for the Metropolitan Police.[8]

If there was an outcome from the May 1993 meeting it was the construction of some plywood single-storey building façades on an unused part of the grass at Lippitts Hill. These too were supposed to represent a 'street', although in appearance the result was an enlarged version of what the instructors had put together themselves in 1985.

### THE MURDER OF CONSTABLE PATRICK DUNNE

At just after 9 o'clock in the evening on 20 October 1993 at 31 Cato Road, Clapham, in south London, three black men armed with two handguns and a baseball bat shot and killed William Danso. Constable Patrick Dunne was unarmed when he heard the shots while he was dealing with an unconnected incident in a house opposite. He went to investigate. He was shot in the chest, receiving fatal injuries. The three men walked away laughing. The main suspect was Gary Nelson but the case against him was not proceeded with because of insufficient evidence. However, he was sentenced to eight years in prison in 1994 after a 'road rage' shooting incident and released in 1999.

It was discovered that, while in prison, Nelson had told another inmate that he had committed the murders. In 2001 the enquiry was reopened and previous evidence was re-examined. In early 2003 Nelson was followed to the United States where he bought a laser-aiming device for a handgun. When he returned to his home in Woolwich in south-west London it was raided by a specialist team and he was caught in possession of a loaded 9mm Browning pistol, a silencer and ammunition. In February 2004 Nelson was sentenced to life imprisonment for firearms offences and in October he was charged with the murders of William Danso and Constable Dunne. At Woolwich Crown Court in February 2006 he was convicted and again sentenced to life with a recommendation that he serve at least thirty-five years.

Constable Dunne had served at Clapham police station and was described by many as being a 'Dixon of Dock Green type of policeman'. He had been a teacher prior to joining the police at the age of forty only three years earlier, and his murder added yet more fuel to the debate on arming the police. At the annual meeting of the Metropolitan branch of the Police Federation shortly after Dunne's death, Sir Paul Condon told the audience:

> Of course I favour and support our traditional unarmed officers but that does not mean that I shall allow history to stand in the way of your safety. At the moment we believe the balance of advantage remains in favour with the majority of police officers not carrying firearms. But I will keep the position under constant review and I tell you now, I will not hesitate to arm more of you if that will add to your safety and security and lower the threat to you.

In fact, the Commissioner was also to decide that his force would no longer comply with the 1983 Home Office guidelines on the issue of firearms to police.

Chapter 14

# THE DIVIDING LINE

## FACILITIES

In 1994 some of the residents living close to Lippitts Hill decided that it was time to complain about the noise from the camp and on 22 March Epping Forest District Council served a notice restricting firearms training to four hours a day, four days a week. After a period of stunned disbelief, the MoD rifle ranges at Milton near Gravesend in Kent were urgently leased, Rainham and Purfleet having already been sold, and much of the training was moved to the PERME and RSAF sites, although the latter would also soon be sold for redevelopment.

Next door to Milton ranges stood the National Sea Training College, opened in 1967. This consisted of a four-storey block of dormitories to the south and west, a classroom block to the north facing the River Thames, and a large dining area, a gymnasium, administration offices and a library to the east, all arranged around a central quadrangle. On top of the western end of the north block was a fully equipped mock-up of a ship's bridge that even included a working radar installation. There was separate residential accommodation for seventy-two staff and the principal of the college (referred to as the 'captain'). A jetty allowed access to the river. It could accommodate 576 students. The British Merchant Navy fleet was already in serious decline and it was becoming increasingly difficult to maintain the facility. By the early 1990s the college was taking only a handful of teenage trainees a year.[1]

*Dwight Atkinson*
[Constable] Alan Papworth, one of the Unit's rifle instructors, told me that Milton ranges were closing and that they were to be sold by

the MoD. At the time we were talking about finding other sites and I mooted the idea of the Metropolitan Police purchasing the site as a rifle and carbine range. We then became aware that the National Sea Training College was also in the throes of closing down. I made a personal approach to the captain and he confirmed that the college was closing, apart from the occasional requirement to train fifteen or twenty personnel. I suggested that both Milton ranges and the National Sea Training College would be ideal for the Met.

On 10 June 1994 the Firearms Unit formally proposed that the college and the ranges be combined to become the purpose-built site it had asked for in November 1993, although in September 1994 the restrictions on Lippitts Hill were eased to allow the camp's use for four and a half hours a day, five days a week. Nevertheless, by the end of the year the Metropolitan Police had accepted that it would have to find somewhere else for its training, and in January 1995 a provisional estimate for the work needed at Gravesend was put at about £8 million plus the cost of buying the two sites. After examining various other possibilities, the policy committee agreed that PSD should acquire the ranges and the college and 'the Gravesend complex was to be developed to provide relief to the Lippitts Hill site as soon as possible'.

Formal negotiations started for the purchase of the two sites, but the Royal Society for the Protection of Birds (RSPB) also had its eye on the ranges and the huge danger area behind them for conservation purposes. The RSPB objected to the sale and insisted that the MoD transfer ownership of the land to the society, which in turn would lease out the ranges. A similar arrangement already existed between the MoD and the RSPB on a number of military ranges and so the Metropolitan Police saw no reason to object. What had not been anticipated was that the resulting negotiations would drag on for the next six years.

## THE MURDER OF SERGEANT DEREK ROBERTSON

During the evening of 8 February 1994, Robert Eades, Christopher Snelling and Snelling's brother Terence broke into the unoccupied flat above a post office at 99 Calley Down Crescent, New Addington, in south London. At just after 8 o'clock the following morning Albert Britton opened up the post office and felt a hand cover his mouth. The three, who were by now wearing full-face balaclava helmets, waved a knife in his face and told him not to make a sound. They stole about £2,750 in coins that were in a safe but another safe containing £31,000 was fitted with a time lock and could not be opened until 9 o'clock. They had just decided to wait when the telephone rang. It was Mr Britton's wife, Barbara, and the three, not wishing to arouse suspicion, allowed him to speak to her. The tone of her husband's voice told her that something was wrong and she called the police.

Two unarmed officers from the local police station, Constable Stephen Wilson and Sergeant Derek Robertson, arrived first. Seeing nothing wrong at the front of the building, they both went to the rear, but they became disorientated and had trouble identifying the correct premises. Sergeant Robertson waited while his colleague went back to the front where Constable Robert Brown joined him. The robbers heard a noise and Eades grabbed Mr Britton from behind. Holding the knife at Britton's throat, Eades ordered him to open the back door. They were confronted by Sergeant Robertson who reported over his radio that: 'There are three suspects all with balaclavas coming out of the rear of the post office. One is armed with a knife.' Seeing Sergeant Robertson, the Snelling brothers ran off, but Eades pushed his captive away and stabbed Sergeant Robertson six times before making good his escape. Mr Britton called for help using the sergeant's radio.

Constables Wilson and Brown had raced around to the back to help their sergeant and ran straight into the Snellings. The brothers gave up when Constable Wilson pointed his hand at them and shouted: 'Armed police. Get down.' Both were arrested, but Eades had disappeared. ARV officers arrived within a few minutes of the original call and sought authority to remove their weapons from the gun-safe in the car. While the Force Control Room started the process of trying to contact a senior officer, the officers took matters into their own hands and armed themselves. Eades was found hiding in an out-building where he was arrested at gunpoint.

Desperate attempts were made to save Sergeant Robertson's life, including open-heart surgery at the scene. He was taken to the Royal Middlesex Hospital by helicopter but he died a short time later. At the Old Bailey in January 1995 Eades was found guilty of murder and sentenced to life imprisonment with a recommendation that he serve a minimum of twenty-five years. The Snelling brothers were found guilty of manslaughter and sentenced to twelve years each.

## ARMED RESPONSE

The reaction to the deaths of Constable Dunne and Sergeant Robertson was such that, in April 1994, it was announced that there would be a further increase in both ARVs and specialist teams. Recruiting and training started immediately using whatever temporary facilities the instructors could lay their hands on, and on 20 June the number of constables on ARVs increased from 75 to 120 (as had been suggested by the Roach Report four years earlier) and the number of teams increased to six.

On 22 May the *Sunday Telegraph*, under the heading 'Too little, too late, say police on the beat', had reported:

South Norwood police station on the fringe of the Croydon commuter-belt looks an unlikely front line for the police. But the officers at this station have suffered a series of stabbings and shootings. Last February they culminated in the murder of Sgt Derek Robertson who was stabbed after disturbing two robbers [*sic*] at a post office in New Addington. The whole station went into mourning. Morale was among the lowest in the Metropolitan Police. It was a significant factor in last week's decision by Paul Condon, the Commissioner, to offer the police more armed protection. . . . As a result there will be 12 armed response vehicles on the streets by June and, from tomorrow, officers patrolling in them may carry handguns on the belt.

The increase in the size of the Firearms Unit was indeed accompanied by a decision to end the situation where the granting of authority to remove weapons from the vehicles was a lottery that depended on the availability and attitude of the senior officer concerned. There had been complaints from some senior officers that the ARV crew should have waited for permission to arm themselves before their search for Eades and this proved to be the last straw. The Commissioner gave approval for ARV crews to wear their handguns overtly and to deploy with weapons without the need to get separate authority each time. The new regulations came into effect on 23 May.

This started a chain reaction. Authority for the overt carriage of firearms was given to the DPG on 8 August and to royalty protection officers (uniform) on 12 September. By now both departments had officers trained in the use of the MP5 and, as at Heathrow, it was senseless to continue trying to hide the fact that they were armed. ARV crews in Greater Manchester were given similar authority by their chief constable on 6 September to join a few other forces that were already openly carrying firearms after seeing the introduction of this measure at airports.

## SHOTS FIRED IN PUTNEY

On 2 August at about 4.50 in the afternoon, Kevin Gregory, armed with a shotgun, and Robert Knapp, armed with a revolver, raided a jeweller's shop in Putney High Street, south-west London. After firing a shot the pair left with jewellery worth over £120,000. Constable Mark O'Brien, an unarmed local officer, watched as the two men walked to their first getaway vehicle parked nearby. A police van driven by Constable David Boyce then arrived and Constable O'Brien got into the passenger seat. Gregory saw them, approached the van, and fired into it through the windscreen. Both officers were hit and although neither was seriously injured, Constable O'Brien fell out of the passenger side of the vehicle. Gregory walked up to him and pressed the muzzle of the shotgun into his forehead. He said nothing and then walked back to the getaway vehicle. The pair sped off.

Despite his injuries, Constable Boyce started the police van and gave chase. The local duty officer and a sergeant arrived in a car and picked up Constable O'Brien. After being told what had happened, they joined in the chase as the robbers headed towards the River Thames. Knapp crashed the vehicle in Merrivale Road and after firing at police again, the pair split up. Knapp advanced on foot towards the duty officer's car, and Constable O'Brien and the duty officer hastily left it, but the sergeant tried to take cover in the footwell. When Constable O'Brien realised the danger he held up his baton as though it was a firearm and shouted: 'Armed police. Put the gun down.' Although this had worked on the Snelling brothers, it did not fool Knapp. He forced the sergeant out at gunpoint. As Knapp tried to start the car, Constable Boyce rammed it with the police van.

An ARV crew arrived just as Knapp managed to get the police car moving with Constables Boyce and O'Brien in hot pursuit in the van. Two of the crew had left their vehicle and so it was the ARV with just its driver that joined the chase, although one of the crew managed to board another police vehicle that also joined in. Knapp crashed the police car in Putney Bridge Road. He left the vehicle through the driver's window – handgun first – but this time the two ARV officers were there as well. Knapp dropped the revolver and gave up.

Meanwhile, Gregory had been firing at TSG officers who were chasing him in a personnel carrier. The third ARV officer had managed to get a lift in another carrier as members of the public directed the officers along the route taken by Gregory. Eventually they saw several people pointing towards an alley leading to a footbridge running beside the railway line that crossed the Thames to Fulham. The ARV officer entered the alley and saw Gregory about halfway across the bridge. As the officer called out a warning that he was armed, Gregory turned and fired. He then took a hostage and walked down the steps at the other end of the footbridge.

Gregory was heading towards where the two robbers had previously left another getaway vehicle, but more unarmed officers had already reached the other end of the bridge. Another ARV soon joined them and the driver, Constable Barry Oldroyd-Jones, said in a television interview several years later:

We made our way to the north side of Putney bridge and from that location we spoke to local officers who were on scene and we were directed to go down towards Hurlingham Gardens. As we carried on walking down, searching the gardens . . . a figure appeared from behind the wall. I saw a large coat, a flash of a gun going off, and I heard the loud bang. I felt burning and pain in my groin and legs down to my feet and I went down. There was a bit of a gunfight going on. [Then] the suspect reloaded . . . and shot himself in the head. . . . The hostage, who had to watch all this, was still in the gardens by the door and he was led away after that.[2]

Gregory had killed himself.

Five days later, on 7 August, an article written by Sir Paul Condon appeared in the *News of the World*. 'Bang 'em up for Years' was the heading, and the article went on to ask:

Was this cops-and-robbers chase that ended up in tragedy just a warning to us of what it might be like on our streets unless we do something fast? I took no pleasure earlier this year in having to order more cars with the officers in them wearing guns to be available in London. And I gave authority for the officers in those cars – known as armed response vehicles – to wear the guns openly instead of having them hidden away. Some said I was overreacting to the tragic deaths in quick succession of two police officers and the maiming of others. I believe I was doing the best possible to make the people of London safer from armed criminals and to protect my police officers who can be asked to take only so much. I certainly do not want to see a fully armed police service, because I think the unique relationship between the British bobby and our public is what sets us apart from any other police service in the world. But I have been back to London as Commissioner for 18 months, having been away for just over three years. It has got more violent.

## ST KITTS AND NEVIS

It seemed to be getting more violent elsewhere as well. On 13 October 1994 at about 7.40 in the morning Superintendent Jude

Matthew, the head of Special Branch on the island of St Kitts, was shot and killed. He had just left his home and was on his way to meet officers from New Scotland Yard's SO1 International and Organised Crime Group who had flown to the island the day before to help with an investigation he was conducting.

The two islands of St Kitts and Nevis are in the eastern Caribbean about 1,300 miles south-east of Miami. With a population of about 39,000, their traditional mainstay until the 1970s had been the islands' sugar crop. They gained independence within the British Commonwealth in 1983, and while other activities such as tourism and offshore banking became an increasingly significant factor in their economy, they also became a 'transhipment point for South American drugs destined for the US and Europe'.[3] Bundles of drugs with a flotation collar attached would be dropped into the sea from a low-flying aircraft to be picked up by a local fishing boat.

Superintendent Matthew had been investigating the drug trafficking and also the disappearance of ten people, including the Deputy Prime Minister's son, Vincent Morris, and his girlfriend, Joan Walsh. Six men had been arrested and charged with conspiracy to murder the couple and a court hearing was in the process of being heard on the day of Matthew's death. The officer's murder was seen as an attempt to undermine the legal process with the kind of ruthlessness that the Medellin cartel had used so successfully in Colombia. The Firearms Unit in London was asked to provide support. Inspector Rawlings and Sergeant, later Inspector, Brian Howat, flew out to St Kitts.

*Clive Rawlings*
Two of us were sent out there on the same plane as three officers from SO1. Before going out we were told that weapons would be supplied to us over there. Not knowing what to expect we both took our Glocks and it was fortunate that we did because what they tried to give us was rubbish. It was just an assortment of rusty stuff – old revolvers – you couldn't even put them in a museum. We had to be sworn in as special constables on the island and we teamed up with an SO1 detective superintendent who was already over there.

We formed into a little squad but we decided early on that, because of the situation, we needed more manpower and that the SO1 officers should also be armed. That was when [Constables] Tony Gray and Keith Shaw came out to join us. Tony gave them a quick reauthorisation on an excuse for a range. I was out there for a week or ten days and from then on the Unit covered it with a kind of rolling posting.

*Tony Gray*
We provided some training for the local police support group as well. Their headquarters was an old British Army camp and it still had the black and white British Army signs and an old armoured car rusting away in the entrance. You could see what it used to be but it was a bit derelict. The range was just a field with some targets propped up out the back of the camp. There was no formal range complex and no proper training in the use of firearms that I could see. To be fair to them, they said that what they dearly needed was training.

The operation lasted for a couple of months after which there were several returns to the islands for the trials of those arrested. St Kitts and Nevis are still on the list of locations involved in drug trafficking.

SHOTS FIRED IN ENFIELD

Back in London it had been decided that the ideal structure for the Metropolitan Police would be for it to have five areas, each under an assistant commissioner. (In 1999 another reorganisation would reduce these to three.) On 2 November 1994 a meeting of the Service Restructuring Project Board was held at New Scotland Yard chaired by the Deputy Commissioner, Sir John Smith. Present were the five new area assistant commissioners, together with the assistant commissioners from Territorial and Specialist Operations departments. One of the subjects they had gathered to discuss was the future of the force's Firearms Unit.

They decided that it should remain centralised within Specialist Operations department and that it would retain responsibility for firearms training, the specialist firearms teams and the armed response vehicles. It was the end of nearly three and a half years of morale-sapping uncertainty, internal politics and rumour.

Christmas 1994 saw its usual crop of out-of-control family breakdowns. In March 1992 Sarah Miles had met Alan McMinn and by the November they were living together. After the birth of their daughter the relationship deteriorated, and by June 1994 Sarah was the subject of both verbal and physical abuse. In August Sarah moved with her daughter to 33A Ordnance Road, Enfield, north-east London, to get away from McMinn, but it was not long before he discovered her address. He visited her several times, and on 24 December they fought again during the course of which Sarah sustained a fractured nose.

Sarah spent Christmas Day at her sister's house, returning to Ordnance Road on Boxing Day. Another argument developed and Sarah fled, leaving McMinn and their daughter inside the flat. She returned to her sister's house and, together, the two women went to Ponders End police station. On being told that McMinn had a gun, the local duty officer, an inspector, sent for ARV assistance. One of those to attend was Constable Helen Barnett who had only joined the ARVs the previous June. She and another officer put on civilian jackets and carried out a reconnaissance of the house before joining the rest of their colleagues at a rendezvous point that had been established close by. Suddenly there was a shout of 'That's him', and they saw a man pushing a child in a pushchair along the pavement. He walked into the middle of the road, said 'Yeah, it's me', and drew a handgun from his jacket pocket. At first he put the muzzle in his mouth, but he then deliberately pointed the gun at Constable Barnett and fired.

The officer was hit and went down. Four other officers returned fire. McMinn was taken by air ambulance to the Royal London Hospital where he was given emergency surgery. He recovered and on 22 September 1995 he was sentenced to just eight years in prison after being convicted of unlawful wounding, assault occasioning actual bodily harm, possessing a firearm with intent to endanger life, and having a firearm and ammunition in a public place. Constable Barnett also recovered from her physical injuries, but the incident had a more insidious effect. The officer had already nearly been killed by a mentally ill man with a knife and had been blown off her feet by the force of a PIRA bomb explosion. Being shot finally tipped the balance and Constable Barnett decided to resign from the force.[4]

## SHOTS FIRED IN HAMMERSMITH

Two months after the incident in Enfield, on 28 February 1995, three officers were on routine patrol in south-west London in an ARV. As the three drove along Castelnau towards Hammersmith Bridge at about 1 o'clock in the afternoon, the radio operator spotted a Toyota MR2 sports car coming towards them. The vehicle had been reported stolen and they saw it pull into the side of the road. When the driver got out and went into a nearby shop, two of the officers approached the vehicle. Then the driver suddenly ran from the shop, climbed back into the car, slammed the door and started the engine. Constable Patrick Hodgson ran to the driver's door and told him to stop the vehicle but, with the engine racing, the man began to shunt the car backwards and forwards.

The officer tried to break the windscreen of the Toyota with his handgun, but when this did not work he pulled open the driver's door and took hold of the man by the shirt. The driver's shirt tore and so the officer got hold of him around the neck. The man said nothing but frantically continued to work the gear lever until suddenly the Toyota sped forward again. The officer was dragged along until the car crashed into a vehicle parked in front of it. He had to let go as the Toyota reversed and then shot forward again. This time it crashed into a white van that had been driven across the road, partially blocking its escape route.

The driver of the ARV drove her car to block the Toyota in from the side, and when the Toyota reversed, Constable Hodgson had to leap out of the way to avoid being hit. The second officer had by now managed to get a passenger out of the vehicle, and Constable Hodgson opened the passenger door and again challenged the driver to stop the car. Many witnesses were later to say that the car seemed as though it was 'being driven by a maniac'. The tyres were billowing smoke and became so hot that the tarmac underneath melted.

Constable Hodgson fired two shots at the driver, David Ewin, who was then taken by air ambulance to the Royal London Hospital in Whitechapel where he died eighteen days later. Ewin had previously been arrested for armed robbery and sentenced to eight years in prison. After his release he had been arrested, again for armed robbery, and sentenced in July 1992 to five years. He had only been released on licence some eight weeks before he met up with the ARV crew in Castelnau, and he was therefore liable to recall, a factor that probably played a significant part in his determination to escape at all costs.

On 17 October Constable Hodgson was arrested and became the first police officer in Britain to be charged with murder because of his actions while on duty. His first trial opened at the Old Bailey on 3 December 1996. The prosecution's case was that it was reasonable neither to draw the gun against the driver of a stolen car nor to use the gun to break the windscreen. The officer's behaviour, it was said, was at least partly responsible for causing Ewin to drive recklessly and the jury was told that if shooting Ewin was the only option then that was tantamount to saying that any car thief could be shot dead by police. By 10 December the trial was just ending when shouts were directed at the jury from the public gallery and the judge declared a mistrial. A second trial opened at the Old Bailey on 14 April 1997 but the jury could not agree on a verdict. A third trial was ordered and this opened six months later at the Old Bailey on 6 October with an alternative charge of manslaughter being added to the original one of murder.

This trial followed much the same format as the previous two, but this time there was a subtle difference. Instead of it not being 'reasonable to draw the gun against the driver of a stolen car', the prosecution told the jury that if the officer had shot Ewin while he was on the driver's side of the vehicle 'he may never have been prosecuted'. Even the trial judge, Sir Lawrence Verney, repeated the assertion that 'shooting on the offside may have been justified'. Such is the flexibility of the dividing line between prosecution and exoneration. Nevertheless, the trial continued and the jury retired on

14 October to consider its verdict. A short time later Constable Hodgson was declared not guilty.

Up to the date of the incident in Castelnau fourteen police officers had been killed in England and Wales by someone deliberately using a car as a weapon. By the end of 2003 there would be a further nine officers unlawfully killed by vehicles, more than twice as many as died as a result of being shot or stabbed during the same period. Many years later Constable Hodgson would say in a television interview:

I put my uniform on that day, gone to work to do a professional job. I'd done it. I had no intention of killing anybody that day and on that basis, that there was no intent, I felt that the end result would be in my favour. I felt they were going through the system and I had to take part in it. It's made clear as a police firearms officer that it is an individual decision to shoot and if it goes wrong then you have to take responsibility, and that's where it stops.[5]

Few people, including few police officers, will ever understand the true meaning of such a simple statement of fact.

### THE DEATH OF CONSTABLE PHILIP WALTERS

The stakes in the debate about arming the police had been raised once again on 18 April 1995 when police were called to a disturbance at a house divided into flats in Ilford in north-east London. A woman had hired three men to beat-up a former boyfriend. When four officers arrived, one man was caught as he tried to run away. As Constable Derek Shepherd went to arrest him, and Constable Philip Walters prepared to handcuff him, a struggle ensued during which the man suddenly produced a gun which was discharged twice. One bullet hit Constable Walters in the chest and he died of his injuries.

The man gave his name as Ray Lee, although he was found to have at least seven different aliases and three different passports. A jury was unable to agree a verdict at the Old Bailey in January 1996 and a second trial was ordered. In June Lee was found not guilty of murder but he was sentenced to eight years in prison for firearms and other offences and to ten years for manslaughter. The sentence provoked a strong reaction with Constable Walters' girlfriend who was reported as saying: 'I do not think any member of the public should expect an answer to a distress call if they are placing such a disgustingly low value on police officers' lives.' The officer's father broke down in tears and his mother reportedly said: 'My son deserved better justice than that. He was prepared to give his life, and he did give his life, and that is what the justice system did for him.'[6]

Once again there were calls that it was time to arm the police and on 24 May 1995 the policy committee in London agreed to another increase in ARVs. On 5 June, a second base from which ARV crews could operate was introduced in south London and by the time all of the changes had been made the Firearms Unit had a strength of 11 inspectors, 30 sergeants and 256 constables.

## NATIONAL DEVELOPMENTS

Constable Walters was the eleventh officer in five years to be killed as a result of a criminal act, and by June 1995 the calls for police to be armed had become so persistent that the Police Federation decided to ballot its 123,660 members. The Electoral Reform Society oversaw the process and the return rate was a respectable 73,379, thereby providing the first independently validated view of the police service nationally on the subject. Only 21 per cent of officers from constable to chief inspector voted for full arming.

At the same time, HMIC conducted an inspection of a representative sample of forces. The subsequent report found that all now had either full- or part-time firearms teams (usually called Tactical Firearms Units (TFUs), again to avoid the SWAT acronym) but only a few were trained in hostage rescue despite the 1989 Home Office circular.[7] In May 1992 the ACPO JSC had agreed to a three-week hostage rescue course being run at the National Centres but the take-up had been low. The HMIC report noted that:

The difficulty may stem from costs in financing and resourcing the capability. Some forces have not been able to place [hostage rescue] above other issues in terms of priority. Additionally, there appears to be reluctance on the part of some chief officers to develop what they perceive as a military-style capability. However, there is a responsibility for chief officers to ensure they can take action when life is in immediate peril and not undertaking the training required is failing to meet that responsibility.

Even today there are forces that have chosen not to have the capability. However, the report did find examples of good practice, particularly in those forces that had started armed response vehicles (or variants). Forces that were still uncertain about whether or not to start an ARV system did so as a result of the HMIC report.

Having an immediate armed response was all very well but it was of limited value if it had to jump through a series of bureaucratic hoops before being deployed. There was widespread criticism directed at the high level of authority officially required before firearms could be issued and a complete review was ordered. At a special meeting of selected members of the ACPO JSC and HMIC on 6 June 1995 the guidelines were rewritten making the authority to issue firearms the responsibility of the officer in charge of an operational command unit (superintendent of a division), or an inspector in urgent cases. Furthermore, it was recognised that trying 'to achieve a greater degree of consistency of practice' for ARVs was pointless. It was therefore decided that each force should be allowed to decide for itself the authority levels required for armed response. The Metropolitan Police had already been doing so for more than a year anyway. The category of armed response was added to that of protection to which a standing authority could be given when firearms were issued regularly, thereby making it official. A full meeting of the ACPO JSC agreed the changes, as did the Chief Constables Council.

## ANNUAL STATISTICS

Although the Home Office also agreed to the new measures, it felt a sense of unease about what the effect would be on the annual statistics. Ever since 1973 it had been keeping records of the issue of firearms to police and over the years the publication of part of the annual total had come to be seen by politicians and the media as a kind of barometer of armed crime. There was still no mention of the fact that only one of the three categories was being made public, thereby perpetuating the belief that it represented the totality of police arming, but in 1995/6 the worst fears were realised when this figure jumped by nearly 70 per cent to 8,476.

The reasons for the increase were urgently sought and there was some relief when it was discovered that the explanation lay not in the new guidelines but in the way the figures were being calculated. For example, in forces that still kept weapons in a safe in a vehicle, if the incident was dealt with before the officers arrived and the call was cancelled, it usually did not count. On the other hand, given the same circumstances in forces that had officers carrying firearms all of the time, it usually did count. They argued that just the sending of permanently armed officers, whether they were needed or not, must implicitly include the issue of firearms.

There was also by now another ingredient in the debate – a growing requirement to measure performance against cost to demonstrate value for money. That meant producing figures, preferably high ones, to justify expenditure. Armed response was no different to any other police function in having to prove its continuing worth, and some forces had started to include all calls that were in any way firearms related in their annual return, whether firearms were issued or not. The 'authority to prepare' or 'arm up' also had to be fitted in somewhere, and the result of the diverse methods of calculation was that between 1990 and 1995/6, eleven forces reported a doubling of the number of 'operations' for which firearms were issued. Four forces reported an increase by a factor of 3 and four forces by 4. Six forces reported a 5-fold increase, four a 6-fold increase, two a 9-fold increase, one a 10-fold increase and two an increase by a factor of 11. Leicestershire increased 14-fold, Bedfordshire 17-fold, Derbyshire 18-fold, Warwickshire 55-fold, Nottinghamshire 57-fold and Cleveland by a factor of 487.

The Metropolitan Police had also started to record the overall number of calls. In 1995 there were 500 team operations and 879

ARV deployments (when officers had to take some action after they reached the scene), but there were 8,666 ARV calls – all responded to by officers who were now permanently carrying firearms. Only the number of operations and deployments had so far been included in the force's return, but if it now copied what some other forces were doing and changed to recording the number of calls then the total 'operations' for the whole country would appear to double overnight. The Home Office suggested that politically this would be hard to explain and the force agreed not to change its reporting method.

However, when there was a similar release of figures in the House of Commons in December 1998 it included advice that: 'Firearms . . . were not necessarily issued to officers on each occasion.'[8] The Home Office had evidently decided that if some forces were using all calls in their return, even if firearms were not issued, then this should be pointed out since it showed that the continuing increases were not as bad as they looked. No one seems to have questioned why the statistics for firearms issue now officially included an unknown number of operations for which they were not issued, and the impression given was that all forces were doing the same. It was a shambles that would have entirely unforeseen consequences.

In January 2003 the Police Complaints Authority (PCA) made headline news when it presented the House of Commons with a review of shooting incidents that had resulted in death or injury.[9] A draft produced in May 2002 had used the total number of incidents to claim that 'the Metropolitan Police Service (MPS) experienced a disproportionate volume of incidents in relation to other forces . . . if the number of incidents were spread pro-rata across all forces'. When it was explained that this methodology failed to take account of the different levels of armed crime and terrorism that each force had to deal with, the PCA switched to using the published annual statistics to claim a 'higher rate of shootings in the MPS area' instead.

The unsuitability of these figures as a means of comparing forces was also explained, but this time the PCA could see its newsworthy 'conclusion' going out of the window and refused to budge. Intriguingly, the final version of the review did contain a comparison of 'violent crime', presumably to head off criticism that this had not been taken into account, but even this was not what it seemed. The statistics used were taken from the British Crime Survey (BCS) in which 'violent crime' meant 'domestic violence, acquaintance violence, stranger violence and mugging'.[10] An entirely separate annual report[11] showing that over 40 per cent of armed crime (excluding air weapons) occurred in London was excluded, leading to suggestions of bias. The Metropolitan Police said that: 'the conclusions drawn in this section of the report are partial and statistically dubious.'[12]

In April 2004 the PCA was scrapped and replaced by the Independent Police Complaints Commission (IPCC). Nevertheless, opportunities for further statistical mischief-making still remain: in 2004 HMIC found that: 'Insofar as the number of armed operations is concerned, evidence was found of widespread variations in recording practices between forces.'[13]

*Chapter 15*

# INTO A NEW CENTURY

## DOMESTIC TERRORISM

In August 1994 the PIRA declared a 'cease-fire', but this did not mean that planning and preparation for attacks also ceased. On 9 February 1996, a few minutes after an announcement that the 'cease-fire' was over, a device detonated outside the Canary Wharf tower resulting in two deaths and more than thirty people injured. Damage was estimated at £85 million. Just over a week later a PIRA terrorist, Edward O'Brien, was killed when a bomb he was carrying exploded in his lap (another own goal) while he was travelling on a London bus in the Aldwych. Nine people were injured. Other attacks included a lorry bomb in Manchester. When this went off on 15 June more than 200 people were injured and the city centre had to be rebuilt.

As the level of security in city centres increased, the PIRA turned to infrastructure targets, and as a result the Firearms Unit, the Anti-Terrorist branch, the Special Branch and the Security Service were involved in one of their largest combined operations to date. About 300 officers, under the codename 'Operation Airlines', tracked a PIRA active service unit (ASU) operating in London and the surrounding area.

The two leading members were Gerard Hanratty and John Crawley. Hanratty had been sentenced to four years in prison in 1983 for possessing a firearm. After his release in 1984 he had been arrested again for firearms offences but he disappeared while on bail. He next turned up in Germany where he was sentenced to two and a half years in prison for firearms offences. He was returned to Northern Ireland where he was sentenced to eight years for the offences for which he had jumped bail.

Crawley was an ex-member of the US Marine Corps and had served ten years in prison for his involvement in the shipment of arms in 1984. An armed prison escape attempt earned him another three years. Both he and Hanratty had been released during the 'cease-fire' despite concerns over the threat that they both still posed. The other members of the ASU included Robert Morrow, who had been sentenced to seven years in prison in 1987 for firearms offences, Donal Gannon, whose fingerprints had been found in a PIRA bomb factory in Clapham in 1988, Patrick Martin and Francis Rafferty.

The terrorists were followed as they made reconnaissance trips to National Grid power sub-stations in Buckinghamshire, Hertfordshire, Essex, Kent and Surrey. It was clear that a campaign of attacks was about to start and the arrest of the ASU was ordered. The Firearms Unit raided the addresses where the men were likely to be found during the night of 14 July 1996. Seven were arrested and a large quantity of terrorist paraphernalia was recovered, including thirty-seven timer and power units, documentation such as maps, large quantities of cash and false identities.

The main six, including Hanratty and Crawley, were convicted of conspiracy to cause explosions in July 1997 after a three-month trial at the Old Bailey. Each was sentenced to thirty-five years in prison. Commander John Grieve, head of the Anti-Terrorist branch, was reported as saying: 'I am very proud of this operation which was the result of excellent teamwork. . . . We have got six of the most dangerous men I think I have ever seen off the streets of London.'[1]

A month after the arrests, in August 1996, the Firearms Unit in London was involved in another combined operation, codenamed 'Operation Tinnitus', which in the end proved to be even larger than 'Airlines'. James Murphy, Patrick Kelly, Diarmuid O'Neill, Brian McHugh and a fifth man were the subject of almost continuous surveillance for a six-week period during which police accumulated over 50,000 hours of surveillance evidence and thousands of hours of CCTV material. By the end of that time, during which Firearms Unit officers travelled as far afield as Staffordshire, it became apparent that preparations for a bombing attack using a lorry packed with home-made explosives were nearing completion.

On 23 September at 4.30 in the morning officers from the Metropolitan and the City of London Firearms Units simultaneously raided a number of addresses in London. Kelly, McHugh and O'Neill were all together in one room at the Premier West Hotel, Glenbourne Road, Hammersmith. O'Neill was shot during the raid, and despite being given first aid he died before reaching hospital. The others were arrested. Police searches recovered over 6 tons of home-made explosive. There were also twenty-five timer and power units, 22lb of Semtex explosive, two under-car booby traps, seventeen electric detonators, three AKM assault rifles, two handguns and a large amount of ammunition. Police recovered pagers, false identity documents, tools, clothing, keys, numerous receipts and vehicle registration documents. The ASU had access to three self-storage units, a number of hire cars and two lorries, one of which was the intended bombing vehicle. At their trial at the Old Bailey in December 1997, Murphy, Kelly and McHugh were sentenced to seventeen, twenty and twenty-five years in prison respectively after being convicted of conspiracy to cause explosions.

The PIRA had declared another 'cease-fire' the previous July, but there were still various dissident republican groups to deal with. The 'Real' IRA (RIRA) was responsible for a rocket-propelled grenade attack on the Secret Intelligence Service HQ in 2000 and car bombs in Shepherds Bush and Ealing in 2001. The 'Irish Question' has still not been answered to the satisfaction of everyone.

## THE DUNBLANE MASSACRE

As Michael Ryan had shown in Hungerford, a disturbed individual with a gun can do as much harm as a terrorist.

Born in Glasgow in 1952, Thomas Hamilton had been authorised to act as an assistant scout leader in July 1973, but this authorisation was withdrawn in May 1974 as a result of suspicions about 'his moral intentions towards boys'. He became increasingly bitter about his dismissal, and to prove how wrong the decision had been he organised and operated fifteen separate boys' clubs for varying periods over the next twenty years or so in the area around Dunblane, one of the smallest and most picturesque cities in Scotland. At the same time he developed a keen interest in firearms and was granted his first firearm certificate in 1977.

There were suggestions that Hamilton was getting something 'unnatural' out of dominating the boys and by 1996 fewer were attending his clubs. He was also being refused access to premises in which to hold meetings and he believed that the primary school staff in Dunblane were telling parents not to send their children to him. On 13 March 1996, at about 8.15 in the morning, Hamilton drove to Dunblane where he cut the telephone wires that he believed, wrongly, served the primary school. Carrying two 9mm Browning self-loading pistols, two .357 Smith and Wesson revolvers and over 700 rounds of ammunition, he walked into the school building and fired 105 shots, killing a teacher and sixteen children. Another twelve children were injured together with three adults. Hamilton then committed suicide.

One result of the tragedy was a ban on the civilian ownership of handguns.[2] This also applied to weapons privately owned by police officers. The divisional pistol clubs, together with members of the public who were invited in as guests, were still regular users of the indoor ranges in London. Since the early 1970s the Firearms Unit had even organised its own annual shooting competition for police and civilian clubs, but that now had to stop.[3] The Metropolitan Police had once officially encouraged the clubs as the only means of providing any form of training at all. Their disbanding in October 1997 marked the unheralded end of a forgotten age.

## GUN CRIME

A Firearms Unit report in January 1998 identified that there had been eleven murders and thirty-nine attempted murders involving a firearm in London in 1996, and twenty-five murders and forty-four attempts in 1997. Moreover, of the twenty-five murders in 1997, fifteen involved black victims who had been killed by black assailants.[4] The response was to set up 'Operation Trident' in March 1998 as an intelligence-based initiative to investigate black gun crime in and around the areas of Lambeth and Brent.

In August 1999 the operation was implemented across the whole force with a separate command unit being set up within the Specialist Operations Serious Crime Group at New Scotland Yard, a degree of centralisation that was starting to become acceptable again. By July 2000 three senior detectives supported by 160 officers were working on 'Trident' murder cases, and as of January 2002 130 guns had been seized, 500 kilos of drugs recovered and 200 arrests made, most with the help of the Firearms Unit.

A culture has developed among some young men in which a firearm is seen as something that enforces power and 'respect' but from media reports it is easy to get a distorted perspective on the nature and extent of gun crime. It tends to be localised with more than 60 per cent of all firearms offences (excluding air weapons) in 2003/4 occurring in just three police areas – the Metropolitan Police, Greater Manchester and the West Midlands. Two other forces, Durham and Cleveland, with 171 authorised officers between them and an equal share in a new state-of-the-art training facility built at a cost of £6.8 million, had to contend with less than 0.6 per cent. In North Wales, a force with just eighty-three authorised officers and another excellent new training facility, the figure was 0.1 per cent. The extent to which you are likely to be affected by gun crime depends on where you happen to live.

## FELTHAM

The number of incidents dealt with annually by the Firearms Unit in London reached 1,000 in 1993. In 1999 it topped 2,000 for the first time, and only occasionally would one call stand out from all the others. Such a call came during the evening of 28 April 1999 when two unarmed traffic officers in a Land Rover saw a Vauxhall Cavalier with an out-of-date vehicle excise licence and signalled the driver to pull over. When the driver got out he opened fire with a Glock 9mm self-loading pistol. He then sped off with the police car in hot pursuit. He continued to fire at police, and when he stopped his car for a second time he took up a Bushmaster .223 calibre assault rifle which he used to riddle the police car with bullet holes. Unarmed officers from Twickenham police station took up the chase and armed response vehicles raced to the scene.

The driver of the car, George Knights, soon abandoned his vehicle but he then hijacked a couple of others. By the time he reached what turned out to be his home he had disabled several more police vehicles with rifle fire. Officers laid siege to Knights' address at 121 Shaftesbury Avenue in Feltham, not far from Heathrow airport, and a specialist team was called. Knights occupied a ground-floor flat and above him lived a family, including a young child, who were terrified by what was going on underneath them. Effectively they were his hostages: the only way into their flat was through a door on the ground floor and Knights could see it should he happen to be looking out through his window.

The Firearms Unit was directed to perform a rescue and, while part of the team distracted Knights, the remainder got the family to safety. Knights then gave up. Inside his flat police found an array of weapons, ammunition and military-style clothing. He later led police to an arms cache he had buried in a wood and he also had a store of weapons and ammunition in Florida. In March 2000 he was convicted at the Old Bailey of nineteen offences, including kidnapping and endangering life, and given nine life sentences.

The legislation introduced after the Hungerford and Dunblane massacres does not mean that firearms are no longer available to someone intent on getting hold of them.

FACILITIES

By January 1996 the cost of developing the training site at Gravesend was estimated at £8.8 million. On 8 May the Metropolitan Police purchased the National Sea Training College for £3.2 million and in October the force announced that the rest of the funding would be by way of the government's Private Finance Initiative (PFI). By April 1997 the Firearms Unit had drawn up a technical specification, and the force then received a very nasty shock. Independent building consultants were asked to provide an estimate of the cost if the site was built and run by a private company and on 7 July they produced a figure of £21 million.

PSD declared the specification 'not affordable' and pointed to the policy committee agreement for the development of the Gravesend site 'to provide relief to Lippitts Hill'. Since it was just the noise from gunfire that was left causing a problem at Lippitts Hill, all that was needed was ranges! Fortunately, this time the Firearms Unit had the support of the ACSO, now David Veness, and despite PSD's spirited defence of its position, all the required facilities were restored to the plan. The specification was finalised on 22 September; two days later notification was received that the PERME site was to become a golf course with some housing and a retail park. The force had to leave its only remaining tactical training area by 27 February 1998. By now the training site at Hounslow was also suffering from the problems associated with noise, and in February 1999 a public order specification was included in the requirements for Gravesend at an estimated added cost of £9.7 million.

By 2001 the Firearms Unit had more than 400 officers. It moved its headquarters to the former Leman Street police station which had a new purpose-built range taking up the whole of the top floor. Greenwich range had been lost when the building which housed it was sold, but Stoke Newington range was being refurbished at last, and on 11 April the contract for Gravesend was signed. At the same time, a lease was agreed with the RSPB and Milton ranges finally became an integral part of the project.

The finished product was a refurbished college with a new two-storey building housing a variety of indoor ranges surrounded by a tactical training area made up of streets complete with buildings, building fascias, roads, and junctions controlled by traffic signals. Milton ranges next door provided a 600-metre rifle range and a 100-metre carbine/pistol range. A separate public order training area was located on what used to be the college football pitch and tennis court.

Lippitts Hill closed in January 2003 and Lord Toby Harris, Chair of the Metropolitan Police Authority (MPA), and Sir John Stevens, Commissioner of the Metropolitan Police 2000–5, later Lord Stevens, officially opened the new site on 15 April. It had cost another £55 million to complete. The Commissioner described the cutting-edge facilities 'as some of the most advanced in the world'.

SO19 became CO19 on 1 April 2005 after another force reorganisation, and British police firearms training is still being exported as far afield as Jordan, Greece, China, Sierra Leone, East Timor, Montserrat and Guyana.

## NATIONAL DEVELOPMENTS

Since 1990 an international agreement has required that governments and law enforcement agencies develop 'non-lethal incapacitating weapons for use in appropriate situations, with a view to increasingly restraining the application of means capable of causing death or injury to persons'.[5]

The search for effective 'incapacitating weapons' had in fact been going on ever since 1977 in London after Stuart Brickell nearly managed to climb over the top of the restraining cage with his machete. Police forces have no research budget and so they rely on private companies producing suitable devices although, in most cases, Home Office authority is required before any of them can be used. In the late 1970s the latest development was a small handgun-shaped device fitted with a tube that fired a squash ball. Anyone who has played the game will know how much one of these can hurt, but all that was needed to defeat it was a few layers of clothing. Since then, producing something that will work under all conditions has become something of a quest with a potential fortune awaiting the inventor.

Serious national research started after a report by Colin Burrows, by now a superintendent in the Royal Ulster Constabulary on attachment to the Police Scientific Development Branch (PSDB) of the Home Office. He had studied the investigation reports into twenty-three incidents in England and Wales over a three-year period and the resulting document, to become known as the Burrows Report, was published in 1996.[6] Of the incidents examined, seven had resulted in a fatality. In nearly 40 per cent of the cases the person concerned had engaged in behaviour that suggested they deliberately caused the shooting, and the term 'provoked shooting' was introduced to describe them. The report also found that 'whilst less than lethal weapons are generally inappropriate when faced with the lethal threat, there were a few cases where the availability of a less than lethal device may have made pre-emptive action by the police a possibility'. The use of baton rounds had been discussed at one post-incident debrief but there had been 'uncertainty regarding the efficacy of their use'. The report recommended that 'the use of kinetic energy rounds be explored for use in appropriate situations and that the Police Scientific Development Branch continue to actively monitor less than lethal technologies'.

The misgivings over the use of baton rounds had mainly centred on the inaccuracy of the weapon and its ammunition, although the Heckler and Koch 37mm baton gun had replaced the Type L67 in 1994. In 2001 a new, more accurate round would be introduced and there was also an improved optical sighting system. The Home Office gave authority in June for the baton gun to be taken into use in situations other than public disorder as a 'less-lethal option', and its first operational use came in North Wales on 27 February 2002 against a man armed with a knife. The Metropolitan Police put the weapon out in its ARVs five months later on 19 July. In June 2005 yet another new baton round would be introduced, known as the 'attenuating energy projectile' (AEP).[7]

The financial incentive has resulted in no shortage of suggestions for suitable devices and they have usually fallen into one of three categories – impact, chemical or electrical – although these categories are occasionally found in combination. Impact devices, as the name suggests, rely on some kind of blow, and today they come in the form of water jets, bean bags (containing lead shot, not beans), socks (similar to bean bags only larger), rubber or plastic balls, and batons. The most accurate and least likely to cause serious injury is the AEP, but at best it will only knock someone off their feet. It is not an 'incapacitating weapon'.

Chemical devices usually contain CS (see Chapter 3), OC (also known as capsicum or pepper), PAVA (a synthetic form of pepper), CN (the original 'tear gas') or CR (stronger than CS but much more dangerous). Since the mid-1990s most police officers in Britain have routinely carried a hand-held CS spray, although in 2001 some forces started to use PAVA instead. The most misunderstood chemical device is the tranquilliser dart. We have probably all seen a wild animal rendered unconscious by one on television and it is tempting to assume that the same process can be applied to a person. Unfortunately it can't. It would probably kill. Moreover, if we go into hospital for an operation we expect an anaesthetist (a qualified doctor who has then specialised in anaesthesia) to watch over us. It is only in films that a police officer with a first-aid certificate can happily knock someone out with a dart.

There are a few other variations on the 'less-lethal' weapon, including smoke, acoustic and electromagnetic waves, nets and glue-guns (firing a sticky foam that expands and then rapidly solidifies with the accompanying risk of suffocation), but electrical devices hold the most promise with the Taser currently being the most favoured. The word 'Taser' is said to be an acronym of Thomas A. Swift's Electric Rifle[8] and the device is shaped like a handgun. It fires two barbs attached to wires 21 feet long and on contact with a person an electrical discharge of 26 watts passes between the two barbs, causing loss of muscle control. In November 2001 the PSDB produced a report on 'less-lethal devices',[9] followed by a second in 2002,[10] and the research was then incorporated within another project set up to identify alternative public order equipment suitable for use in Northern Ireland. This reported favourably on the Taser in December 2002, although it noted that: 'In considering the suitability of taser devices for use in the UK, it must be borne in mind that there is currently a ban on the export of electro-shock devices, including tasers, from the UK.'[11]

What the report had tactfully avoided saying was that in July 1997 the Foreign Secretary, Robin Cook, had announced his intention of adding 'an ethical dimension' to UK foreign policy. When asked in the House of Commons 'What action is being taken to ban the export of electro-shock weapons?' he had replied: 'We are committed to preventing British companies from manufacturing, selling or procuring equipment designed primarily for torture and to press for a global ban.'[12] The measures had become law in December when 'stun guns and electric shock dart guns (tasers)' were added to the list of goods that could not be exported.[13]

The Home Secretary, David Blunkett, therefore found himself in the curious position of being advised by his officials to allow police forces to adopt a device that the Foreign Secretary and his officials had been trying their best to outlaw for nearly six years. In January 2003 the police service tried to avoid a wry smile at the paradox of the Home Office agreeing to a twelve-month operational trial of Tasers in the UK, and the following April they were issued in five forces – Northamptonshire, Thames Valley, Lincolnshire, North Wales and the Metropolitan Police.

In London they were carried in the Firearms Unit's ARVs and the political sensitivities surfaced at once. Amnesty International announced on 16 April that: 'New electro-shock "taser" weapons being trialled by UK police forces from tomorrow must be treated as lethal weapons. . . . These controversial weapons have not been proved safe for general use. There is great potential for abuse of taser weapons. The UK Government recently banned the export of tasers to other countries, because of concerns that they are used to torture people.' In the same month, the first use of a Taser occurred in Hounslow, south-west London, when a man who was believed to be armed was first hit by a baton round and, when he tried to get up, disabled with a Taser and arrested. Although the trial of the device had been due to end after twelve months, a Taser had only actually been fired fourteen times during that period, and so on 15 September 2004 the Home Office extended the trial to all forty-three forces in England and Wales. By January 2006 the weapon was in use in thirty-four of them.

When Sir John Stevens had been asked in July 2004 'Would you like to see the routine arming of officers?' he had replied:

We have had to look at that recently. . . . However, there is at the moment no need to arm our officers overall. . . . Taser needs to be introduced on a wider basis. It has been a real success and real consideration needs to be given to doing that. I would extend it to most of the units we have got, certainly have it available in the [unarmed] response cars. . . . I think that that is probably a way of doing things without going to full arming.[14]

The issuing of Tasers is likely to increase, but only time will tell whether a device that can truly replace a gun will ever be found.

Meanwhile, a completely revised ACPO Manual of Guidance on Police Use of Firearms had been produced for England, Wales and Northern Ireland in January 2001 and adopted in Scotland (for the first time) the following July. The first six chapters of it were made available on the Internet and a new Code of Practice on Police Use of Firearms and Less Lethal Weapons came into effect in December 2003. A National Police Firearms Training Curriculum, covering everything from abseil to waterborne operations, was introduced in February 2004 to standardise police training still further, and in September 2005 Strathclyde police became the first force north of the border to introduce Tasers.

## INTERNATIONAL TERRORISM

The north tower of the World Trade Center in New York was hit by a hijacked 767 commercial airliner on 11 September 2001 at 8.45 in the morning and a similar hijacked jet hit the south tower 18 minutes later. A hijacked 757 hit the Pentagon building near Washington DC at 9.43 the same morning, and less than half-an-hour later a fourth hijacked aircraft crashed in Pennsylvania. The south tower of the World Trade Center collapsed 62 minutes after being hit, followed by the north tower a few minutes later. A 47-storey office building that had been damaged by the collapsing towers caught fire and fell later in the afternoon. Over 2,800 people were killed. The British Army was temporarily called back to Heathrow to provide additional security.

The world had suddenly become a disturbingly different place and there was a new name to conjure with – al-Qaeda (The Base). Militant Islamic terrorism had assumed centre stage and the security of airports, aircraft and passengers once again became a priority. In February 2003 the Transport Secretary, Alistair Darling, announced that: 'Armed undercover police have been trained for use on UK passenger flights.' Gravesend had been used before its official opening for the training of sky marshals – police officers drawn from forces around Britain which had airports within their jurisdiction. There was also training in how to conduct operations while wearing clothing designed to reduce exposure to chemical, biological, radiological and nuclear (CBRN) material.

Suicide bombers posed a threat never before encountered in the UK and national contingency plans, codenamed 'Operation Clydesdale' and 'Operation Kratos', were drawn up to deal with someone about to commit 'a determined and deadly attack'. These recognised that officers commanding an operation may have information that would not be available to officers on the ground and so, for the first time, they included provision for a senior officer to order when shots will be fired.

On 11 March 2004 there were bombing attacks on the train system in Madrid, killing more than 190 people and injuring over 2,000. During an attempt to arrest some of those responsible on 3 April in south Madrid, the terrorists killed themselves by detonating a device in a flat being raided by a specialist police team. A police officer was also killed and eleven others were injured. Sir John Stevens warned that an attack in the UK was 'inevitable'.

At just before 9 o'clock in the morning of 7 July 2005, suicide bombers set off devices on London Underground trains at Liverpool Street, Edgware Road and Kings Cross stations, and on a double-decker bus in Tavistock Square. Fifty-six people were killed and over 700 were injured. Two weeks later there was an attempt to repeat the attacks, although this time the devices failed to detonate. The Commissioner, now Sir Ian Blair, said that his force faced 'its largest operational challenge since the war' and security was stepped up to an unprecedented level. Hundreds of additional officers were drafted into central London and the sight of heavily armed police officers became a regular feature of television news programmes. Then, during a counter-terrorist operation on 22 July, Jean Charles de Menezes was mistaken for a terrorist and shot dead, a dreadful event with repercussions that have yet to be fully felt.

On the first anniversary of the 7/7 bombings Sir Ian Blair was asked whether he could prevent further attacks. He replied that: 'I fear that it is almost inevitable that there will be further attacks and almost inevitable that some of those attacks will get through. That is the new reality in which we are operating.' Left unsaid was that it will be many years before this particular battle can be declared finally over.

## ARMING THE POLICE – THE FUTURE

As the new century dawned there were 5,776 officers authorised to carry a firearm in England and Wales out of the total police strength of over 127,000, but the debate on police arming was still just as active as it had been for the previous decade. Between 1990 and the end of March 2003 the criminal use of firearms had resulted in the deaths of four officers with another 135 injured[15] and the Police Federation decided it was time for another arming survey. ERS Market Research canvassed the views of a representative sample of 26,476 officers, of whom 12,114 responded.

The result, announced in May 2003, was that about 78 per cent did not want to be routinely armed, but three of the four officers killed had been in London and Metropolitan officers were therefore asked separately in August whether they would carry a firearm if it were decided that all officers should be suitably trained and armed.[16] Three-quarters of the 11,635 respondents were constables and 91 per cent said that they would, although one in ten said that they would only do so if ordered. Only 4 per cent said they would resign rather than accept an order to carry a firearm. In the most recent national survey, in May 2006, 77 per cent of the 47,328 officers who responded were still against routine arming, showing a remarkable degree of consistency since 1995.[17]

As many commissioners and other chief officers have realised over the years, arming the police is essentially an issue of morale. If officers feel that their safety is not being taken seriously, they will demand that they be given the means of defending themselves. The Patten Report on policing in Northern Ireland said in 1999 that: 'Provided policing can be delivered effectively without significant risk to police officers, it is plainly much to be preferred if they can be routinely unarmed.'[18] There had been 302 RUC officers murdered as a result of terrorist activity since the Hunt Report in 1969, and the proviso is of the utmost importance. So far the existence of an immediate armed response has satisfied the need in the rest of the UK, but if full arming is ever considered necessary, it would not simply mean buying a lot more guns. Additional training facilities would be required and these would take years to build to cope with what would be a 22-fold increase in numbers. Even a doubling would stretch the financial resources of most forces and inevitably hard decisions would have to be taken about what else would no longer be done in order to pay the bill.

## THE SHEPHERDS BUSH MURDERERS

It is forty years since the killings of Constable Geoffrey Fox, Detective Constable David Wombwell and Detective Sergeant Christopher Head in Braybrook Street, Shepherds Bush, an event that precipitated modern moves to arm police officers. John Duddy died in prison in February 1981. John Witney was freed on licence in June 1991 after serving twenty-four years. His sentence had been reduced after a review in 1983 because he had not actually fired a shot during the killings. He died in August 1999 while living in Bristol. Harry Roberts was refused parole when his thirty-year tariff expired in 1996 and in 2001 he challenged a decision that he should not be allowed to see evidence filed by the Home Secretary opposing his release. In December 2003 the High Court in London upheld the decision, as did the Court of Appeal in April 2004 and the House of Lords in July 2005. In December 2006 Roberts was again refused parole.

What perhaps gives pause for thought is the realisation that, despite all the developments since that horrific crime so many years ago, it could happen again tomorrow. The police service faces the first half of the twenty-first century with absolutely no idea of just how much it may still have to change.

# NOTES

## CHAPTER 1: THE GOOD OLD DAYS

1. H. Scott, *Scotland Yard* (Middlesex, Penguin, 1957), p. 100
2. Ibid., p. 89
3. Ibid., p. 90
4. Internal memorandum from the Assistant Commissioner 'A' department to the Commissioner, 2 February 1938
5. W.G. Gould and M.J. Waldren, *London's Armed Police* (London, Arms and Armour, 1986), p. 11
6. Metropolitan Police Orders, 30 June 1884
7. Essex Constabulary Regulations, 1 June 1885
8. Metropolitan Police Order 2, 28 July 1936
9. Metropolitan Police Order 10, 8 March 1955

## CHAPTER 2: A FIREARMS TRAINING WING

1. D. McNee, *McNee's Law* (London, Collins, 1983), p. 44
2. Metropolitan Police Order 20, 2 December 1966

## CHAPTER 3: TEETHING PROBLEMS

1. Metropolitan Police Order 19, 13 October 1967
2. Report to the Commissioner, 26 April 1973
3. Confidential Memorandum 4/72, 17 February 1972

## CHAPTER 4: CRIME AND TERRORISM

1. Metropolitan Police Order 19, 5 January 1973
2. R. Mark, *In the Office of Constable* (London, Collins, 1978), p. 165
3. Ibid., p. 141
4. Extract from the minutes of the 109th Central Conference of Chief Constables, Thursday 3 May 1973, Item 7

## CHAPTER 5: SIEGES

1. Mark, *In the Office of Constable*, pp. 188–9
2. Ibid., pp. 183–4
3. 'Report of the Working Party on Firearms for Police Use in Peacetime'. Part I covered conventional weapons. Part II covered CS and similar weapons. Part III covered 'Maintenance of consistent high standards in weapons and training'

## CHAPTER 6: TEAMWORK

1. Metropolitan Police Order 25, 28 May 1976
2. G. Kelland, *Crime in London* (London, The Bodley Head, 1986), p. 255

## CHAPTER 7: VICTORY AND DISASTER

1. From 'Bobbie to Bullets', *Coppers*, Historic Films, for Channel 4, 1999
2. McNee, *McNee's Law*, pp. 160–1
3. From a children's television programme feature called 'Anneka and the Hot Seat' with Anneka Rice, 1985
4. Metropolitan Police Order 11, 29 July 1980
5. 'D11 Branch, Firearms Training, Review of Training, Staff and Future Requirements', 1 June 1982
6. Kelland, *Crime in London*, p. 249

## CHAPTER 8: NEW RULES AND A CONVENTION

1. Home Office Circular 47/1983
2. 'Report of the Working Party on the Selection and Training of Police Authorised Firearms Officers', November 1983
3. 'Force Organisation and Management Review', October 1983. The remaining changes were contained in 'Force Reorganisation – Implementation Planning Guidelines', March 1985
4. Vienna Convention on Diplomatic Relations, 14 April 1961, United Nations Conference on Diplomatic Intercourse and Immunities, Articles 22 (1) and 31
5. Ibid., Article 29
6. Ibid., Article 27
7. C. Stern, *Dr Iain West's Casebook* (London, Warner, 1997), pp. 44–5
8. J. Porter and H. Murdock, 'Selection and Assessment of Authorised Firearms Officers', internal Metropolitan Police report, September 1984

9. C. Mirrees-Black, *Using psychometric personality tests in the selection of firearms officers*, Home Office Research Paper (No. 68), 1992

## CHAPTER 9: A MORE SENSIBLE CARTRIDGE

1. *Public Disorder in Tottenham – 6 October 1985*, a report for the Haringey Police Community Consultative Group
2. 'Sten Machine Carbine', *Small Arms Training*, volume 1, pamphlet 22 (The War Office, 1942)
3. 'Wanted: a national police firearms school', *Police*, July 1986
4. 'On the Use of Bullets which Expand or Flatten Easily in the Human Body', First Peace Conference at The Hague, 29 July 1899, Declaration III
5. 'Means of Injuring the Enemy, Sieges, and Bombardments', Laws and Customs of War on Land (Hague IV), 18 October 1907
6. Professor Alexander Ogston, 'The Dum-dum Bullet', *British Medical Journal*, 29 July 1899, pp. 278–81. Ogston, a distinguished surgeon, argued that some European countries escaped censure despite their use of bullets that caused far greater injury than did the 'dum-dum'. Furthermore, the 'Continental Powers' had successfully conspired to use the Hague Conference to 'exhibit England as introducing a bullet too cruel for any other nation to employ' in order to get the 'Dum-dum' and the 'Woolwich Bullet' prohibited, thereby putting Britain at a disadvantage before the next war.
7. 'Basic Principles on the Use of Force and Firearms by Law Enforcement Officials', Article 11(c), Eighth United Nations Congress on the Prevention of Crime and the Treatment of Offenders, Havana, Cuba, 27 August–7 September 1990
8. Lords Hansard, 6 April 1998, Column WA99
9. 'Report of the Home Office Working Group on the Police Use of Firearms', December 1986

## CHAPTER 10: UNAUTHORISED AND UNORTHODOX

1. Metropolitan Police Order 11, 29 July 1980
2. Metropolitan Police Order 18, 10 July 1987
3. Metropolitan Police working group's final report, 'Selection and Training of Authorised Firearms Officers', October 1987
4. Metropolitan Police working group's final report, 'Proposals for establishment of additional firearms teams and tactical advisers for areas and Specialist Operations department', March 1986

5. At the time, the Firearms Acts 1968 and 1982 controlled civilian possession of firearms. These and other controls were added to the 1968 Act by the Firearms (Amendment) Act 1988
6. C. McLachlan, Her Majesty's Inspector of Constabulary, 'The Hungerford Incident', July 1988

## CHAPTER 11: MORE WORKING PARTIES

1. Metropolitan Police Notices 2/98, 2 September 1998
2. M. Manolias and A. Hyatt-Williams, 'Study of Post Shooting Experiences in Firearms Officers', Police Scientific Research and Development Branch (Home Office), May 1986

## CHAPTER 12: INDECISION

1. 'Working Party Report on Armed Response Vehicles', 31 January 1989
2. 'Report of the Working Party on the Metropolitan Police Use of Firearms', March 1990
3. Parliamentary Intelligence and Security Committee Annual Report 1999/2000
4. Metropolitan Police Order 20, 13 September 1985
5. Metropolitan Police Operational Reference Document 21/91

## CHAPTER 13: TO ENCOURAGE THE OTHERS

1. P. Southgate, 'The Management and Deployment of Armed Response Vehicles', Home Office Research and Planning Unit (Paper 67), May 1992
2. Commissioner's Annual Reports
3. 'Implementation plan for the devolvement of Armed Response Vehicles to area. Report of the Steering Group on the Metropolitan Police Use of Firearms', October 1992
4. J. Shatford and W. Doyle, *Dome Raiders* (London, Virgin, 2004)
5. Metropolitan Police Firearms Unit, 'The employment and training of Authorised Firearms Officers in the Metropolitan Police Service. 1 July 1991–30 June 1992', 23 August 1992
6. Metropolitan Police Firearms Unit, 'Proposals to improve the quality and quantity of training given to Authorised Firearms Officers in the Metropolitan Police Service', 7 September 1992
7. Metropolitan Police Firearms Unit, 'The Future of Firearms Training. A paper for the Operations Executive highlighting current problems and seeking agreement in principle on proposed resolutions', April 1993

8. Metropolitan Police Firearms Unit, 'The Provision of a Purpose Built Firearms Training Site for the MPS', November 1993

## CHAPTER 14: THE DIVIDING LINE

1. R. Derham, *School for Seamen* (Buckingham, Baron, 2000), pp. 89–125
2. Interview with Trevor Phillips on a special edition of *The London Programme* which focused on officers shot while on duty, LWT, 2002
3. CIA, https://www.cia.gov/cia/publications/factbook/index.html, select St Kitts and Nevis
4. H. Barnett and H. Armitage, *Urban Warrior* (London, Blake, 1999), pp. 17–21
5. *London Tonight*, ITV, 2 November 2004
6. *Police Review*, June 1996
7. 'Facing Violence – The Response of Provincial Police Forces', Her Majesty's Inspectorate of Constabulary, 1995
8. Hansard, 15 December 1998, vol. 322, no. 14, p. 17
9. 'Review of shootings by police in England and Wales from 1998 to 2001', Police Complaints Authority, ordered by the House of Commons to be printed 30 January 2003
10. *Home Office Statistical Bulletin*, 'Crime in England and Wales 2001/2002', Home Office, July 2002, p. 51
11. *Home Office Statistical Bulletin*, 'Crime in England and Wales 2002/2003: Supplementary Volume 1: Homicide and Gun Crime', p. 55
12. Metropolitan Police press release, 'Met Welcomes Scrutiny of Police Use of Firearms', 30 January 2003
13. 'Guns, Community and Police. HMIC Thematic Inspection into the Criminal Use of Firearms', Home Office Communication Directorate, May 2004, p. 72.

## CHAPTER 15: INTO A NEW CENTURY

1. *Police Review*, 11 July 1997
2. Firearms (Amendment) (No. 1) Act 1997 and Firearms (Amendment) (No. 2) Act 1997
3. Metropolitan Police Notices 41/97, 15 October 1997
4. 'The Criminal Use of Firearms. A Paper prepared for the Metropolitan Police Committee', January 1998
5. 'Basic Principles on the Use of Force and Firearms by Law Enforcement Officials', Eighth United Nations Congress on the Prevention of Crime and

the Treatment of Offenders, Havana, Cuba, 27 August–7 September 1990, General Provision 2

6. 'A Review of the Discharge of Firearms by Police in England and Wales 1991–1993', Police Scientific Development Branch, September 1996

7. Hansard, 4 April 2005, column 122WS

8. Victor Appleton [Howard R. Garis], *Tom Swift and His Electric Rifle* (Stratemeyer Syndicate, 1911)

9. T. Donnelly, 'Less Lethal Technologies. Initial Prioritisation and Evaluation', Police Scientific Development Branch publication 12/01

10. T. Donnelly, K. Douse, M. Gardner and D. Wilkinson, 'PSDB Evaluation of Taser Devices', Police Scientific Development Branch publication 9/02

11. 'A Research Programme into Alternative Policing Approaches towards the Management of Conflict, the third report prepared by the Steering Group led by the Northern Ireland Office, in consultation with the Association of Chief Police Officers', December 2002

12. Hansard, 28 July 1997, column 66

13. Export of Goods (Control) (Amendment No. 3) Order 1997: Statutory Instrument 1997 No. 2758

14. *Police Review*, 23 July 2004

15. 'Intelligence and Security Committee Annual Report 1999/00' and 'Crime in England and Wales 2002/2003: Supplementary Volume 1: Homicide and Gun Crime'

16. *Police Review*, May 2003, 28 November 2003

17. *Police Review*, 19 May 2006

18. *The Report of the Independent Commission on Policing for Northern Ireland*, 1999, p. 49

# SELECT BIBLIOGRAPHY AND FURTHER READING

Ascoli, D., *The Queen's Peace* (London, Hamish Hamilton, 1979)

Barnett, H. and Armitage, H., *Urban Warrior* (London, Blake, 1999)

Bishop, P. and Mallie, E., *The Provisional IRA* (London, Transworld, 1988)

Derham, R., *School for Seamen* (Buckingham, Baron, 2000)

Dobson, C. and Payne, R., *War Without End* (London, Harrap, 1986)

Fairbairn, W.E. and Sykes, E.A., *Shooting to Live* (1942; repr. Colorado, Paladin, 1987)

Gould, W.G. and Waldren, M.J., *London's Armed Police* (London, Arms & Armour, 1986)

Gray, R., *The Trojan Files* (London, Virgin, 2000)

Ingleton, R., *Arming the British Police* (London, Frank Cass, 1996)

Kelland, G., *Crime in London* (London, The Bodley Head, 1986)

McNee, D. (Sir), *McNee's Law* (London, Collins, 1983)

Mark, R. (Sir), *In the Office of Constable* (London, Collins, 1978)

Scott, H. (Sir), *Scotland Yard* (Middlesex, Penguin, 1957)

Shatford, J. and Doyle, W., *Dome Raiders* (London, Virgin, 2004)

Stern, C., *Dr Iain West's Casebook* (London, Warner, 1997)

Waddington, P.A.J., *Arming an Unarmed Police* (London, Police Foundation, 1988)

——, *The Strong Arm of the Law* (Oxford, Oxford University Press, 1991)

# INDEX